MIKE MEYERS' CERTIFICATION

Passport ✦

MSCE Windows® 2000

Directory Services Administration

EXAM 70-217

STEVEN D. KACZMAREK

OSBORNE

New York • Chicago • San Francisco
Lisbon • London • Madrid • Mexico City
Milan • New Delhi • San Juan
Seoul • Singapore • Sydney • Toronto

Osborne/**McGraw-Hill**
2600 Tenth Street
Berkeley, California 94710
U.S.A.

To arrange bulk purchase discounts for sales promotions, premiums, or fund-raisers, please contact Osborne/**McGraw-Hill** at the above address. For information on translations or book distributors outside the U.S.A., please see the International Contact Information page immediately following the index of this book.

Mike Meyers' MSCE Windows® 2000 Directory Services Administration Certification Passport

1 2 3 4 5 6 7 8 9 0   DOC   DOC   0 1 9 8 7 6 5 4 3 2 1

Book p/n 0-07-219595-9 and CD p/n 0-07-219594-0
parts of
ISBN 0-07-219471-5

Publisher	**Acquisitions Coordinator**	**Design and Production**
Brandon A. Nordin	Jessica Wilson	epic
Vice President &	**Technical Editor**	**Illustrators**
Associate Publisher	Alan Gardner	Michael Mueller
Scott Rogers		Beth Young
	Copy Editor	Lyssa Wald
Editorial Director	Bart Reed	Kelly Stanton-Scott
Gareth Hancock		
	Proofreader	**Series Cover Design**
Acquisitions Editor	Sossity Smith	Ted Holladay
Nancy Maragioglio		
	Indexer	
Senior Project Editor	Valerie Perry	
Pamela Woolf		

This book was composed with Quark XPress™.

Information has been obtained by Osborne/**McGraw-Hill** from sources believed to be reliable. However, because of the possibility of human or mechanical error by our sources, Osborne/**McGraw-Hill**, or others, Osborne/**McGraw-Hill** does not guarantee the accuracy, adequacy, or completeness of any information and is not responsible for any errors or omissions or the results obtained from use of such information.

This book is dedicated to my partner William, for whose support and encouragement I am grateful, and to our cairn terrier Scruffy, who let me know when it was time to take a break, and started to snore loudly when I got too techie. Thanks, also, to my parents for their on-going support and help when we need it.

About the Author

Steven D. Kaczmarek has been a trainer, author and consultant since 1991, providing enterprise networking, administration, consulting and training support through his company ENACT Solutions Corporation. He holds training and professional certifications (MCT and MCP) from Microsoft Corporation for Windows NT and Windows 2000, Systems Management Server 1.2 and 2.0, as well as the Microsoft Certified Systems Engineer (MCSE) certification.

He is the author of the *Systems Management Server 2.0 Administrator's Guide* published by Microsoft Press. He is also the author or contributing author of three books published by Que: *Windows NT Workstation 4.0 Exam Guide*, *Windows NT Server 4.0 Exam Guide*, and *Windows NT Server 4.0 in the Enterprise Exam Guide*.

In prior positions, Steve provided a variety of client PC support services through the IS departments of several large corporations, which included purchasing and installation of PC hardware and software, network management, maintenance and help desk support, and customized training.

Steve has a Master of Science degree from Loyola University with a specialization in computational mathematics.

Steve can be reached through e-mail at skaczmarek@enactcorp.com and more information about his background and services can be located at his Web site: www.enactcorp.com.

About the Technical Editor

Alan Gardner, MCSE, MCT, MSF trainer, MCSD, MCNI, MCNE, CCNA, CCNP, CCDP, CCDA, A+, Network +, CTT+, has more 17 years of experience working in the IT industry, including 12 years training experience with Microsoft and Novell, and 9 years as a director of technology and telecommunications at the U.S. Courts. He is a well-recognized speaker at such national and worldwide events as Microsoft Tech-Ed, Microsoft Exchange Conference (MEC), and Computer Associates CA World. Alan is regarded as an expert at enterprise consulting. He holds extensive experience in all flavors of operating systems including Microsoft, starting at DOS and Windows 1.0 through Windows XP and the .NET Framework; Novell Netware 2.2 and above; and Sun Solaris System V. He is a Cisco Certified Network Professional (CCNP) and Cisco Certified Design Professional (CCDP) specializing is wide area network design and implementation as well as network infrastructure switching. Alan possesses a Bachelor's degree in Computer Information Systems from Calumet College of St. Joseph.

Acknowledgments

Special thanks must go to Nancy Maragioglio for snagging me to work on this book in the series and for her dogged support throughout the process. Thanks, too, to Gareth Hancock for his efforts to make the process run smoothly, and to Jessica Wilson, Alan Gardner, Pamela Woolf and the other editors for their assistance in producing a quality book. My thanks to all of them for recognizing and sharing my determination to produce a book of high quality and value.

Contents at a Glance

Contents

Check-In

May I See Your Passport?

What do you mean you don't have a passport? Why, it's sitting right in your hands, even as you read! This book is your passport to a very special place. You're about to begin a journey, my friend, a journey toward that magical place called *certification*! You don't need a ticket; you don't need a suitcase—just snuggle up and read this passport—it's all you need to get there. Are you ready? Let's go!

Your Travel Agent—Mike Meyers

Hello! My name's Mike Meyers. I've written a number of popular certification books and I'm the president of Total Seminars, LLC. On any given day, you'll find me replacing a hard drive, setting up a Web site, or writing code. I love every aspect of this book you hold in your hands. It's part of a powerful new book series called the *Mike Meyers' Certification Passports*. Every book in this series combines easy readability with a condensed format. In other words, the kind of book I always wanted when I went for my certifications. Putting this much information in an accessible format is an enormous challenge but I think we have achieved our goal and I am confident you'll agree.

I designed this series to do one thing and only one thing: to get you the only the information you need to achieve your certification. You won't find any fluff in here—your author, Steven D. Kaczmarek, packed every page with nothing but the real nitty-gritty of the certification exam. Every page is packed with 100% pure concentrate of certification knowledge! But we didn't forget to make the book readable, I hope you enjoy the casual, friendly style—I want you to feel as though the author is speaking to you, discussing the certification—not just spewing facts at you.

My personal e-mail address is mikem@totalsem.com. Please feel free to contact me directly if you have any questions, complaints or compliments.

Your Destination—MCSE Windows 2000 Directory Services Administration

This book is your passport to the Microsoft MCSE Windows 2000 Directory Services exam. The MCSE Windows 2000 Directory Services exam tests your skills in advanced Windows 2000 features—particularly implementation and management of Active Directory. You'll learn about installing and configuring DNS for Windows 2000 and Active Directory, implementing Active Directory, managing and troubleshooting network environments using Active Directory features such as group policy and remote installation services, and optimizing and securing the networking environment. You will understand these technologies and appreciate how and when to use them.

Your Guide—Steven D. Kaczmarek

Steven D. Kaczmarek is one of those folks you never want to invite to a Quake or Half-Life party—he'll get you so interested in the network itself that you'll forget all about fragging your fellow players and instead find yourself having fun creating Active Directory integrated forward lookup zones. (Of course who *doesn't* enjoy making Active Directory integrated forward lookup zones - but you catch my drift). Wait a cotton-pickin' minute—don't tell me you don't know Steven Kaczmarek! Well, he's the author of the *Systems Management Server 2.0 Administrator's Companion*—a book considered standard issue for those who deal with SMS, including the Microsoft Systems Management Server development team! Plus, you may know Steven from his popular conference sessions as well as from the classroom. Steve has adopted Active Directory as an area of great personal interest and it won't take you many pages into this book to see that when it comes to Active Directory, Steve is your one-stop source!

Steve wants you to know that your input is very important. You can contact him at skaczmarek@enactcorp.com to discuss any issues or questions relating to this book.

Why the Travel Theme?

One of my favorite topics is the parallel of gaining a certification to a taking a trip. All the elements are the same: preparation, an itinerary, a route—even mishaps along the way. Let me show you how it all works.

This book is divided into 11 chapters. Each chapter begins with an Itinerary of objectives covered in each chapter and an ETA to give you an idea of the time involved learning the skills in that chapter. Each chapter is broken down by real exam objectives, either those officially stated by the certifying body or if the vendor doesn't provide these, our expert takes on the best way to approach the topics. Also, each chapter contains a number of helpful items to bring out points of interest.

Exam Tip

Points out critical topics you're likely to see on the actual exam.

Travel Assistance

Points you to you additional sources such as books and Web sites to give you more information.

Local Lingo

Describes special terms in detail in a way you can easily understand.

Travel Advisory

Warns you of common pitfalls, misconceptions, and downright physical peril!

The end of the chapter gives you two handy tools. The Checkpoint reviews each objective covered in the chapter with a handy synopsis—a great way to quickly review. Plus, you'll find end of chapter questions and answers to test your newly acquired skills.

But the fun doesn't stop there! After you've read the book, pull out the CD and take advantage of the free practice questions! Use the full practice exam to hone your skills and keep the book handy to check answers. When you're passing the practice questions, you're ready to take the exam—go get certified!

The End of the Trail

The IT industry changes and grows constantly—and so should you. Finishing one certification is just a step in an ongoing process of gaining more and more certifications to match your constantly changing and growing skills. Read the Career Flight Path (Appendix B) at the end of the book to see where this certification fits into your personal certification goals. And remember, in the IT business, if you're not moving forward, you're way behind!

Good luck on your certification! Stay in touch!

Mike Meyers
Series Editor
Mike Meyers' Certification Passport

Installing, Configuring, Managing, Monitoring, and Troubleshooting DNS for Active Directory

Implementing Domain Name Service (DNS)

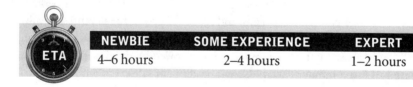

	NEWBIE	SOME EXPERIENCE	EXPERT
ETA	4–6 hours	2–4 hours	1–2 hours

3

Install and Configure DNS for Active Directory

Objective 1.01

Your journey toward studying for and passing the Windows 2000 Directory Services exam begins with *Domain Name Service*, more commonly referred to as DNS. Microsoft expects you to have more than just a working knowledge of DNS. Microsoft devotes an entire section of the exam to the installation, configuration, and management of DNS, especially as it relates to Active Directory. If you are not comfortable with basic DNS concepts or have not implemented a DNS server before, you should probably start your training by setting up a Windows 2000 Advanced Server computer as a DNS server to gain the hands-on experience necessary to pass any of the Windows 2000 MCSE exams.

DNS Basics

Think of DNS as a distributed database system that provides name resolution within an IP (Internet Protocol) network. It consists of a hierarchically structured namespace, top-level domains and subdomains, and one or more administrative zones, similar to what you see in Figure 1-1. The topmost domain is called the *root domain* or *root zone*, and it hosts the database of all the top-level domains. It is typically represented by the notation " . ". The top-level domains include some you are already familiar with, such as com, org, and edu. Second-level domains are those you would be familiar with from surfing the Web. For example, when you enter **www.xyz.com** in your Internet browser, you are querying for the Internet service provider's DNS server for the domain "xyz.com".

Within an organization, there can be one or more subdomains used to further structure and organize access to resources within the organization's network. In Figure 1-1, it.xyz.com, sales.xyz.com, and accounting.xyz.com all represent subdomains of xyz.com. Computers within the Sales domain would be referred to in the DNS database by their computer name followed by the domain name. In Figure 1-1, the computer called PC1 within domain sales.xyz.com is stored in DNS as PC1.sales.xyz.com. This is known as the computer's *fully qualified domain name* (FQDN).

A zone represents a contiguous portion of the namespace over which a particular DNS server or servers have authority to provide name resolution. A zone can store information about one or more DNS domains or portions of a DNS

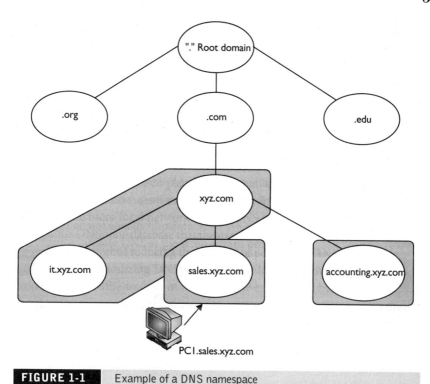

FIGURE 1-1   Example of a DNS namespace

domain. The shaded areas in Figure 1-1 show possible zone configurations for xyz.com. Zones are used to determine authority over DNS domains or to delegate responsibility for administering portions of the namespace.

Local Lingo

FQDN   An object's FQDN, or fully qualified domain name, represents that object's location in the domain relative to other objects. In a DNS zone database, the FQDN of a computer begins with its computer name, also called the host name. The computer's location in the DNS hierarchical namespace is appended to the computer's name to form the FQDN. In Figure 1-1, the computer called PC1 resides in the DNS domain sales.xyz.com. Therefore, its FQDN is PC1.sales.xyz.com.

You can configure three basic types of zones: standard primary, standard secondary, and reverse lookup. A standard primary zone is created every time you create a new zone and is required before you can implement Active Directory. It is also referred to as a *forward lookup zone* because its records map computer names to IP addresses and thus performs name resolution. A secondary zone can also be though of as a "fall back" zone. The secondary zone maintains a copy of the primary zone database. Any changes to the primary zone are periodically replicated to the secondary zone so that DNS servers in either the primary or secondary zone can be used to resolve names to IP addresses.

A reverse lookup zone contains the same records as a standard primary zone. However, these records map IP addresses to their corresponding computer names so that a computer query can be resolved through its IP address rather than the more familiar computer name.

A fourth type of zone can also be configured and is pertinent to this book's main focus. This zone type is the Active Directory integrated zone, which is a standard primary zone that has been incorporated into Active Directory and whose records are maintained as Active Directory objects. An Active Directory integrated zone provides the following benefits for DNS:

- Because Active Directory replicates its objects to all domain controllers within the Active Directory domain, there is no single point of failure for DNS name resolution.
- For the same reason, all Active Directory domain controllers are considered primary zones, thus providing fault tolerance.
- Updates to DNS records are performed as part of the regular Active Directory replication, so there is only one replication topology to maintain.
- Active Directory integration allows for the implementation of secure dynamic updates, which ensures that record updates are performed as authorized.

DNS domains and zones are administered through the DNS administration utility on the Windows 2000 server. Once a zone is Active Directory integrated, it is stored in Active Directory, although it is still administered through the DNS administration utility.

In preparation for implementing DNS for Active Directory, you should consider what your DNS structure should look like. For example, a root zone is used to resolve a FQDN on the Internet by providing forward lookup records for servers in top-level domains, such as com and edu. You may need to configure a root zone for your DNS hierarchy if your organization does not host an Internet server. In other words, if your company's intranet is strictly internal, or if it connects to the Internet through a proxy server, you should configure a root zone.

Exam Tip

If the DNS server is not a domain controller, you must be a local administrator on that server to administer DNS. To administer DNS on a domain controller in Windows 2000, you must be a member of the DNS Admins, Domain Admins, or Enterprise Admins group.

Travel Assistance

For more technical background on DNS for Windows 2000, refer to the Microsoft whitepaper titled "Windows 2000 DNS," which can be found at Microsoft's Windows 2000 Web site: www.Microsoft.com\windows2000.

DNS Setup for Active Directory

In order to install Active Directory, it is necessary to have a DNS server established. In fact, if you try to install Active Directory without DNS, the Active Directory installation process will install the DNS service for you. You can install the DNS service on any server in the Windows 2000 domain, but you will need to install it on a Windows 2000 domain controller in order to enable an Active Directory integrated DNS zone. You can also install DNS as part of your installation of Active Directory. One way or another, you will need to have DNS installed and configured appropriately.

DNS Server is installed as a service on the designated Windows 2000 server through the Add/Remove Programs application in Control Panel. When you choose to install the DNS Server service, the following actions are carried out:

- The DNS Server service is loaded and set to start automatically whenever the server boots.
- The DNS administration tool is added to the Administrative Tools program group.

- The DNS folder is added to the *systemroot*\System32 folder, where *systemroot* refers to the Windows 2000 operating system folder (which is typically WINNT).
- The DNS key is added to the Hkey_Local_Machine\System\ CurrentControlSet\Services key in the Registry.

Four DNS database files are added to the *systemroot*\System32\DNS folder. The main zone database file that is used for forward lookup query resolution is maintained in *domainname*.dns, where *domainname* is the name you assigned to the domain. The reverse lookup file is maintained in x.y.z.in-addr.arpa. The file cache.dns contains host records for hosts outside the domain (for example, xyz.org) or the root servers on the Internet. Finally, and optionally, the Boot file contains startup information for the DNS Server service. This file is optional because the boot settings for DNS under Windows 2000 are stored in the Registry. However, if you were intending to migrate a DNS server that was running BIND (Berkeley Internet Name Domain) to Windows 2000 DNS, you would want to copy and use the Boot file used with that DNS server to help facilitate the migration.

Travel Advisory

UNIX-based DNS servers that use BIND follow a different file-naming convention than the Windows 2000 DNS servers. As part of your migration, you need to copy and rename the zone files appropriately. The Boot file on the UNIX DNS server is called "named.boot" and should be copied and renamed to "Boot". The forward lookup zone file called "db.domainname" should be copied and renamed to "domainname.dns". The reverse lookup file called "db.x.y.z" should be copied and renamed to "z.y.x.in-addr.arpa.dns".

Once the service and accompanying support files are installed, the DNS server can be configured through the DNS administration tool found in the Administrative Tools group on the Start | Programs menu.

The first time you launch the DNS administration tool, you will be prompted to start the Configure DNS Server Wizard. This is a fairly straightforward wizard that will prompt you to create forward and reverse lookup zones. Then, the New Zone Wizard can be launched whenever you need to create additional forward or reverse lookup zones (or secondary zones) by right-clicking the DNS server icon in the DNS administration tool and then choosing New Zone. Figure 1-2 shows the DNS administration tool for a company called "Cairncorp". Notice the forward and reverse zone entries.

The DNS server is required to have a static IP address configured before you install the DNS service. If you are installing DNS before installing Active Directory, you must provide a primary suffix for the domain as well. Because Active Directory and DNS share an identical namespace, the primary suffix should represent the forest root name of Active Directory. This would be something like "xyz.com". You will also need to create a standard primary forward lookup zone, making the DNS server authoritative for that zone if it is the first DNS server for the Active Directory domain. In addition, it is recommended, though not required, that you create a corresponding primary reverse lookup zone. Finally, you should enable dynamic updates for the DNS server.

The Active Directory Installation Wizard allows you to install DNS as part of the installation process. If you choose to have the wizard install DNS, the wizard will create the primary suffix and the standard primary forward lookup zone as well as enable dynamic updates. You will still need to create the recommended reverse lookup zone.

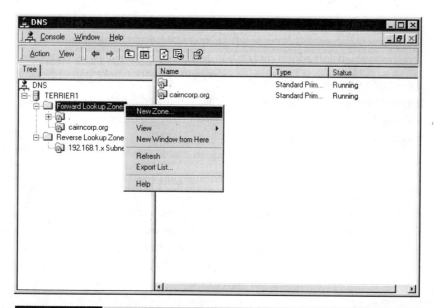

FIGURE 1-2 DNS Administration Tool

DNS servers that support Active Directory provide three main functions

- They respond to queries for the location of a computer by resolving the computer's *host* name with that computer's address as it is listed in the DNS server's database. This is known as *name resolution*.
- They maintain a common naming structure that extends into the Internet and that corresponds to the structure used by Active Directory.
- They respond to requests for the location of computers that run specific services, such as a domain controller.

Specifically for the exam, you should know that Active Directory requires the DNS server to support SRV (service) records, the dynamic update protocol, and, optionally, incremental zone transfers.

Exam Tip

Throughout this book, lists such as those just presented contain key facts that Microsoft expects you to know for the exam. You will rarely have to select these facts from a list of multiple choice options. Rather, a typical question may present a list of goals to be attained, followed by actions taken by an administrator to achieve those goals. Your job in answering the question will be to identify the goals actually accomplished by the actions taken by the administrator. Studying lists of key facts will allow you to more easily discern when a goal is accomplished by a particular action. More importantly, however, you will be expected to understand the interrelationships and impact of these actions when resolving problems presented within the many scenario-based questions that Microsoft prefers in its exams.

A computer's host information is stored in DNS as a resource record. There are many types of resource records, and they are explored in more detail in Chapter 2. However, three resource records in particular are of interest now.

The first is the "A" resource record. This is the main computer record that contains the computer's fully qualified domain name (FQDN) and the IP address associated with that computer. When a DNS server is configured to allow dynamic updates to its database, Windows 2000 computers are able to register their A records automatically when they boot up and are assigned an IP address by a Dynamic Host Configuration Protocol (DHCP) server.

Travel Assistance

To become more familiar with the implementation and function of DHCP servers, see the Microsoft whitepaper "Dynamic Host Configuration Protocol for Windows 2000 Server", available from Microsoft's Web site (www.microsoft.com\Windows2000), or read Module 2 in Microsoft Certified Course 2153: Implementing a Microsoft Windows 2000 Network Infrastructure. However, elements of DHCP that you need to know for the exam are covered in this book.

The second record type is the "SRV" (service) record. This record is similar to the A record, but it also contains service or component information as it relates to the computer in question. Required for Active Directory, DNS uses SRV records to locate:

- Domain controllers specific to a Windows 2000 domain or forest
- Domain controllers in the same site as the client computer
- Global catalog servers
- Kerberos Key Distribution Center (KDC) servers

For example, when a user at a Windows 2000 computer searches for an object in the Active Directory, the computer might need to query DNS for a domain controller that is functioning as a global catalog server that can respond to the user's query with information about printers in the domain.

The third resource record is the "PTR" (pointer) record. Usually referred to as a *reverse lookup record*, the PTR record is used to map an IP address to a computer name so that a computer can be located by searching for its IP address alone. PTR records are not registered automatically by Windows 2000 computers. However, you can configure DHCP to register the PTR record for a Windows 2000 computer when that computer has been assigned an IP address by the DHCP server.

All Windows 2000 domain controllers register both A resource records and SRV resource records. The A record contains the FQDN and IP address of the domain controller in question. The SRV record contains the FQDN of the domain controller and the name of the service that the domain controller provides (global catalog, authentication for a site, and so on). This information is essential for a user to be able to log on to a Windows 2000 domain.

When a user logs on, the Net Logon service on the user's Windows 2000 computer queries DNS for a domain controller in the domain and/or site that the computer belongs to. The DNS server looks for SRV records in the zone database that match the services required by the computer—in this case, domain controllers that can authenticate the user. The DNS server creates a list of domain controllers that fit the criteria and their corresponding IP addresses and sends the list to the computer.

The Net Logon service on the computer contacts the domain controllers in the list and authenticates with the first domain controller that responds back. The connection information is then cached on the user's computer so that it can more easily connect the next time the user needs to perform a similar function. This process is generally the same whether the user is logging on, searching for an object in Active Directory (for which it would need to contact a global catalog server), or performing any other task that requires the intervention of a domain controller.

Integrate Active Directory DNS Zones with Existing DNS Infrastructure

Objective 1.02

When you configure DNS servers for use within your organization, you will consider several factors. For example, you will want to be sure that your users can quickly and easily—and with a minimum expense of bandwidth—contact a DNS server to perform name resolution and provide service information.

In Windows NT, backup domain controllers were used to authenticate users when they logged on to the network. Typically, you would want to place a backup domain controller on the same subnet as the users' computers to facilitate authentication and to minimize bandwidth usage across the WAN. In a similar fashion, you will want enough DNS servers to adequately service your computers' requests, and you will want them located "near" the computers they will be serving.

You can accomplish this by creating primary and secondary zones, standard primary DNS servers, and standard secondary DNS servers. Zones can be used not only to delegate administrative authority but also to "group" resource records to facilitate query resolution. Recall that a zone can include one or more DNS domains or portions of a DNS domain.

Within a zone you will always have one standard primary DNS server, which will have authority over that zone. You may also implement one or more secondary DNS servers for the zone, which will host the secondary zone database. You create the secondary zone the same way you create a primary zone—by launching the Configure DNS Server Wizard in the DNS administration tool (if this is the first zone you are creating) or by launching the New Zone Wizard (if this is an additional zone) and then selecting Standard Secondary Zone on the Zone Type page, as shown in Figure 1-3.

When you create the secondary DNS zone, you are prompted to designate a primary (or *master*) DNS server from which to obtain the primary zone database, as shown in Figure 1-4. When you designate the master DNS server, the master DNS server sends a copy of its zone database to the secondary DNS server, creating the secondary zone database. Any given secondary DNS server can host additional secondary zones. To do this, you simply need to add additional master DNS servers to the list and place the servers in the order in which you want the primary zones to be replicated.

Because the secondary DNS server maintains a copy of the primary zone's database, that DNS server can also respond to queries from computers that reside within that zone. Furthermore, any modifications or updates made to the primary DNS server are periodically replicated to the secondary DNS server so that DNS servers in either the primary or secondary zones can be used to resolve names to IP addresses.

Setting this all up requires a certain amount of planning, hardware and software installation to support the structure, and a fair amount of ongoing maintenance. Within a Windows 2000 Active Directory domain hierarchy, the DNS

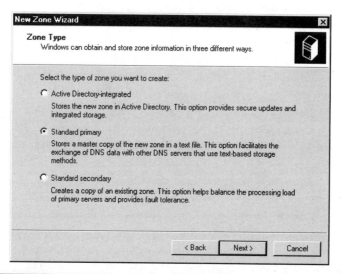

FIGURE 1-3   The Zone Type page of the New Zone Wizard

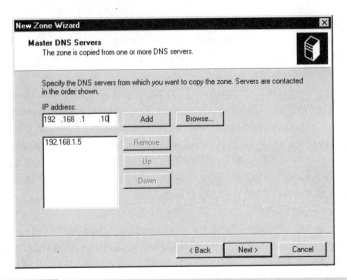

FIGURE 1-4   The Master DNS Servers page of the New Zone Wizard

structure is integral to the successful, efficient, and effective use of Active Directory. If any DNS server goes "down," you want to have enough redundancy (secondary zones and servers) to continue to service user and computer requests for resources. As you saw earlier in this chapter, if the user cannot locate a Windows 2000 domain controller, that user will not be able to log on to the network.

Having multiple DNS servers in play ensures that there is redundancy for servicing user and computer requests for resources. Nevertheless, if the primary DNS server becomes unavailable for whatever reason, the secondary zones cannot be updated and changes to the DNS namespace may not be recorded. In other words, the primary DNS server represents a single point of failure.

One of the many benefits of Active Directory is that every domain controller in the domain acts as a "primary" domain controller. All the domain controllers maintain a copy of the Active Directory, and all can accept changes and updates to the Active Directory. All the domain controllers periodically replicate their Active Directory changes to all the other domain controllers in the domain in what is called a *multimaster model*. Therefore, no single point of failure exists for Active Directory.

It seems logical, then, to take advantage of this benefit and let Active Directory also host the DNS zone databases. This is, of course, the fourth type of zone mentioned earlier in this chapter—the Active Directory integrated zone. DNS servers that are Windows 2000 domain controllers can have their zones configured to Active Directory integrated zones.

Another benefit of the Active Directory integrated zone is the ability to perform standard zone transfers from the Active Directory integrated zone to DNS servers that are not configured as domain controllers. These servers can nevertheless still function as secondary DNS servers within the Active Directory environment or within a mixed domain environment.

Exam Tip

An Active Directory integrated zone cannot be replicated to other Windows 2000 domains because the Active Directory itself is replicated only to domain controllers within the same domain. If you need to extend an Active Directory integrated zone to include other Windows 2000 domains, you will need to create at least one secondary DNS server in the other domain to host the secondary zone.

Local Lingo

Mixed domain   A mixed domain environment is one in which not all domain controllers have been upgraded to Windows 2000 Active Directory domains. Some domains may, for various reasons, still be running Windows NT 4.0.

Assuming that the DNS server is running on a Windows 2000 domain controller and meets the prerequisites for Active Directory (support for SRV resource records and the dynamic update protocol), you can create a new Active Directory integrated zone by initiating the New Zone Wizard and selecting Active Directory Integrated on the Zone Type page. Alternatively, you can convert an existing zone to an Active Directory integrated zone by opening the Properties dialog box for the zone you want to convert, selecting Change on the General tab to display the Change Zone Type dialog box, and choosing Active Directory Integrated, as shown in Figure 1-5. When the zone is converted to an Active Directory integrated zone, the old primary zone is deleted from the DNS server and copied into Active Directory.

Windows 2000 DNS servers can be secondary DNS servers for Windows NT 4.0 primary DNS servers, and vice versa. If you are migrating from Windows NT 4.0 DNS to Windows 2000 DNS and want to retain the current zone information, you can install and configure a new Windows 2000 server as a secondary DNS server to the Windows NT 4.0 DNS server. After the Windows NT 4.0 DNS server transfers its zone database to the Windows 2000 DNS server, you can configure the Windows 2000 DNS server to become the primary DNS server and the Windows NT 4.0 DNS server to become the secondary DNS server. You can then take advantage of the benefits of Active Directory integrated zones.

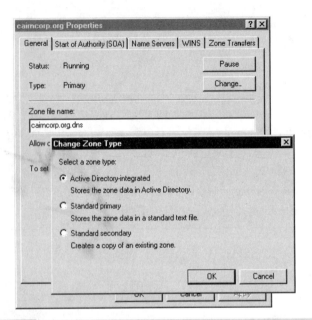

Exam Tip

The zone type option Active Directory Integrated is not available on the Change Zone Type dialog box on the DNS server unless Active Directory has been implemented on the server.

 **Objective 1.03**

Configure Zones for Dynamic Updates and Secure Dynamic Updates

As you'll recall, one of the DNS components strongly recommended by Microsoft for Active Directory is support for the dynamic update protocol, which allows Windows 2000 clients to automatically register and update their A resource records with DNS servers, but not their PTR records. Non-Windows 2000 clients cannot interact with the dynamic update protocol at all. However, Windows 2000 DHCP servers can be configured to interact with the dynamic update protocol to accommodate automatic registration and updating of Windows 2000 PTR records and non-Windows 2000 client records.

In addition, dynamic updates can be made secure so that the DNS server only accepts new registrations from client computers that have an account in Active Directory and only accepts updates from the computer that initially registered the resource records. Update records must first be encrypted by the Windows 2000 client, using IPSec (IP Security protocol) and/or the DHCP server before the DNS server will accept them.

Secure dynamic updates provide two key benefits:

- Zone records can be protected from unauthorized modifications.
- Authorization of updates can be assigned to specific users and groups.

Enabling Dynamic Updates

As you have seen, dynamic updates, although not strictly required to implement Active Directory, nevertheless are strongly recommended by Microsoft. There are three actions to perform when enabling dynamic update protocol:

- Configure the DNS servzer to allow dynamic updates
- Configure the DHCP server to perform dynamic updates
- Configure the clients to perform dynamic updates

Configuring the DNS server to allow dynamic updates is relatively straightforward. In the DNS administration tool, you must open the Properties dialog box for the zone you want to configure and select Yes in the Allow Dynamic Updates list box, as shown here.

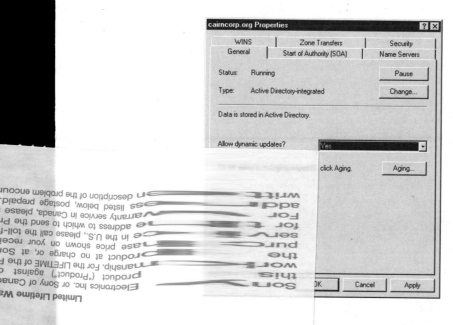

Exam Tip

The zone type does not have to be Active Directory integrated in order to enable dynamic updates.

A DHCP server can be configured to perform dynamic updates in order to register and update PTR records for Windows 2000 clients, to register and update both A and PTR records for all clients, and to register and update both A and PTR records for non-Windows 2000 clients.

Again, configuration of DHCP for dynamic updates is relatively easy. Using the DHCP administration tool in the Administrative Tools program group, you must open the Properties dialog box for the server you want to configure. On the DNS tab, select the option Automatically Update DHCP Client Requests (enabled by default) and then choose the option or options that are appropriate. The three main choices are Update DNS Only If DHCP Client Requests (enabled by default), which will cause DHCP to register the PTR record for a Windows 2000 client if the client is so configured; Always Update DNS, which will cause DHCP to register the A and PTR records regardless of how the Windows 2000 client is configured; Enable Updates for DNS Clients That Do Not Support Dynamic Update, which causes DHCP to register the A and PTR records for non-Windows 2000 clients.

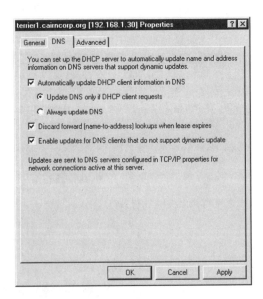

Exam Tip

A DHCP server that has been authorized in Active Directory is set to use dynamic updates by default. The options Automatically Update DHCP Client Information In DNS and Update DNS Only If DHCP Client Requests are both selected

---

Windows 2000 clients are configured to use dynamic updates by default. If you want to modify these options, you must open the Properties dialog box for the Networking and Dial-up Connection you want to configure, select Internet Protocol, and then select Properties. In the advanced settings on the DNS tab, you need to select one of two options: Register This Connection's Addresses in DNS, which causes the client to register the A record using the full computer name and IP address of the connection, or Use This Connection's DNS Suffix in DNS Registration, which causes the client to register the A record using the first label of the computer name plus the DNS suffix for the connection if the DNS suffix is different from the DNS domain name. The client settings can be seen here.

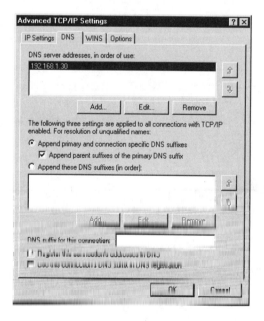

Enabling Secure Dynamic Updates

Once again, configuring the DNS server to accept only secure dynamic updates is relatively straightforward. In the DNS administration tool, you must open the Properties dialog box for the zone that you want to configure and select the option Only Secure Updates in the Allow Dynamic Updates list box, as shown here:

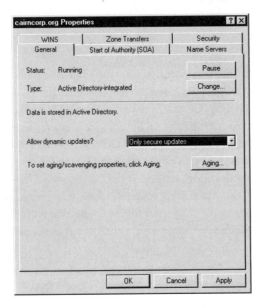

Exam Tip

In this case, the zone type zmust be Active Directory integrated in order for the Only Secure Updates option to be available.

CHECKPOINT

✔ **Objective 1.01: Install and Configure DNS for Active Directory** DNS is a distributed database system that uses a hierarchically structured name-space to provide name resolution in an IP network. The namespace is organized using domains, subdomains, and zones and is identical to the namespace used by Active Directory.

You can configure three types of zones: standard primary (or *forward lookup*) zones, which map a computer's name to its IP address and are required for Active Directory; standard secondary zones, which maintain a copy of the primary zone and are used for load-balancing name resolution requests; and reverse lookup zones, which map a computer's IP address to its computer name.

✔ **Objective 1.02: Integrate Active Directory DNS Zones with Existing DNS Infrastructure**   Active Directory integrated zones maintain the DNS zone information in Active Directory, thus eliminating any one single point of failure and providing fault tolerance, because the Active Directory is periodically replicated to all domain controllers within the Active Directory domain, simplifying administration and allowing for secure dynamic updates to resource records. Active Directory integrated zones cannot be replicated to other Windows 2000 domains.

Active Directory requires that the DNS server support SRV records, dynamic updates, and optionally incremental zone transfers. Active Directory uses DNS records not only for name resolution but also to find domain controllers that perform network functions, such as authentication and location of resources through a global catalog.

DNS does not have to be installed on a Windows 2000 domain controller. However, if it is not, it cannot take advantage of Active Directory integrated zones. Nevertheless, it can function as a secondary zone server for an Active Directory integrated zone. This allows you to extend the Active Directory integrated zone to include other domains.

✔ **Objective 1.03: Configure Zones for Dynamic Updates and Secure Dynamic Updates**   Dynamic updates allow Windows 2000 clients to regis-ter their A resource records and updates with the DNS server to minimize administration of those records. DHCP servers can use dynamic updates to register PTR records for Windows 2000 clients as well as A and PTR records for non-Windows 2000 clients. Configuration of dynamic updates occurs on the DNS server, the DHCP server, and on the Windows 2000 clients, if necessary, because Windows 2000 clients are configured to use dynamic updates by default. Dynamic updates to a DNS zone do not require that the zone be an Active Directory integrated zone.

Secure dynamic updates provide an extra level of protection for Active Directory integrated zones. Only authorized users and groups can perform updates, and updates from clients and DHCP servers are encrypted when using IPSec.

Travel Assistance

For Microsoft's take on DNS for Active Directory, or if you feel that you need
more instruction, refer to these sections in the following Microsoft Certified
Classes: Module 3, MOC 2153, "Implementing a Microsoft Windows 2000
Network Infrastructure," and Module 2, MOC 2154, "Implementing
and Administering Microsoft Windows 2000 Directory Services."
Also, read Chapters 1 and 3 in the "Distributed Systems" book in
the Microsoft Windows 2000 Resource Kit.

REVIEW QUESTIONS

1. Your organization is migrating from an Windows NT 4.0 network environment to a Windows 2000 environment. One Windows NT 4.0 server is hosting a primary DNS zone, and you would like to retain its zone information.
   You intend to implement Active Directory in the near future. What steps do
   you need to perform for DNS to retain your current zone information and
   prepare for Active Directory?

   A. Do nothing.
   B. Upgrade the Windows NT 4.0 DNS server with the Windows 2000 DNS
   service.
   C. Install a Windows 2000 server, configuring the DNS server as a secondary
   server to the Windows NT 4.0 DNS server. After the zone transfer com-
   pletes, make the Windows 2000 DNS server the primary zone.
   D. Install the Active Directory client for Windows NT 4.0 on the Windows
   NT 4.0 DNS server.

2. You are the DNS administrator for xyz.com. Your organization's DNS namespace includes a sales division named sales.xyz.com and an IT division
   named it.xyz.com. Each has its own zone and DNS server. The DNS namespace is identical to the Active Directory namespace already implemented.
   The DNS server for it.xyz.com is installed on a Windows 2000 member
   server. You would like to delegate the administration of DNS for it.xyz.com
   to Jo, a network manager in the IT division. Jo is already a member of the
   Domain Users group for the it.xyz.com Windows 2000 domain. What else
   do you need to do to give Jo authority over the it.xzy.com DNS zone?

A. Do nothing.

B. Make Jo a member of the DNS Admins group.

C. Make Jo a member of the local Administrators group on the DNS server for it.xyz.com.

D. Create a group policy that delegates authority over the it.xyz.com DNS zone to Jo.

3. Which of the following are required before you can install Active Directory?

A. DNS must support SRV resource records.

B. DNS must support the dynamic update protocol.

C. DNS must support incremental zone transfers.

D. DNS must be installed on a Windows 2000 domain controller.

4. You have implemented DNS for your Active Directory domain on a Windows 2000 domain controller. You want to ensure that Windows 2000 clients register their A and PTR records with the DNS server and that the updates are encrypted and protected. You want Active Directory to host the DNS zone database. You decide to make the DNS zone an Active Directory integrated zone, and you enable dynamic updates on the DNS server itself. Which of the goals have you accomplished?

A. Do Windows 2000 clients register their A records.

B. Windows 2000 clients register their PTR records.

C. Record updates are encrypted and protected.

D. Active Directory hosts the DNS zone database.

5. You have decided to make all DNS zones in your Windows 2000 network Active Directory integrated zones. Which of the following is not true regarding Active Directory integrated zones?

A. Active Directory integrated zones eliminate a single point of failure for DNS.

B. All domain controllers within the Active Directory domain are primary zone servers.

C. The DNS topology is maintained within the DNS server.

D. An Active Directory integrated zone can include domain controllers from other domains.

6. You are the DNS administrator for a large global organization called xyz.com. You have implemented a DNS namespace for your organization, and for the

time being you have decided not to implement Active Directory integrated zones. You have also decided to create zones that map to your organization's regional locations: na.xyz.com (North America), as.xyz.com (Asia), eu.xyz.com (Europe), and sa.xyz.com (South America). Each of these DNS zones consist of subdomains in which users are located. You would like to facilitate DNS query resolution for your users throughout the organization as well as reduce the amount of WAN traffic generated and maintain redundancy. Which of the following actions will you take to accomplish this goal?

A. Create at least one secondary server for each zone.
B. Create multiple primary servers for each zone.
C. Place a secondary server on each local network.
D. Make the zones Active Directory integrated zones.

7. You are the DNS administrator for xyz.com. Your organization's DNS namespace includes a sales division named sales.xyz.com and an IT division named it.xyz.com. Each has its own zone and DNS server. All zones are Active Directory integrated zones. Because of a restructuring within your organization, you need to have the xyz.com zone include some computers in the it.xyz.com zone. Which of the following actions will you take?

A. Do nothing. The Active Directory integrated zone databases are automatically replicated to all domain controllers in all Active Directory domains.
B. Configure the Active Directory integrated zones so that they replicate between xyz.com and it.xyz.com.
C. Create a secondary DNS server for the xyz.com Active Directory integrated zone in the it.xyz.com domain.
D. Active Directory integrated zones cannot extend to include other Windows 2000 domains.

8. You have enabled your DNS server to use the dynamic update protocol. Although most of your clients are running Windows 2000 Professional, some clients are still running Windows NT Workstation and Windows 98. Which DNS resource records will be registered by default if you do nothing else?

A. A resource records for all clients
B. A and PTR resource records for all clients
C. A resource records for Windows 2000 clients only
D. A and PTR resource records for Windows 2000 clients only
E. No resource records for any clients

9. You are the DNS administrator for your organization. Your DNS namespace consists of three primary DNS zones, corresponding to each of three Active Directory domains. All your DNS servers are running on Windows 2000 domain controllers, and you have enabled them to accept dynamic updates. A Windows 2000 DHCP server has been configured to register PTR records for Windows 2000 clients. You want to ensure that all updates made to the DNS server dynamically are encrypted and protected. What two actions must you take?

   A. Modify the zones to be Active Directory integrated zones.
   B. Enable the Only Secure Updates option for the DNS zone.
   C. Enable DHCP to only send secure updates.
   D. Enable the Send Secure Updates option on all Windows 2000 clients.

10. You are the DNS administrator for xyz.com. Your organization's DNS namespace includes a zone for the sales department, a zone for the IT department, and a subzone for sales called accounts. A server named ACCT1 resides in the accounts domain. What is its FQDN?

   A. acct1.xyz.com
   B. acct1.sales.xyz.com
   C. acct.accounts.xyz.com
   D. acct1.accounts.sales.xyz.com
   E. acct1@accounts.sales.xyz.com

REVIEW ANSWERS

1. **C** is correct because a Windows 2000 DNS server can be a secondary server to a Windows NT 4.0 DNS server. After the zone transfer takes place, you essentially reverse the roles of the two. This gives you a Windows 2000 primary DNS server that is compatible for Active Directory. A is incorrect because the Windows NT 4.0 version of DNS server will not support Active Directory just as it is. You would need to upgrade the NT server to Windows 2000 and then install Windows 2000 DNS. B is incorrect because the Windows 2000 DNS service can only be installed on a Windows 2000 server. D is incorrect because the Active Directory client will only enable the Windows NT 4.0 server to be able to take advantage of some Active Directory features, such as the application of group policy. The client will not affect the installation of DNS nor make it compatible for Active Directory.

2. **C** If the DNS server is not installed on a Windows 2000 domain controller, you must be a member of the local Administrators group on that server to administer DNS. If DNS was installed on a Windows 2000 domain controller, then A, B, and C would be correct because you must be a member of the DNS Admins, the Domain Admins, or the Enterprise Admins group to administer DNS in this circumstance.

3. **A** and **B** Active Directory requires that your installation of DNS support SRV resource records because it uses SRV records to find domain controllers that perform specific functions for the Windows 2000 domain. Also, DNS supports dynamic updates to the zone database from Windows 2000 clients and from DHCP. C is incorrect because although Active Directory prefers that the DNS server support incremental zone transfers, this is only an optional requirement. D is also incorrect. DNS can be installed on any Windows 2000 member server or domain controller.

4. **A** Enabling dynamic updates on the DNS server allows it to accept A records from Windows 2000 clients, which register these records by default. B is incorrect. Windows 2000 clients do not register their PTR records by default, even with dynamic updates enabled on the DNS server. You must additionally configure a DHCP server to register the PTR records for the Windows 2000 clients. C is incorrect. Dynamic updates alone do not encrypt and protect updates to the DNS zone. You must enable secure dynamic updates. Making the zone an Active Directory integrated zone makes the Secure Dynamic Updates option available but does not enable it automatically. D is correct. Making the zone an Active Directory integrated zone moves the zone database into Active Directory and deletes it from the DNS server.

5. **C** and **D** When you make a zone an Active Directory integrated zone, it becomes part of Active Directory and is maintained there. It is deleted from the DNS server. Also, because Active Directory is replicated only to domain controllers within the domain, the Active Directory integrated zone cannot include domain controllers from other domains. A and B are incorrect in this case. All domain controllers within the domain do become primary zone servers for the Active Directory integrated zone. As a result, the zone database is replicated to all domain controllers within the Active Directory domain when Active Directory itself is replicated. Therefore, you do eliminate the single point of failure associated with a regular DNS structure.

6. **A** and **C** Creating a secondary server does provide for redundancy because the primary server replicates and maintains a copy of the zone at each of its designated secondary servers. Also, placing a secondary server on each local network will help to reduce the amount of network traffic generated across the WAN as well as potentially decreasing response time for users' DNS queries. B is incorrect because each zone can have only one primary server. Although making the zone Active Directory integrated may accomplish some or all of these goals, you don't have enough information in the question. D is also incorrect because, according to the question, you have already decided not to implement Active Directory integrated zones at this time.

7. **C** If you need to extend an Active Directory integrated zone to include other Windows 200 domains, you need to create at least one secondary DNS server in the other domain to host the secondary zone. A and B are incorrect because Active Directory integrated zones cannot extend to include other Windows 2000 domains (Active Directory itself is only replicated to domain controllers within the same domain). They cannot be configured to replicate across domains. D, although a correct statement, is an incorrect answer for this question for the same reason given for C.

8. **C** is correct; D is incorrect because Windows 2000 computers register only their A resource records, and this option is enabled by default. However, you can configure a Windows 2000 DHCP server to register PTR records for Windows 2000 computers. A and B are incorrect because Windows NT and Windows 98 clients cannot register any DNS records automatically. However, you can configure a Windows 2000 DHCP server to register A and PTR records for these clients with the DNS server. E is obviously incorrect.

9. **A** and **B** Secure dynamic updates are configured through DNS, but the DNS zone must be an Active Directory integrated zone before that option is made available for selection. C is incorrect because secure updates are configured through DNS, not through DHCP. Enabling secure updates in DNS will cause DHCP to send updates encrypted. D is incorrect, again, because secure updates are configured through DNS, not at the Windows 2000 client. Enabling secure updates in DNS will cause Windows 2000 clients to send updates encrypted and ensure that new registrations will come only from clients that have accounts in Active Directory.

10. **D** can be the only correct answer. An object's FQDN, or fully qualified domain name, represents its location in the DNS namespace. The FQDN begins with the computer's name, and its location in the namespace is appended with a dot to its name. In this case, the computer named ACCT1 is located in the accounts domain (zone), which is itself a member of the sales zone, which is, in turn, a member of xyz.com. ACCT1's FQDN then must be acct1.accounts.sales.xyz.com. E actually represents an e-mail address rather than a FQDN and is therefore incorrect. A, B, and C are incorrect.

Maintaining DNS

	NEWBIE	SOME EXPERIENCE	EXPERT
ETA	4 hours	3 hours	2 hours

Create and Configure DNS Records

As you learned in Chapter 1, resource records are used by DNS to resolve client queries for the locations of other computers. Chapter 1 introduced you to three record types that are of particular importance for Active Directory: the A resource record, the PTR (reverse lookup pointer) resource record, and the SRV (service locator) resource record. These three can be dynamically updated in Windows 2000. However, you can create several other kinds of records to configure the DNS server or to assist with the name-resolution process. Table 2-1 defines the most common of these.

TABLE 2.1   Common Resource Record Types for DNS

Record Type	Description
CNAME (alias or canonical name)	Specifies another name by which a computer can be known so that you can use more than one name to refer to a single computer. For example, the computer acct1.xyz.com may, among other things, host your company's Internet Web site. Outside users generally don't know the specific computer name that hosts a Web site. Users typically type **www.xyz.com** to reach a Web site. In this case, a CNAME record can be created that maps "www" as an alternate way to refer to acct1.xyz.com.
MX (mail exchanger)	Specifies the server that receives e-mail messages. E-mail applications use this record to find the e-mail server associated with a user's e-mail address (that is, the "xyz.com" in user@xyz.com).
NS (name server)	Specifies a server that is authoritative for a zone or contains the zone file for the domain.

(Continued)

TABLE 2.1	CONTINUED
Record Type	**Description**
SOA (start of authority)	The first resource record created for a new zone that specifies which DNS server is authoritative for the zone. It also specifies how updates and zone transfers occur and how long information is maintained.

These records generally are maintained by you, the DNS administrator. They are not dynamically updated like the A, PTR, and SRV records are in Windows 2000. You can add these records to a zone through the DNS administration tool by right-clicking the zone and choosing the option Other New Records. You can then select the record from the list and provide the appropriate record information.

> **Exam Tip**
>
> Be sure that you understand how the dynamic update process works and how each of these records is registered. A and **PTR** records and the dynamic update process are discussed in Chapter 1. SRV records are discussed next in this chapter.

SVR Records

In Windows 2000 networks, SRV records are used by clients to locate servers that can perform specific network-related tasks, such as authenticating users when they log on, supplying users with security credentials or keys, and searching Active Directory for object information (such as the location of a printer). SRV records map a service to the corresponding server's computer name, as registered in the server's A record. Windows 2000 domain controllers dynamically register their SRV records with the DNS server.

Here is an example of an SRV record. Table 2-2 provides a brief description of each record field.

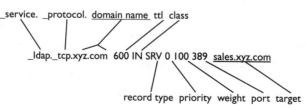

TABLE 2.2	SRV Field Definitions
SRV Field	**Description**
_service	Name of the service provided by the server, such as _LDAP, _GP, or _Kerberos.
_protocol	Indicates the protocol transport type (generally TCP or UDP).
domain name	DNS in which the server providing the service resides.
ttl	Indicates the time to live value for the record.
class	Standard DNS resource class (generally "IN").
priority	Number used to indicate the priority of the server relative to other servers providing the same service. Clients choose the server with the lowest priority.
weight	Number used to place this server's importance for providing this service among other servers providing the same service. Clients choose SRV records with higher weights.
port	Port number the server uses to "listen" for the service.
target	FQDN of the computer providing the service.

Figure 2-1 shows the properties of an SRV record viewed through the DNS administration tool.

In Windows 2000 networks, LDAP servers and global catalog servers do not have to be Windows 2000 domain controllers, and their records will look similar to the earlier example. However, Windows 2000 domain controllers register additional SRV records unique to their role within Active Directory. Two additional fields are added after the _protocol field: DcType and _msdcs.

The DcType field indicates whether the server is a domain controller, indicated by the value "dc", or a global catalog server, indicated by the value "gc". The _msdcs flag is a suffix specific to Microsoft that allows clients to locate Windows 2000 domain controllers that perform specific functions in Active Directory. For example, the following record would indicate that the server is a Windows 2000 domain controller functioning as a global catalog server:

```
_ldap._tcp.gc._msdcs.xyz.com
```

_ldap Properties   ? ✕

Service Location (SRV) | Security |

Domain: dc._msdcs.cairncorp.org

Service: _ldap

Protocol: _tcp

Priority: 0

Weight: 100

Port number: 389

Host offering this service:

terrier1.cairncorp.org.

[OK   ]   [Cancel]   [Apply]

FIGURE 2-1   Example of an SRV record viewed through the DNS tool

---

Exam Tip

Windows 2000 servers are referred to by their SRV records as *LDAP*
(Lightweight Directory Access Protocol) servers because they run
the LDAP service, which is used to search for or modify objects in
Active Directory.

Objective 2.02   Manage, Monitor, and Troubleshoot DNS

This section of the test primarily concerns your familiarity and ability to work
with DNS support tools in order to maintain and troubleshoot DNS in your
Active Directory domain. Although not entirely necessary, a hands-on working
knowledge of the tools discussed in this section would be to your advantage.

Perhaps one of the foremost concerns of a network administrator is the
successful containment of network traffic and the aggressive management of

applications and servers that generate network traffic. DNS servers, by their very nature, generate network traffic. The primary function of a DNS server is to respond to client computers' requests for the location of network resources (this is known as *name resolution*). As you learned in the last chapter, Active Directory uses DNS to find domain controllers that perform specific functions, such as hosting the global catalog and authenticating users.

Managing DNS Network Traffic

Requesting information from a DNS server necessarily involves the generation of network traffic. Basically two kinds of queries can be generated for DNS: iterative and recursive.

An iterative query is one that is initiated at the client computer for the location of another computer or server. The DNS server searches its zone database for the information and returns the IP address of the requested computer or server back to the client. If the DNS server does not have the requested computer in its zone database, it gives the client the address of a DNS server that might be able to respond to the request. This server might be higher or lower in the DNS namespace. The client then sends the request to the other DNS server. If that DNS server can respond, it does; if it cannot respond, it might refer the client to yet another DNS server. The process continues until the client's request can or cannot be resolved.

Here is an example using Figure 2-2 in which a client in xyz.com needs to access the server acct1.sales.xyz.com:

1. The client begins by querying its DNS server in xyz.com.
2. The DNS server for xyz.com searches its zone database for the record acct1.sales.xyz.com.
3. The DNS server for xyz.com cannot find the record, but it does have a record for the zone sales.xyz.com. It sends the IP address for a DNS server in sales.xyz.com to the client.
4. The client sends its query to the DNS server in sales.xyz.com.
5. The DNS server for sales.xyz.com finds the records in its zone database and sends the IP address for acct1.sales.xyz.com to the client.

A recursive query, like an iterative query, is one that is initiated at the client computer for the location of another computer or server. The DNS server searches its zone database for the requested computer and responds back to the client's request with that computer's IP address. Unlike an iterative query, however, if the

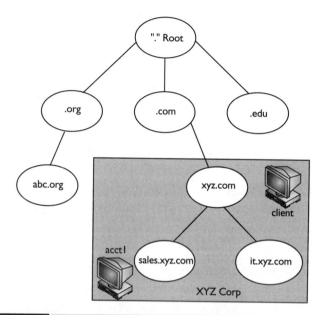

FIGURE 2-2   Sample DNS hierarchy

DNS server does not have the computer in its database, it may be configured to forward the request to another DNS server or servers using iterative queries. In this case, the DNS server does all the work on behalf of the client. Recursive queries are the more common type of query.

Here is an example using a recursive query rather than an iterative query from the client in which the client in xyz.com needs to access the server acct1.sales.xyz.com. Again, use Figure 2-2 as your guide as you follow along:

1. The client begins by querying its DNS server in xyz.com using a recursive query.
2. The DNS server for xyz.com searches its zone database for the record acct1. sales.xyz.com. If it cannot find a matching record, it will look for a record for a DNS server in sales.xyz.com.
3. The DNS server for xyz.com sends an iterative query to the authoritative DNS server for the sales.xyz.com zone.
4. The DNS server for sales.xyz.com finds the record in its database and sends the IP address for acct1.sales.xyz.com to the DNS server for xyz.com.
5. The first DNS server, in turn, sends the information to the client that originated the request. The DNS server then caches the request based on a TTL value.

All in all, this may not sound like all that much traffic. However, in a large organization, this traffic begins to grow proportionally to the number of users and resources in the network—especially depending on the location of the clients and the DNS servers.

Local Lingo

Bandwidth Network traffic is also referred to by the term *bandwidth*. Bandwidth actually refers to the amount of traffic that a network infrastructure can reasonably handle. For example, a 10BaseT network can accommodate up to 10Mbps of network traffic. Fast Ethernet networks can accommodate up to ten times as much traffic as 10BaseT networks. Consequently, the same application (DNS, for example) generating the same amount of traffic on both types of networks can be perceived to be running more "slowly" on a 10BaseT network than a Fast Ethernet network because there is less bandwidth—or space on the wire, if you will—on a 10BaseT network.

Here is a more complicated example involving a wider search. Again, referring to Figure 2-2, suppose that a user in xyz.com needs to access the Internet site www.abc.org:

1. The user types **www.abc.org** in their Internet browser screen.
2. The client will generate a recursive query to its DNS server in xyz.com.
3. If the DNS server for xyz.com cannot find a record for abc.org in its zone database or its cache, it sends an iterative query to a DNS server that is authoritative for the root domain.
4. The DNS server for the root likewise cannot locate a matching record, so it sends the IP addresses of servers that are authoritative for the org domain back to the DNS server for xyz.com.
5. The DNS server for xyz.com sends an iterative query to a server that is authoritative for the org domain.
6. If the DNS server for the org domain cannot find a record for www.abc.org in its database, it sends the IP address for a DNS server that is authoritative for abc.org back to the DNS server for xyz.com.
7. The DNS server for xyz.com sends an iterative request to a DNS server for abc.org.

8. The DNS server for abc.org finds a matching record in its zone database and returns the IP address for www.abc.org to the DNS server for xyz.com.

9. The DNS server for xyz.com sends the IP address back to the client that originated the query in the first place and then caches the request based on its TTL value.

Using Secondary DNS Servers

One way to manage the amount of network traffic that is generated by the DNS name-resolution process is to place DNS servers "close" to the users who need to use them. This was first mentioned in Chapter 1. You could install secondary DNS servers on the users' local networks. These DNS servers would host a secondary zone for the DNS zone database that the users would be most likely to query. This action has the effect of reducing the amount of potential WAN traffic that might be generated by localizing DNS queries to the local network. In addition, this action can reduce the amount of response time experienced by the users.

Exam Tip

Microsoft is fond of presenting scenarios that include references to minimizing or optimizing network traffic or bandwidth utilization. Be sure to read these questions carefully, especially if goals and solutions are presented. Also, be sure to study any diagram that might be presented to see what types of servers (such as DNS servers) could affect network traffic or bandwidth utilization.

Using Caching-Only Servers

Another way to reduce and manage DNS network traffic generated by client queries is to implement caching-only servers, as shown in Figure 2-3. Caching-only servers are DNS servers that do not host a zone database. Rather, they perform name resolution on behalf of a client by sending recursive queries to an authoritative DNS server and then caching the responses before sending a reply to the client. When a caching-only server receives a name resolution request from a client, it first checks its cached names. If it finds a match, it sends the information back to the client, and no other DNS traffic is generated.

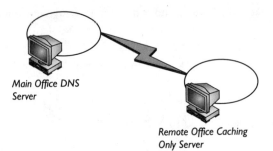

Main Office DNS
Server

Remote Office Caching
Only Server

FIGURE 2-3   Example of the placement of a caching-only server

Caching-only servers are particularly useful for remote offices connected to a main office by a slower WAN link. Because such a server caches the most frequently requested names and does not generate any zone transfers, it only needs to utilize the WAN connection to send recursive requests to resolve names not found in its cache.

Local Lingo

WAN   WAN stands for *wide area network*. Like a local area network, or *LAN*, the WAN also has a given amount of bandwidth available to handle all the traffic that needs to flow across the WAN connection. Slow WANs typically are considered to have a speed of 512 Kbps or less. Fast WANs, such as T1 or T3 lines, are considered to have high-speed connection links. The less bandwidth you have, the more significant it becomes to optimize the traffic that needs to use that connection.

You configure a caching-only server by installing DNS on any Windows 2000 server. However, you will not configure any forward or reverse lookup zones. Instead, you will configure your server to another caching-only server, your designated authoritative DNS server, or your ISP DNS server. The authoritative DNS server is called the *forwarder*. These two steps, in effect, make the server into a caching-only server.

You configure forwarders through the DNS administration tool. On the Properties dialog box for the caching-only server, select the Forwarders tab and then select the Enable Forwarders check box, as shown in Figure 2-4. Enter the IP address of the server that you will forward requests to and then click OK.

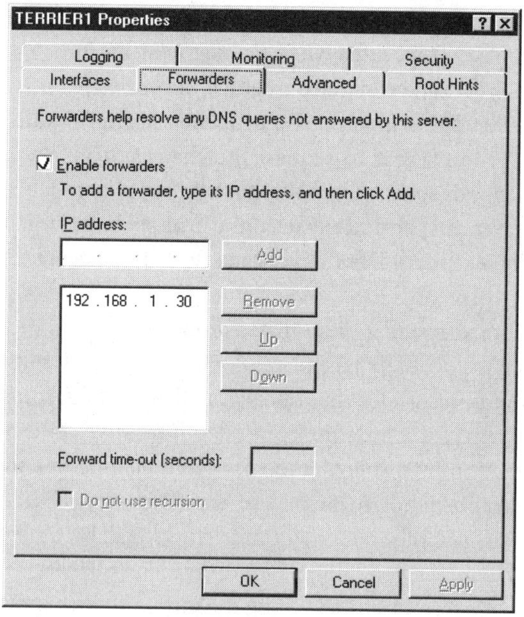

FIGURE 2-4   Enabling a forwarder for a caching-only server

Exam Tip

Forwarders can also be configured on DNS servers that host a zone. In effect, you are designating a specific DNS server that you will forward requests to in the event that the first DNS server cannot resolve the query. This is another way to manage network traffic between DNS servers.

Managing Zone Transfers

A third way to manage DNS traffic is through the effective implementation and scheduling of zone transfers. Zone transfers take place between primary and secondary DNS servers within a domain and occur whenever "name to IP address" mappings change or records are created or deleted within the primary zone database file.

Recall from Chapter 1 that Windows 2000 Active Directory recommends that DNS servers support incremental zone transfers (IXFR). An incremental zone transfer only replicates record information that has changed in the primary zone file. If the DNS servers do not support incremental zone transfer (IXFR), the entire zone database is replicated when a zone transfer is initiated.

The zone transfer can be initiated by either the primary DNS server or the secondary DNS server. The primary server can send a change notification to the secondary server, prompting it to request the changes from the primary server. Pending the receipt of such a notification from the primary DNS server, the secondary DNS server can periodically "ask" the primary server for any changes that it may have. The secondary DNS server can also request changes based solely the "start of authority" records.

You can modify several zone transfer properties to gain more control over how and when zone transfers take place. Zone transfer information is contained in the SOA resource record for the zone. Recall that the SOA record identifies the domain or domains for which the zone is authoritative. You can modify zone transfer information by displaying the Properties dialog box for the zone and selecting the Start of Authority (SOA) and Zone Transfers tabs.

Figure 2-5 displays the Start of Authority (SOA) tab for a zone. Most of these fields are self-evident, but you can get a more detailed explanation using the online help available with Windows 2000. Only the more significant of these fields are discussed here.

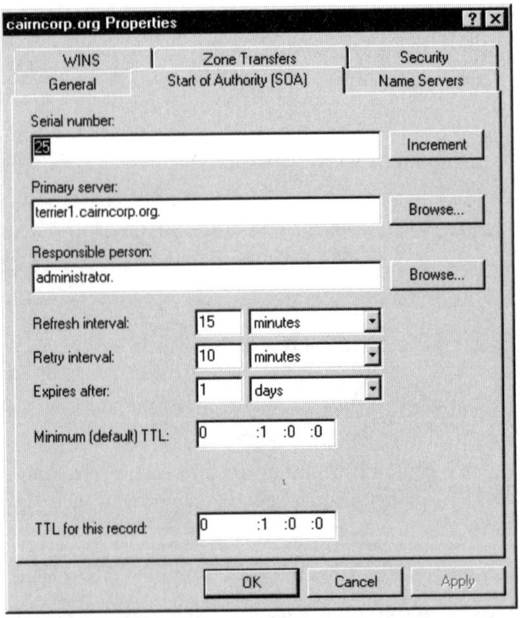

FIGURE 2-5   Start of Authority tab

The Serial Number field is used to assign a number increment to database modifications. When a change occurs, the serial number is updated. A secondary DNS server uses the serial number to determine whether its copy of the zone database needs to be updated. If the number has changed, the secondary server initiates a zone transfer.

Travel Advisory

You can force a zone transfer to take place by increasing the serial number increment for the zone.

The Primary Server field identifies the FQDN of the primary DNS server. The Refresh Interval fields specify the frequency at which the secondary server checks with the primary server to see whether the changes have occurred (that is, whether the serial number has changed). If the zone database does not change frequently, you can consider increasing this value to decrease network traffic. This is the most likely field you will modify when optimizing zone transfer traffic.

The Expires After fields specify how long the secondary server will continue to respond to client queries if the primary server becomes unavailable for zone transfers for whatever reason. At the end of this interval, the secondary server considers its zone database to be outdated, and it stops responding to client queries. If you experience long network outages or congested WAN connections and your zone database remains fairly static, you might consider increasing this value to ensure that clients can continue to resolve names.

The Minimum TTL field represents the minimum length of time that zone information can be cached on the secondary server. If network names do not change frequently, you could increase this value to improve performance.

Figure 2-6 displays the Zone Transfers tab for a zone. The options in this tab allow you to secure zone transfer information by designated which DNS servers are authorized to receive zone transfers from the primary DNS server.

Three main options can be found here:

- **To any server**   Zone transfers can be sent to any secondary DNS server (default).
- **Only to servers listed on the Name Servers tab**   The Name Servers tab displays a list of all the servers that are in the same domain as the primary zone. Selecting this option means that secondary servers in subdomains will not receive zone transfers.

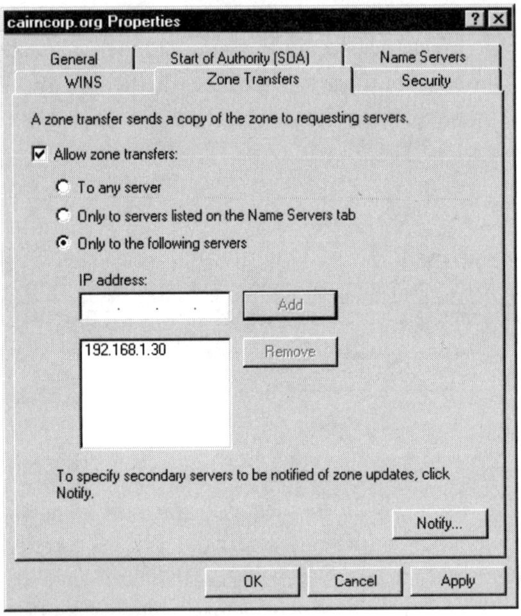

cairncorp.org Properties   ? ✕

| General | Start of Authority (SOA) | Name Servers |
| WINS | Zone Transfers | Security |

A zone transfer sends a copy of the zone to requesting servers.

☑ Allow zone transfers:

   ○ To any server

   ○ Only to servers listed on the Name Servers tab

   ◉ Only to the following servers

     IP address:

     [.   .   .   ]   [Add]

     [192.168.1.30]   [Remove]

To specify secondary servers to be notified of zone updates, click
Notify.

                     [Notify...]

     [OK]   [Cancel]   [Apply]

FIGURE 2-6   Options on the Zone Transfers tab

- **Only to the following servers**   You supply the IP addresses of the
  servers that should receive zone transfers.

Earlier in this chapter, you read that a primary DNS server can initiate a zone
transfer by notifying a secondary server that a change has taken place. You identify which, if any, secondary DNS servers should initiated a zone transfer by receiving a notification from the primary DNS server by creating a notify list. You do
this by clicking the Notify button shown in Figure 2-6 and entering the IP
addresses of the secondary servers that should be notified.

Monitoring and Troubleshooting DNS

Because the purpose of a DNS server is to respond to client queries to locate computers on the network, your main concern as a DNS administrator is to determine
whether the DNS server is performing its query resolution tasks successfully. There
are three main actions you can take to check the integrity of your DNS server:

- Test the query-resolution process
- Monitor DNS events
- Enable logging

You can monitor the query-resolution process through the DNS administration tool by performing two query tests: simple and recursive. A simple query test uses the DNS resolver (client) on the server to make a local iterative query to find the DNS server that is on the same computer. A recursive query test generates a recursive query to another DNS server. You can perform these tests manually as needed, or you can choose to schedule them to recur at a designated interval.

To configure simple and recursive query tests, you need to open the Properties dialog box for the DNS server you are going to test. On the Monitoring tab, in the section Tests Performed, you can select the simple query option or the recursive query option (or both) and then click the Test Now button. Test results appear in the Test Results frame on this tab, as shown in Figure 2-7. The results show the time each query was performed and whether it was successful.

Notice in Figure 2-7 that you can choose to schedule the tests to recur periodically by enabling the Perform Automatic Testing at the Following Interval option and then designating an interval.

Like all other Windows 2000 services, the DNS service reports elements of its activity to the Windows 2000 Event logs, which can be viewed using the Event Viewer tool. Several types of logs can be viewed through the Event Viewer. The

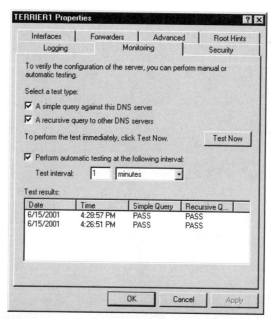

FIGURE 2-7 Query test options on the Monitoring tab

main logs are the Service, Application, and Security logs. However, other logs are added as you install additional services on the Windows 2000 server. The DNS service's Event log, created when you install the DNS service, is the most useful. This is where DNS service errors and other DNS events are commonly reported. If there is a problem with the DNS server, such as the error event shown in Figure 2-8, it will be reported here. Common errors could include the inability to perform a zone transfer to a secondary server or an incorrectly formatted resource record that caused a query to fail.

Travel Advisory

You should already be familiar with the administrative tools provided with Windows 2000 Server, which include the Event Viewer. In all its exams, Microsoft expects your understanding of these tools to be a given. If you are not comfortable with these tools, stop reading now and take some time to familiarize yourself with how they are used and what they can do for you.

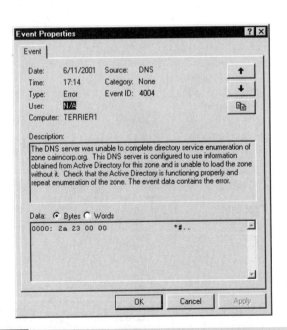

FIGURE 2-8   Sample DNS service Event log error message

You might find DNS entries in other logs as well. Figure 2-9 shows an error generated by the Net Logon service and recorded in the system's Event log. In this case, the message clearly shows that records cannot be registered because dynamic updates have not been enabled on the DNS server.

If you are having a particularly tricky problem with your DNS server on which query tests and/or the Event Viewer are not shedding any light, you could choose to enable detailed logging of DNS events through the DNS administration tool. As you know, monitoring and recording events in this manner can use a lot of system resources and affect your server's overall performance, and DNS logging is no different. Nevertheless, for advanced troubleshooting purposes, it can be a very useful tool to help identify and rectify a DNS problem. DNS logging is not enabled by default and should not be confused with the DNS service events recorded in Event Viewer.

In the Properties dialog box for the DNS server you want to monitor, select the Logging tab. Then select the DNS events you want to monitor, as shown in Figure 2-10. As the events take place, the DNS server will write its logging data to the file dns.log, which can be found in the *systemroot*\system32\dns folder on the server. Table 2-3 explains the various logging options.

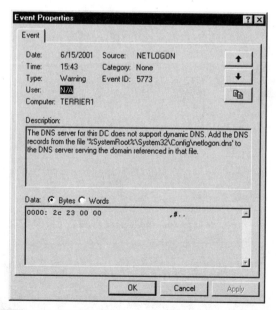

FIGURE 2-9   Sample server Event log message relating to DNS

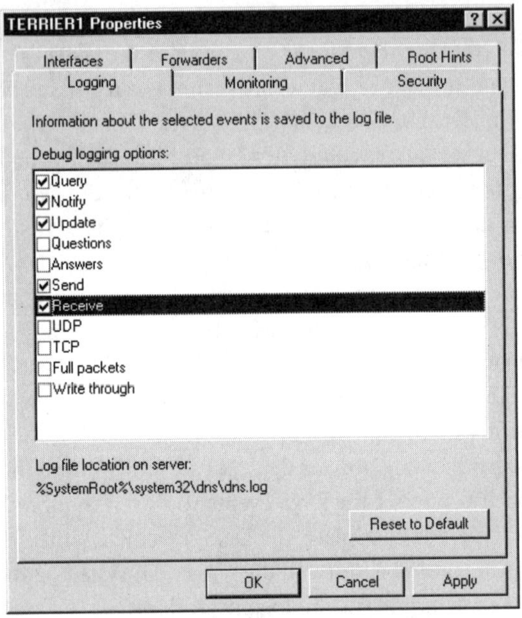

FIGURE 2-10   Logging options for DNS server

TABLE 2.3   DNS Logging Options

Log Option	Description
Query	Records queries received by the DNS server from clients
Notify	Records notification messages received by the DNS server from other servers
Update	Records dynamic updates received by the DNS Server service from other computers
Questions	Records the contents of the question section for each DNS query message processed by the DNS server

(Continued)

TABLE 2.3 CONTINUED	
Log Option	**Description**
Answers	Records the contents of the answer section for each DNS query message processed by the DNS server
Send	Records the number of DNS query messages sent by the DNS server
Receive	Records the number of DNS query messages received by the DNS server
UDP	Records the number of DNS requests received over a UDP port
TCP	Records the number of DNS requests received over a TCP port
Full packets	Logs the number of full packets written and sent by the DNS server
Write through	Logs the number of packets written back to the zone by the DNS server

Troubleshooting Using Command-Line Functions

Two very useful command-line functions are available to help you troubleshoot name-resolution issues in DNS: Nslookup and Ipconfig.

The **nslookup** command is used to verify the integrity of resource records and can be entered with a set of parameters either in a Windows 2000 command prompt window or as part of a batch file to return a specific piece of data. Here is the basic syntax of the **nslookup** command:

```
nslookup <-option> <computername_or_IP_address> <-server>
```

Table 2-4 explains each parameter.

TABLE 2.4   Nslookup Parameters

Parameter	Explanation
-option	One or more **nslookup** commands that you would like to perform as part of this task. Commands include ls, which lists information about a domain, and set type, which lets you specify the information query type (NS, SOA, and so on). A complete list of commands can be displayed by typing **nslookup?**.
computername_or_IP_address	The name or IP address of the computer you are trying to find. Entering an IP address returns the computer name. Entering the computer name returns the IP address. Entering the computer name without a trailing period assumes you are searching the default DNS domain. Entering the computer name with a trailing period finds a computer outside the default DNS domain.
-server	Designates which DNS server you want to search. By default, it is the DNS server that is specified in the TCP/IP configuration of Network Properties.

Nslookup can also be run in interactive mode in a Windows 2000 command prompt window to allow you to obtain multiple pieces of data. Simply type **nslookup** at the command prompt and then press ENTER. You can then enter **nslookup** commands as you need to and type **exit** when you are done. For example, typing the command **ls -t a sales.xyz.com** displays a list of all the A resource records in the domain sales.xyz.com.

Exam Tip

You can use Nslookup to help troubleshoot zone transfer problems by using the command **set type=soa**. This command displays the start of authority record information for a DNS server, which includes the current zone serial number. You can compare serial numbers of each DNS server that should receive zone transfers to determine whether a server is receiving updates from the primary DNS server.

Travel Advisory

When Nslookup runs, it first performs a reverse lookup using the IP address of the DNS server. If a PTR record does not exist for the DNS server, Nslookup will generate an error and may not return correct information.

Sometimes the problem with resolving names in DNS lies not with the DNS server but rather with the client computers themselves. Windows 2000 adds two parameters to the **ipconfig** command that can help you to troubleshoot name resolution on client computers: **/flushdns** and **/registerdns**.

When a client computer resolves a name from a DNS server, it caches that name locally and uses this information for future queries. Obviously, this is more efficient and generates less network traffic. However, it could happen that the information for a record contained in the client's cache has changed on the DNS server. This can result in the client incorrectly resolving a query involving that record. If you think that might be the problem on a client, you can empty and reset the cache on the client computer by typing the command **ipconfig /flushdns** at a command prompt on the client.

Windows 2000 clients use dynamic updates to register their A records with a DNS server. If you find that a client's DNS records are missing or incorrectly registered, you can force the client to reregister itself by typing the command **ipconfig /registerdns** at a command prompt on the client. This command will also cause the client to renew its DHCP address information as well. Consequently, if DHCP is used to dynamically update the Windows 2000 PTR records, this command will cause those records to be updated as well.

CHECKPOINT

✔ **Objective 2.01: Create and Configure DNS Records**   Although A, PTR, and SRV resource records are significant for supporting Active Directory and can be dynamically registered and updated, there are other resource records that can be used to make the name-resolution process more efficient and practical. The CNAME record, for example, is used to provide alternate names by which a computer can be referred to, such as ftp and www.

When Windows 2000 domain controllers register their SRV records, they include two additional fields that flag them as Windows 2000 domain controllers. The DCType field identifies the server as a domain controller (dc) or global catalog server (gc), and the _msdcs field identifies the server as a domain controller for Active Directory functions.

Exam Tip

To register or update SRV records for a Windows 2000 server, stop and restart the Net Logon service.

✔ **Objective 2.02: Manage, Monitor, and Troubleshoot DNS**   Iterative and recursive queries generated by DNS clients to a DNS server or from one DNS server to another generate network traffic. One way to manage this traffic is to place DNS servers on the same local network as the users who need to query these servers.

Another way to manage DNS network traffic is to implement caching-only servers in remote locations. A caching-only server sends recursive lookup queries to a designated DNS server on behalf of the clients and caches the result. When it receives future client queries, it checks the cached results first to keep the traffic local before making a recursive query across a WAN connection to another DNS server.

Zone transfers also generate traffic between a primary DNS server and secondary DNS servers. However, you can control how and when zone transfers occur to help manage the traffic that is generated. For example, you can specify how often the secondary servers check for zone updates from the primary.

DNS servers can be monitored for performance and errors by running simple or recursive test queries, checking the DNS server and other Event logs in the Event Viewer, and by turning on detailed DNS server logging, when required, for advanced troubleshooting.

The **nslookup** and **ipconfig** commands offer a way to obtain information from a DNS server and troubleshoot potential client issues through the command prompt.

Travel Assistance

For Microsoft's take on DNS for Active Directory, or if you feel you need more instruction, refer to these sections in the following Microsoft Certified Classes: Module 3, MOC 2153, "Implementing a Microsoft Windows 2000 Network Infrastructure" and Module 2, MOC 2154, "Implementing and Administering Microsoft Windows 2000 Directory Services," Also, read Chapters 1 and 3 in the Distributed Systems book in the Microsoft Windows 2000 Resource Kit. For detailed technical information about DNS for Windows 2000, read the Microsoft whitepaper titled "Windows 2000 DNS," which can be found at Microsoft's Windows 2000 Web site: www.Microsoft.com\windows2000.

REVIEW QUESTIONS

1. You are the DNS administrator for xyz.com. The company's CIO has implemented a Microsoft IIS server to host XYZ Corp's Internet Web site. The IIS server name is xyzsrv1.xyz.com. The CIO wants the general public to access XYZ's Web site by typing www.xyz.com. The IIS server is a Windows 2000 domain controller. What do you need to do to facilitate the CIO's request?

   A. Do nothing. When you install IIS on a Windows 2000 domain controller, it automatically registers the server name with the A record alias WWW.

   B. Do nothing. When you install IIS on a Windows 2000 domain controller, it automatically registers the server name with the CNAME record alias WWW.

C. Do nothing. When you install IIS on a Windows 2000 domain controller, it automatically registers an SRV service record for the IIS server with the host name WWW.

D. Create a CNAME record that maps WWW to the host name xyzsrv1. xyz.com.

2. You have installed DNS on a Windows 2000 domain controller and created an Active Directory integrated domain. You have also enabled the DNS servers to accept dynamic updates from clients. All your clients are Windows 2000 DHCP clients. A proprietary application in your company uses IP address lookups to the DNS server to resolve computer names that are displayed in its interface to the user. Will the DNS lookups work as expected?

A. Yes. Windows 2000 clients register their A records and their PTR records.

B. Yes, but only for Windows 2000 servers that register their SRV records.

C. Yes, but only if the DNS server has a PTR record for itself.

D. Yes, but only if DHCP is configured to register the Windows 2000 clients' PTR records.

3. When viewing the SRV records for a DNS zone, you find the following record: _ldap._tcp.dc._msdcs.(Server Name).xyz.com. What is correct interpretation of that record?

A. This is a Windows 2000 member server in xyz.com.

B. This is a Windows 2000 global catalog server for the forest root domain xyz.com.

C. This is a Windows 2000 domain controller for the domain xyz.com.

D. This is a Windows 2000 domain controller for the domain msdcs. xyz.com.

4. You are the DNS administrator for xyz.com. Your users are located in various domains in different regions of the country, some of which are in remote locations connected by slow WAN links. Clients need to be able to locate servers anywhere in the organization. You would like to generate as little network traffic as possible, especially across the WAN links. Which two of the following actions will facilitate your goal?

A. Implement caching-only servers in the remote locations.

B. Implement secondary DNS servers on the local networks within each region.

C. Use iterative queries from the clients.

D. Make each zone an Active Directory integrated zone.

5. As the DNS and network administrator for an organization that consists of several regional office connected by WAN links of varying speeds and reliability, you have already implemented a DNS structure consisting of three DNS zones, each with a primary DNS server and several secondary DNS servers. To control the flow of DNS lookup requests, you would like certain DNS servers to direct lookup requests to a specifically designated DNS server when they cannot resolve these requests. How can you accomplish this goal?

   A. Enable caching-only on the secondary DNS servers.

   B. Configure the SOA record to designate which secondary servers should initiate a zone transfer.

   C. Configure forwarding on the DNS servers in question, designating the desired DNS server as the forwarder.

   D. You can only control how caching-only servers forward lookup requests.

6. While monitoring several DNS servers in xyz.com to ensure that their zone information is up to date, you notice that one secondary DNS server has seemed to cease responding to client requests. You think that the zone information on that DNS server has not been updated from the primary DNS server. Which of the following commands can help you determine whether the secondary zone is out of sync with the primary?

   A. Use the Nslookup command **set type=SOA** to display the serial number of the zone and compare it with the current serial number of the primary zone.

   B. Use the Nslookup command **ls -t a xyz.com** to display the serial number of the zone and compare it with the current serial number of the primary zone.

   C. Use the command **ipconfig /flushdns** to display the DNS zone information on the DNS server.

   D. Use the command **ipconfig /registerdns** to force the DNS server to resync with the primary DNS server.

7. You have implemented a DNS hierarchy and have left the zone transfer configured with default values. After monitoring your DNS servers for some time, you determine that zone updates do not have to take place as frequently as configured. You would like zone transfers to take place when a change occurs to the primary zone but also at least once each day. Which steps do you need to take to accomplish your goal? (Select all that apply.)

A. Modify the SOA Refresh Interval property for the zone so that its interval reflects once each day.

B. Modify the SOA Minimum TTL property for the zone so that its interval reflects once each day.

C. Modify the Zone Transfers transfer options for the zone to replicate only to servers on the Name Servers tab.

D. Modify the Zone Transfers Notify list for the zone to identify the servers that should be notified of changes.

8. As you monitor your DNS servers, you begin to see a pattern of failed lookup requests emerging among some of your DNS servers when requests are forwarded between servers. The problem appears to be intermittent. Which of the following two actions will help you to more closely monitor the lookup process?

A. Enable the DNS servers to perform simple recursive tests.

B. Enable the DNS servers to perform recursive tests.

C. Periodically perform the query test and review the results.

D. Schedule the test to perform periodically over time and view the results.

9. You are the DNS administrator for xyz.com. Your users are located in various domains in different regions of the country. Most enjoy high-speed access across the WAN, but some are in remote locations connected by slow WAN links. Your optimization goals are to minimize DNS network traffic generated from clients, minimize performance impact on DNS servers, track DNS server events in a detailed log, and optimize traffic across slow WAN links. You decide to place secondary DNS servers in all user locations and enable DNS logging events. Which of your goals have you accomplished?

A. Minimize DNS network traffic generated from clients.

B. Minimize performance impact on DNS servers.

C. Track DNS server events in a detailed log.

D. Optimize traffic across slow WAN links.

10. As you monitor your DNS servers, you find that some of your Windows 2000 client A and PTR records are missing. You have checked your dynamic update configurations and see that they are configured correctly. What action can you take on the Windows 2000 clients to fix the problem?

A. Reinstall the DNS client on the Windows 2000 clients.

B. Issue the command **ipconfig /flushdns** on the Windows 2000 clients.

C. Issue the command **ipconfig /registerdns** on the Windows 2000 clients.

D. Issue the command **nslookup -registerdns** on the Windows 2000 clients.

REVIEW ANSWERS

1. **D** You need to create a CNAME record that maps the desired alias—in this case, WWW—to the server's computer name. A is incorrect because although Windows 2000 domain controllers do register their A records, they register them with the actual computer name of the server—in this case, xyzsrv1.xyz.com—not with an alias. B is incorrect because the only records that a Windows 2000 domain controller will register is the A and SRV records. C is incorrect because although Windows 2000 domain controllers do register SRV records, they map a service to the server's computer name—in this case, xyzsrv1.xyz.com—not an alias.

2. **D** is correct because the only way to have Windows 2000 clients' PTR records registered dynamically is through DHCP. In order for a reverse lookup of an IP address for a computer name to work, a PTR record must be created for the computers that need to be located in this way. A is incorrect because Windows 2000 clients register only their A records by default. DHCP must be configured to register the Windows 2000 clients' PTR records using dynamic update. B is incorrect because SRV records have nothing to do with reverse lookups. C is incorrect because although a lookup for the DNS server name would work, any other lookup would fail if PTR records are not registered for the other clients.

3. **C** is correct because the fields "dc." and "_msdcs" (which indicate the server to be a Windows 2000 domain controller). A is incorrect because of the presence of the _msdcs field, which is present only in SRV records registered by Windows 2000 domain controllers. B is incorrect because of the presence of the field "dc." (which indicates a domain controller). If this were a global catalog server, the field would have been "gc." instead. D is incorrect because "msdcs" refers to the server being a Windows 2000 domain controller and is not part of the domain name.

4. **A** and **B** Caching-only servers send lookups to designated DNS servers on behalf of the clients and then cache the results locally to minimize requests outside the local network. Secondary DNS servers function similarly, but they maintain a copy of the zone database and periodically receive updates to the zone database from a primary DNS server. Because this update process can be controlled as well, this is a good way to keep network traffic under control. C is incorrect because iterative queries cause the client to do more of the lookup work than the DNS server; therefore, the client generates more traffic. D is incorrect because no where does the question mention that the network is a Windows 2000 network. Tricky, yes, but this

is representative of how key words—or the lack of them—can change the answer to a question.

5. **C** Any DNS server, other than the root domain, can be configured with a forwarder. For the same reason, D is incorrect. A is incorrect because caching-only servers cannot be configured on current DNS servers. They can have no forward or reverse lookup zones. B is close but still incorrect. Although this would control how and when zone transfers take place, it would really not designate a specific server to which lookups should be directed.

6. **A** is the correct command syntax to display SOA record information, including the serial number of the zone. B is incorrect. This command syntax returns the list of A records for the zone. C is incorrect. This is a command performed on a client computer to delete cached DNS information that may be causing lookup errors. D is incorrect. This is a command performed on a client to reregister its A record with the DNS server.

7. **A** and **D** The Refresh Interval reflects the frequency with which secondary servers check with the primary server to see whether there are any updates. You want secondary servers to check at least once a day for changes. The Zone Transfer Notify list specifies a list of secondary servers that the primary server should contact when a change takes place. This accomplishes the other goal—to let transfers take place when changes occur. B is incorrect because the TTL value represents the minimum length of time that zone information can be cached on the secondary server. Although you might want to increase this value, it does not relate specifically to your stated goals. C is incorrect because the Name Servers list only specifies which servers should receive updates, not which server should perform them or be notified of changes.

8. **D** is correct because the problem is intermittent, and you can schedule the tests to run periodically for you and then review the results later. The idea here is to identify which server is failing to send recursive lookups to other DNS servers. A is incorrect because simple query tests perform a local iterative query to see whether the DNS server itself is responding to requests. B is correct because a recursive test queries another DNS server to see whether a query can be resolved. C is incorrect because the problem is intermittent, and you probably do not want to sit at your DNS server and manually perform a test every few minutes.

9. **A** is correct because placing secondary servers on the same local network as the users is a recommended way to reduce DNS traffic. C is correct because enabling logging does generate detailed tracking of DNS events. However, enabling logging also puts a greater stress on server resources, thus impacting the DNS server to a greater degree, which, by the way, makes B incorrect. D is incorrect because although placing secondary servers in all user locations minimizes traffic from clients, this will not have the same effect of optimizing traffic over the slow WAN links that placing a caching-only server would.

10. **C** is correct because the **/registerdns** switch causes the client to release and renew its IP address and reregister its A records. If DHCP is configured to dynamically register PTR records, the **release/renew** action will cause PTR records to be reregistered as well. A is incorrect. There is no DNS client to install or deinstall. DNS settings are part of the IP address settings configured on the client or assigned through DHCP. B is incorrect because the **/flushdns** switch causes the client simply to delete its local DNS lookup cache in the event that lookups are receiving incorrect responses due to old information in the cache. D is incorrect because there is no such command switch for Nslookup.

Installing and Configuring Active Directory

Installing
Active Directory

CHAPTER 3

	NEWBIE	SOME EXPERIENCE	EXPERT
ETA	5 hours	4 hours	2 hours

In Part I, you studied the role that DNS plays in the Windows 2000 Active Directory infrastructure. You learned how to install and configure DNS for Active Directory, including the enabling of dynamic updates and the configuration of server resource records, as well as how to maintain and troubleshoot DNS servers.

Part II visits the process of installing and configuring Active Directory for your Windows 2000 network and is divided into two chapters. This chapter focuses on the installation process, including how to verify and troubleshoot that process. This chapter also distinguishes among forests, trees, and domains. It introduces organizational units and talks about how to implement a basic organizational structure.

Install Forests, Trees, and Domains

Objective 3.01

Before we discuss the installation process, you should have a good understanding of what Active Directory is all about. Several terms may be new to you, or at least new as they are applied within an Active Directory environment. For example, you will be implementing forests, creating trees and domains, structuring using organizational units, and optimizing communications using sites and links. Therefore, an overview of Active Directory is in order.

Active Directory Overview

Active Directory is a Windows 2000 network service that facilitates the location of network resources for users and applications. Network resources are stored as objects in Active Directory and are grouped by class. Classes of objects include computers, users, servers, and printers. Each class is defined by a consistent set of attributes, such as name, description, location, access permissions, and so on. The classes and their attributes are known as the *Active Directory schema*. Key principles of the Active Directory schema include the following:

- Attributes are defined once for consistency and can be used across object classes.
- End-user applications can access the schema for objects and attributes.
- The schema is extensible and can be dynamically updated.
- Objects can be secured through the use of discretionary access control lists (DACLs).
- There can be only one schema per forest.

Besides providing an easy means to find network resources, Active Directory promotes centralized management of network resources and integration with other network services. Particular to this discussion, Active Directory integrates support for Dynamic Host Configuration Protocol (DHCP), DNS (as discussed in Part I), Lightweight Directory Access Protocol (LDAP), and Kerberos V5 security server services. Clients needing to use one or more of these network services can use Active Directory to locate servers that provide the requested service.

Local Lingo

Lightweight Directory Access Protocol (LDAP)   LDAP is a communication protocol that is used by users and applications to find objects in Active Directory. It identifies an object by its relative distinguished name. In Chapter 1, you were introduced to the term *fully qualified domain name* (FQDN), which refers to the object's full DNS name. In Active Directory, an object's full name is referred to as its *distinguished name* (DN). An object's relative distinguished name is the portion of its DN that identifies the object in question. For example, the relative distinguished name of the computer whose FQDN is acct1.sales.north.xyz.com would be "acct1". The relative distinguished name of the OU whose FQDN is sales.north.xyz.com would be "sales".

Recall from Part I that Active Directory requires at least one DNS server to be installed before you install Active Directory. Furthermore, the DNS server must support server resource (SRV) records, and it is also highly recommended that it support dynamic updates. With those two features in place, Windows 2000 servers can then register themselves and the network services they provide in the DNS database. The DNS database, in turn, can be Active Directory integrated. Subsequently, clients can easily find servers that provide specific network services. Indeed, Active Directory uses DNS for three main purposes:

- Name resolution, by mapping computer names to their IP addresses
- Namespace structure, by using the same naming conventions for the Active Directory domain structure that DNS uses
- Locating servers hosting network services

In addition to DNS configured with support for SRV records, there are other prerequisites that must be met before you can install Active Directory. Active Directory requires the following:

- Windows 2000 Server, Advanced Server, or Datacenter Server installed
- No less than 200MB of disk space for the Active Directory database and 50MB for the transaction log files (Microsoft recommends 1GB)
- A disk partition formatted with NTFS (version 5)
- Dynamic updates (recommended)

Additional benefits that come with the implementation of Active Directory include the ability to group objects such as users, groups, and other network resources that have similar administrative requirements or security needs into container objects known as *organizational units* (OUs). Furthermore, administrators can use group and security policies to control how resources are accessed within the domain, define how users' desktops should be organized, and which applications should be made available or installed on computers.

Active Directory Structure

There are four main elements that compose the logical structure of Active Directory: forests, trees, domains, and organizational units. All four are very specifically defined in the Active Directory schema and serve specific purposes within the structure. A forest consists of one or more trees. Trees consists of one or more domains. Domains consist of one or more organizational units.

> **Exam Tip**
>
> Spend some time understanding the nuances of forests, trees, domains, and organizational units. These are the basic building blocks of Active Directory around which all other Active Directory concepts, such as group policy implementation, revolve. A strong understanding of these elements will ease your study for the harder concepts.

A forest, then, is the highest element of the structure. The first domain created in Active Directory is called the *forest root*. In Figure 3-1, xyz.com is the first domain created in Active Directory and is therefore the forest root. Domains created beneath the forest root share the same contiguous namespace—the name of the domain is combined with that of its parent, as you see with north.xyz.com and

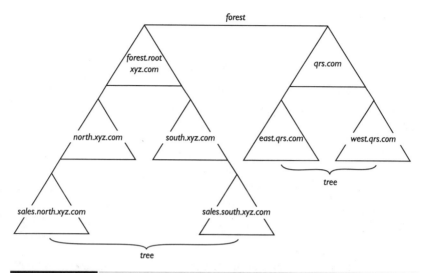

FIGURE 3-1   Example of a forest, trees, and domains

sales.north.xyz.com as well as south.xyz.com and sales.south.xyz.com. The domains that share the same contiguous namespace are known as *trees*.

A forest can have more than one tree. However, each subsequent tree will begin its own namespace. In Figure 3-1, qrs.com is a second tree in the xyz.com forest and has two domains that share its namespace: east.qrs.com and west.qrs.com.

The domain is the main defining element of the Active Directory structure. Each domain defines a centrally managed group of computers, users, and groups that share a common Active Directory database. All domain controllers within a domain maintain a copy of the directory for that domain and replicate changes to each other within the boundaries of the domain. Security—for example, administrative control—is also defined within the boundaries of the domain.

Objects within a domain are often further organized into OUs. OUs simply extend the logical hierarchy of Active Directory to better meet your organization's management needs. For example, you might model your OU structure on the departmental or regional structure of your company or on the administrative needs of the organization.

All Windows 2000 domains within a tree enjoy the benefits of two-way transitive trust relationships. As you should recall from Windows NT domain environments, a *trust relationship* is a security relationship between two domains that defines how network resources in one domain may be accessed by users in another domain. The "how" in the previous statement, of course, refers to the security applied to those objects as assigned to users. A two-way transitive trust also exists by default between trees in a forest.

> **Local Lingo**
>
> **Active Directory**   Active Directory supports two types of domain modes: mixed mode and native mode. Mixed-mode domains are those that consist of Windows 2000 domain controllers as well as Windows NT domain controllers. Native-mode domains consist solely of Windows 2000 domain controllers. The main difference between the modes has to do with functionality. All the features and functionality of Active Directory are available in native-mode domains, whereas only a subset of features is available in mixed mode. These differences will be made manifest throughout this and subsequent chapters.

Because these are two-way, transitive trusts, it is easy for users in domain sales.north.xyz.com in Figure 3-1 to be given permission to use and access resources in sales.south.xyz.com.

Active Directory Installation

Installing Active Directory actually involves promoting a member server running Windows 2000 Server, Windows 2000 Advanced Server, or Windows 2000 Datacenter Server to be a domain controller. In fact, a Windows 2000 server cannot become a domain controller without Active Directory also being installed.

You can promote a Windows 2000 server to be a domain controller and thus initiate the installation of Active Directory by typing the command **dcpromo.exe** in the Start/Run command box and pressing ENTER. The **dcpromo** command launches the Active Directory Installation Wizard, which lets you install a domain controller in several configurations:

- First domain controller in a new forest
- First domain controller for a new domain tree in a forest
- Domain controller for a new child domain of an existing domain
- Additional domain controller for an existing domain

The first choice you have to make, as shown in Figure 3-2, is whether this computer will be a domain controller for a new domain or an additional domain controller for an existing domain. Choose the Domain Controller for a New Domain option if you are creating a new forest, a new domain tree in the forest, or a child domain for an existing domain in the forest. Choose the Additional Domain Controller for an Existing Domain option if you are adding another

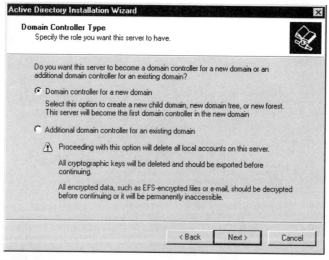

FIGURE 3-2   The Active Directory Installation Wizard's Domain Controller
Type dialog box

domain controller to an existing domain. The choice you make here affects which setup dialog boxes will be subsequently displayed.

In all cases, when you complete the Active Directory Installation Wizard, the Windows 2000 server is converted to the domain controller role, Active Directory is installed on it, the database and support file paths are modified per your choices in the wizard, and the Active Directory administrative consoles (Microsoft Management Console snap-ins) are added to the Administrative Tools program group on the new domain controller. Start by creating the first domain in a new forest.

First Domain Controller in a New Forest

After you select the Domain Controller for a New Domain option on the Domain Controller Type dialog box, the Create Tree or Child Domain dialog box is displayed (see Figure 3-3). Here you can choose to create a new domain tree or create a new child domain in an existing domain tree. Both options are fairly self-explanatory and are described in dialog box. Because you are creating the first domain controller for a new forest and no domain trees yet exist, you will select Create a New Domain Tree and click Next.

On the next dialog box, shown in Figure 3-4, you choose whether you will create a new forest of domain trees or place this domain tree in an existing forest. Because you are creating the first domain controller for a new forest, choose Create a New Forest of Domain Trees and click Next.

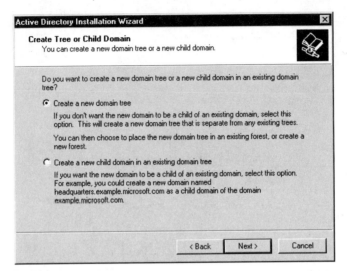

FIGURE 3-3   The Active Directory Installation Wizard's Create Tree or Child Domain dialog box

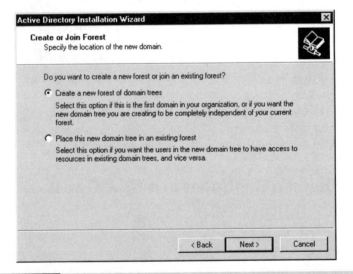

FIGURE 3-4   The Active Directory Installation Wizard's Create or Join Forest dialog box

Subsequent dialog boxes will ask you for additional information to guide and customize the installation. Required choices include the following:

- The DNS name you want to assign to the new domain as well as the user-friendly, NetBIOS name.
- The folder and path where you want to store the Active Directory database and log files. (The default is *systemroot*\NTDS.)
- The folder and path for the shared system volume where support files such as logon scripts and group policy information are stored. (The default is *systemroot*\sysvol.)
- Whether you need to support permissions that are compatible with earlier versions of Windows NT (mixed mode environments) or only with Windows 2000 servers (native mode environments).
- An administrative password when starting Active Directory in restore mode.

If you had not already implemented DNS, you will also be given the option to install and configure DNS as the setup wizard progresses.

Travel Advisory

As an optimization tip, Microsoft recommends placing the Active Directory database and transaction log files on different hard drives to improve overall server performance as well as Active Directory performance.

First Domain Controller for a New Domain Tree in a Forest

Recall that all the trees within a forest share a common Active Directory database schema, although not a contiguous namespace. In Figure 3-1, xzy.com and qrs.com represent two different trees in the same forest. Your reasons for creating one or more additional trees are likely to come from business or organizational decisions.

For example, if your company acquires another company, you may decide to retain that other company's identity within Active Directory by retaining its naming structure (or creating a naming structure for it) and adding it as a new tree in the existing forest of your company. As another example, suppose that your organization is multinational in scope and that each regional business unit maintains its own administrative control over its resources. Once again, you may decide that creating additional trees to represent each regional business unit serves to maintain the identity and administrative control of each business unit while still representing all as part of the same company "forest."

Exam Tip

These kinds of distinctions—when to create a new forest versus a new tree in a forest versus a child domain, and so on—pop up on the exams quite frequently in the form of scenario-based questions, similar to the examples presented in this section. The more comfortable you are with these distinctions, the more easily you will be able to grasp the focus of such a question.

As with the creation of the first domain controller in a new forest, you initiate the creation of a new tree in an existing forest by running the **dcpromo** command on the Windows 2000 server that will become the first domain controller for the new tree.

The first three dialog boxes that display after you launch the Active Directory Installation Wizard are the same as those displayed when you created the first domain controller in a new forest. You would select the option Domain Controller for a New Domain on the Domain Controller Type dialog box, as shown previously in Figure 3-2. You would select the option Create a New Domain Tree on the Create Tree or Child Domain dialog box, as displayed previously in Figure 3-3. However, at this point, the similarity ends. On the Create or Join a Forest dialog box, shown previously in Figure 3-4, you would choose the option Place This New Domain Tree in an Existing Forest.

The next dialog box, Network Credentials (shown in Figure 3-5), asks for the account name, password, and domain name of an account that has authority to create a new domain tree in an existing forest. This account must be a member of the Enterprise Admins group, whose membership is maintained in the forest root domain. You'll then need to supply the DNS name for the new tree, such as "qrs.com" in Figure 3-1.

Subsequent dialog boxes are the same and ask for the same information as those displayed during the creation of the first domain—that is, the DNS and NetBIOS name of the new domain controller, the location of the database and support files, mixed-mode or native-mode permissions support, and the Active Directory restore-mode administrative password.

Domain Controller for a New Child Domain of an Existing Domain

A more likely organizational scenario will involve the creation of one or more child domains of existing domains within a forest. In Figure 3-1, north.xyz.com and south.xyz.com are both child domains of the forest root domain xyz.com.

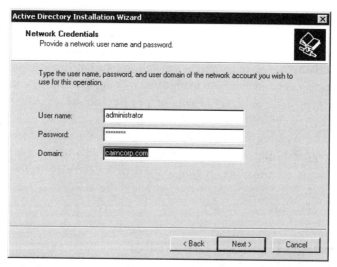

FIGURE 3-5   The Active Directory Installation Wizard's Network Credentials dialog box

Similarly, sales.north.xyz.com is a child of north.xyz.com and sales.south.xyz.com is a child of south.xyz.com.

You initiate the creation of a child domain of an existing domain by running the **dcpromo** command on the Windows 2000 server that will become the first domain controller for the new tree.

Exam Tip

In like fashion, as you see in Figure 3-1, east.qrs.com and west.qrs.com are both child domains of qrs.com, which is the first domain controller in a new tree in the forest whose root is xyz.com. Not too confusing, is it? It won't be if you study the relationships of each of the domain controller options presented in this chapter. Scenarios that use these types of relationships are guaranteed to show up on the exam.

This time, the first two dialog boxes that display after you launch the Active Directory Installation Wizard are the same as those displayed when you created the first domain controller in a new forest. You would select the option Domain Controller for a New Domain on the Domain Controller Type dialog box, as displayed previously in Figure 3-2. However, this time you would select the option Create a New Child Domain in an Existing Domain Tree on the Create Tree or Child Domain dialog box, shown previously in Figure 3-3.

Now the Network Credentials dialog box, shown previously in Figure 3-5, is displayed and prompts you to enter the account name, password, and domain name of an account that has authority to create a new domain tree in an existing forest. Recall that this account must be a member of the Enterprise Admins group whose membership is maintained in the forest root domain. The next dialog box will require you to supply the DNS name of the parent domain as well as the DNS name of the new child domain.

Subsequent dialog boxes are the same and ask for the same information as those displayed during the creation of the first domain—that is, the NetBIOS name of the new domain, the location of the database and support files, mixed-mode or native-mode permissions support, and the Active Directory restore-mode administrative password.

Additional Domain Controller for an Existing Domain

There are two main reasons why you would want to create one or more additional domain controllers for any given domain. The first reason is for fault tolerance purposes. A copy of the Active Directory database is maintained on each domain controller within the domain. Any domain controller can accept changes to the database and will replicate the changes to all other domain controllers. For this reason, if one domain controller becomes unavailable, your clients will still be able to log on, authenticate, and access objects through the remaining domain controller(s).

The other reason to create additional domain controllers is to provide load balancing for your clients. Having additional domain controllers ensures that no one domain controller will have to shoulder the entire load when servicing network requests for logon, authentication, and Active Directory queries.

The **dcpromo** command is used to create additional domain controllers for an existing domain. As you have seen, the dialog boxes that will be displayed when you launch the Active Directory Installation Wizard vary somewhat depending on the options you select. On the Domain Controller Type dialog box, shown previously in Figure 3-2, you would choose Additional Domain Controller for an Existing Domain as your option.

Instead of being asked whether you want to create a new tree or child domain, the next dialog boxes that display will ask first for the network credentials—account name, password, and domain name—of an account that has authority to create a domain controller in Active Directory and then for the name of the existing domain that this domain controller will join.

Subsequent dialog boxes are the same and ask for the same information as those displayed during the creation of the first domain—that is, the DNS and NetBIOS name of the new domain controller, the location of the database and support files, mixed-mode or native-mode permissions support, and the Active Directory restore-mode administrative password.

Travel Advisory

During the installation process, the domain controller's computer account gets moved from the computer's container to the domain controller's organizational unit in Active Directory.

Install Verification and Configuration Process

Throughout each step of the Active Directory Installation Wizard, your options and input are verified before the installation proceeds to the next step. If at any point a verification fails, you are presented with an error prompt so that you can correct the problem, as you see in the example in Figure 3-6. In all, six areas are verified as the installation process progresses.

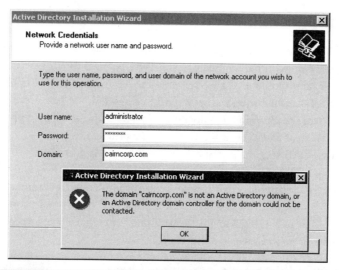

FIGURE 3-6   Example of an error generated during the Active Directory Installation Wizard

Preinstallation Requirement Verification

The first step occurs before the Active Directory Installation Wizard ever starts. Your credentials are verified to be appropriate to run the **dcpromo** command. In order to initiate the installation of Active Directory, the following must be true:

- You are logged on as a local administrator.
- Windows 2000 Server, Advanced Server, or Datacenter Server has been installed.
- A previous install of Active Directory is not waiting for a reboot of the server.
- A previous install or uninstall of Active Directory is not in progress.

If all four of these criteria are met, the wizard launches and proceeds to verify your input.

Server Name Verification

When you create a new domain controller, that server's name must be added to the Sites container in the Active Directory database. All server names, of course, must be unique, and the wizard verifies that the server name does not already exist in the database. If it does, the wizard assumes you are reinstalling Active Directory and removes the existing server from the Sites container.

IP Configuration Verification

The TCP/IP protocol is required for Active Directory domain controllers with an IP address supplied either manually (recommended) or through a DHCP assignment. A properly configured DNS server is also required but can be created during the installation process. The wizard verifies that IP has been properly configured for the server. If it has not been configured, the installation process will end with an error and a request to you to fix the problem.

If this is the first domain controller in a new forest or new domain, the wizard verifies that a DNS server is available that is authoritative for the domain and that supports dynamic updates. If it is not, you are prompted to create and configure such a DNS server during the installation process. If this domain controller is being added to an existing domain, the wizard assumes that a properly configured DNS server already exists.

DNS and NetBIOS Name Verification

As you proceed through the Active Directory Installation Wizard, you must supply a DNS name that is unique within the forest for a new domain as well as a unique

NetBIOS name for the domain that is derived from the first 15 characters of the common name of the FQDN for the domain. For example, if the domain name is northregionaccountingdom.xyz.com, its NetBIOS name would be "northregionacco". Obviously, you will want to choose your domain and NetBIOS names with some thought and common convention.

The Active Directory Installation Wizard verifies that these names are indeed unique within the forest. If either is not unique, the wizard will require that you change the name before you can continue with the installation.

Installation Permissions Verification

As you saw, when you create a new domain tree, a new child domain, or an additional domain controller for an existing domain, you are prompted to enter the user name, password, and domain name for a user who has permissions to create new domains or add a domain controller.

In practice, the Active Directory Installation Wizard first verifies whether the user performing the installation has the appropriate permissions to carry out the task—that is, whether the user has permissions to create new domains or add a domain controller. This is different from the verification that takes place when you first try to launch the wizard.

If the logged-on user does not have the appropriate level of permissions, he or she will be prompted to enter the network credentials of a user who does by supplying an account name, password, and domain for that user.

Exam Tip

A user must be a member of the Domain Admins group to add a domain controller to an existing domain or a member of the Enterprise Admins group to create a new domain tree or a child domain. Account verification, however, is not performed when the first domain controller is installed in a new forest because Active Directory security will not have yet been established in that case.

Path Verification

Finally, the Active Directory Installation Wizard verifies the paths that you entered for the Active Directory database file, log file, and Sysvol folder. You may alter the paths from their defaults, but whatever path you specify for the Sysvol folder must represent a partition formatted with NTFS. If the path you specify does not exist, the wizard will create it assuming there is enough free space available (see the Active Directory requirements earlier in this chapter). If the path does exist, the folder specified must be empty.

In addition to the verifications performed during the execution of the wizard, several post-installation operations take place to complete the conversion of the Windows 2000 server to the domain controller role and configure Active Directory. Any required Registry entries are created and configured, Active Directory–specific performance counters are implemented for use with the System Monitor, the Local Security Authority (LSA) is set with the domain controller role, the Active Directory administration consoles and other tools are added to the Administrative Tools program group, and the Kerberos v5 authentication protocol is loaded. Also, directory partitions that map to containers in the Active Directory are created and include the schema partition, the configuration partition for forest objects, and the domain partition for domain-specific objects, such as users, groups, and computers.

Recall that Active Directory domain controllers require that IP be properly installed and configured. That is because Active Directory is IP centric. It uses IP subnets to define the way domain controllers and domains interact for replication, authentication, and lookup purposes. Active Directory groups domain controllers by sites. Sites are defined by IP subnet addresses.

When you install the first domain controller for a new forest, that domain controller becomes a member of a default site that is defined by the IP subnet in which the domain controller resides. That default site name is Default-First-Site-Name (easy enough to remember). However, as you will see in the next chapter, it is possible, and often desirable, to create additional sites, for example, to control network traffic.

Exam Tip

Although this exam does not test you on your ability to address and subnet networks using the IP protocol, you do need to have more than a passing familiarity with how the IP protocol works and what is meant by "subnetting a network," because question scenarios will frequently include a diagram of a network's subnet structure. For example, a question might ask you to determine the number of sites to create to achieve a certain replication scheme given a particular subnet structure. If you can't decipher what the IP subnet structure looks like, that question is history for you.

If you have defined additizonal sites, the Active Directory Installation Wizard determines which site the domain controller should become a member of based on the IP subnet of that domain controller, and it creates a server object for that domain controller in the Site container for that site.

Six services are loaded and configured to start automatically when the server boots—the most prominent being the following three:

- **Net Logon**   Used to authenticate users and resource access and to dynamically register SRV records in DNS
- **Key Distribution Center (KDC)**   Maintains account information for security principals for Kerberos v5 authentication
- **Windows Time**   Synchronizes the computer system clocks among Windows 2000 clients and servers

Finally, the appropriate default client, user, and group accounts are created, default group policies and security policies are installed, and security passwords are set.

Removing Active Directory

No discussion of any product installation would be complete without also talking about how to get rid of it. As it happens, there may be scenarios in which you will need to remove Active Directory from a domain controller. For example, you might need to upgrade server hardware or reconfigure your domain structure because of a company reorganization or merger.

Removing Active Directory effectively demotes a domain controller to the role of member server or standalone server, and this is accomplished by running the **dcpromo** command once again. When Dcpromo starts, it detects that Active Directory is installed, prompts for your confirmation to remove it, and then proceeds. Basically, the uninstall process reverses everything the install process did. Active Directory tools are removed from the Administrative Tools program group, the Sysvol object and the Sysvol folder structure are removed, the database and transaction log files are removed, the SRV records are removed from DNS, the Local Security Authority (LSA) policy is updated to reflect that the server is no longer a domain controller but rather a member server or standalone server, and Active Directory–specific services are stopped and removed.

If you are demoting one domain controller among others in a domain, these changes are replicated to the other domain controllers and to any parent domains if they exist. If this is the last or only domain controller in the domain, the uninstall process will make sure no child domains exist (if they do, it will notify you of that fact so you can deal with the child domains first). It then replicates changes to a parent domain and updates—or removes—the Active Directory forest objects. You must specify when you run Dcpromo whether this is the last domain controller in the domain, as shown in Figure 3-7. As you can see in the figure, demoting the last domain controller removes all vestiges of Active Directory support for that domain, and the domain will no longer exist.

Travel Advisory

Demoting one domain controller among others effectively makes that domain controller a member server of the domain. Demoting the last domain controller in a domain effectively makes it a standalone server and a member of the default workgroup "Workgroup."

Exam Tip

If you are demoting one domain controller among other domain controllers, you must be a member of the Domain Admins group for that domain to perform the task. If the domain controller you are demoting is the last domain controller in that domain, you must be a member of the Domain Admins group for the domain or the Enterprise Admins group for the forest.

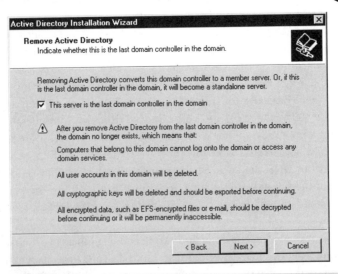

FIGURE 3-7   The Active Directory Installation Wizard's Remove Active Directory dialog box

Automate Domain Controller Installation

Objective 3.02

The promotion of a Windows 2000 server to the domain controller role along with the installation of Active Directory can be automated through the use of an answer file. An *answer file* is a text file that provides the option choices and other information that a setup program requires to successfully carry out its installation tasks to your specifications. In this case, the answer file you create supplies the option choices and other necessary information required by the Active Directory Installation Wizard launched by running the **dcpromo** command.

The typical answer file looks like and is organized very much like an INI file. It is divided into sections, each with one or more parameters listed with their accompanying values. These values map to the options, choices, and other data needed by the setup program to carry out its installation tasks.

The answer file that you would create for the **dcpromo** command will have only one section in it: [DCInstall]. Table 3-1 details those parameters used to perform the four types of domain controller installation, as described in the last section of this chapter.

TABLE 3.1 Dcpromo Answer File Parameter Descriptions

Parameter	Value	Installation Role
AutoConfigDNS	Yes/No	Specifies whether DNS should be installed as part of the domain controller installation if no valid DNS server is available.
CreateOrJoin	Create/Join	Specifies whether the new domain controller is the first domain controller in a new forest or is joining an existing forest as a new tree.
DatabasePath	Path	Identifies the folder location for the Active Directory database files. The default is C:\Winnt\Ntds.

(Continued)

TABLE 3.1   *CONTINUED*

Parameter	Value	Installation Role
DNSOnNetwork	Yes/No	A value of No indicates that this is the first domain in a new forest and that no DNS client has been configured on the server, allowing for the automatic configuration of DNS for the domain.
DomainNetBIOSName	NetBIOS name	Defines the unique NetBIOS name for a new domain being created.
LogPath	Path	Identifies the folder location for the Active Directory transaction log files. The default is C:\Winnt\Ntds.
NewDomainDNSName	DNS name	Identifies the name of the first domain in a new forest—the forest root domain.
ParentDNSDomainName	DNS name	Identifies the DNS name of the parent domain when you are creating a child domain.
Password	Password	Specifies the password of an account with the authority to create a new domain controller when you are creating a new tree, a child domain, or an additional domain controller in an existing domain (as requested in the Network Credentials dialog box in the Active Directory Installation Wizard).

(Continued)

TABLE 3.1   *CONTINUED*

Parameter	Value	Installation Role
RebootOnSuccess	Yes/No	Specifies whether the server should be restarted after installation completes successfully.
ReplicaOrNewDomain	Replica/Domain	Identifies whether the domain controller you are installing is an additional domain controller for an existing domain (replica) or the first domain controller for a new domain (as requested in the Domain Controller Type dialog box in the Active Directory Installation Wizard).
SYSVOLPath	Path	Identifies the folder location for the Active Directory support files. The default path is C:\Winnt\Sysvol.
TreeOrChild	Tree/Child	Specifies whether the new domain controller represents a new tree in an existing forest or a child domain of an existing domain (as requested in the Create Tree or Child Domain dialog box in the Active Directory Installation Wizard).
UserDomain	Domain name	Specifies the domain name of an account with the authority to create a new domain controller when you are creating a new tree, a child domain, or an additional domain controller in an existing domain (as requested in the Network Credentials dialog box in the Active Directory Installation Wizard).

(Continued)

Parameter	Value	Installation Role
TABLE 3.1 *CONTINUED*		
UserName	Account name	Specifies the name of an account with the authority to create a new domain controller when you are creating a new tree, a child domain, or an additional domain controller in an existing domain (as requested in the Network Credentials dialog box in the Active Directory Installation Wizard).

An automated installation of a domain controller can be initiated in several ways. After the installation of a Windows 2000 server, you can run the **dcpromo** command at the Start/Run menu referencing the answer file you created by typing the command using the following syntax:

```
dcpromo.exe /answer:answerfile.txt
```

This command could, of course, also be executed as part of a batch file. Automated installation of a domain controller can also be accomplished as part of a larger automated Windows 2000 server installation by referencing the **dcpromo** command during the installation process. Here is an example of an answer file that would install the first domain controller in a new forest and install DNS:

```
[DCInstall]
AutoConfigDNS=Yes
CreateOrJoin=Create
DatabasePath=C:\Winnt\Ntds
DNSOnNetwork=No
DomainNetBiosName=xyz
LogPath=C:\Winnt\Ntds
NewDomainDNSName=xyz.com
RebootOnSuccess=Yes
ReplicaOrNewDomain=Domain
```

```
SysVolPath=C:\Winnt\Sysvol
TreeOrChild=Tree
```

An answer file can also be used to remove Active Directory and demote a domain controller to either a member server, or, if it's the last domain controller in a domain, to a standalone server. Additional parameters specific to the removal of Active Directory are available for use in the answer file. More information about these and all the answer file parameters can be found in the Microsoft whitepaper "Microsoft Windows 2000 Guide to Unattended Setup," which can be found at Microsoft's Windows 2000 Web site, or in the file unattend.txt, which can be found in the deploy.cab file on the Windows 2000 source CD.

Travel Advisory

The purpose of this book is not to review automated server installations, so you will not be subjected to a detailed discourse describing how to automate a server installation. However, automated installations of Windows 2000 servers also involve an answer file known as the unattend.txt file.

You can have the automated server installation kick off the domain controller installation by referencing the same **dcpromo** command line in the unattend.txt file. In that file, look for the section titled [GuiRunOnce]. In that section, add the line **Commandx = "dcpromo /answer:answerfile.txt"**, where "x" is a number increment beginning with 0. Optionally, the [DCInstall] section of the Dcpromo answer file could be added to the automated server's unattend.txt file, which in effect installs the Windows 2000 server and automatically promotes it to the role of domain controller as part of a complete automated installation package

---

Travel Assistance

If you would like to be subjected to a more detailed discourse describing how to automate the installation of a Windows 2000 server, refer to the Microsoft whitepaper titled "Microsoft Windows 2000 Guide to Unattended Setup," which can be found at Microsoft's Windows 2000 Web site: www.Microsoft.com\windows2000. This whitepaper also describes all the parameters available for configuring a Dcpromo answer file.

Objective 3.03

Verify and Troubleshoot Active Directory Installation

After the Active Directory Installation Wizard completes, the server has been converted to the domain controller role, Active Directory has been configured and installed, and the server restarts, you should verify that the installation completed successfully and according to your specifications. There are two areas to check to verify and troubleshoot the installation.

The first thing to check is the creation of SRV records for the new domain controller. You can verify the SRV records by

- Typing the command **nslookup ls -t SRV domainname** at a command prompt to list the SRV records.
- Opening the DNS administration tool in the Administrative Tools program group and verifying the creation of the following folders in the Forward Lookup Zone for the new domain: _msdcs, _sites, _tcp, and _upd.
- Viewing the contents of the netlogon.dns file in the systemroot\System32\Config folder on the new domain controller for LDAP SRV records.

If the SRV records do not appear in the DNS database, you can force the domain controller to reregister its SRV records by stopping and starting the Net Logon service on the domain controller. However, check to make sure that you have enabled dynamic updates for the DNS server first. That DNS support the dynamic creation of SRV records is not a hard requirement for Active Directory, and if the SRV records do not exist, you might optionally need to create the records yourself.

Next, check that the post-installation configuration tasks described in the last section of this chapter have been carried out. In particular, you want to be sure that the Sysvol folder structure was created successfully and that the Active Directory database file (Ntds.dit) and transaction log files (edb.*) have been created in the systemroot\NTDS folder.

The folder %systemroot%\Sysvol contains the following subfolders: domain, staging, staging area, and Sysvol. The Sysvol subfolder should be shared as "sysvol" and will itself contain a folder that matches the name of the domain (for example, xyz.com). Furthermore, the folder systemroot\Sysvol\Sysvol\domain\scripts should be shared with the name Netlogon and will be used to process logon, logoff, startup, and shutdown scripts assigned to computers and users via a group policy.

Another good place to look to verify that all went well with the installation would be the Event Viewer for the domain controller. Active Directory installation will log events in the System, Directory Service, DNS Server, and File Replication service Event logs.

> **Travel Advisory**
>
> After Active Directory has been successfully installed and configured, you should consider converting your DNS zone to an Active Directory integrated zone and enabling secure DNS updates to protect against unauthorized updates to DNS records. You can review the steps for both in Chapter 1.

Objective 3.04   Implement an Organizational Unit Structure

Although strictly speaking not part of the actual installation process for Active Directory, it is strongly recommended as a post-installation task that you plan and implement an organizational unit (OU) structure. OUs exist within domains and are used to manage domain objects such as users, groups, and computers. These domain objects are generally managed through the use of group and security polices.

Domain objects are managed within the domain to which the objects belong. Similarly, the Active Directory database for that domain is replicated only within that domain with a superset of objects that can be globally located within the forest. For these reasons, it is generally recommended that you try to restrict the number of domains you create. By using organization unit structures, you can organize users, groups, computers and child OUs to support the delegation of administrative authority and group policy objects.

The concept of organizational units as they relate to group policy implementation and object management will be addressed in Part III. Nevertheless, Microsoft includes some questions regarding OUs in this section of the exam, and these initial concepts are covered here.

Organizational units are used mainly to structure and organize your domain to meet the administrative requirements of your company. By creating an OU, you can do the following:

- Delegate control for the administration of that OU and control access to that OU.
- Group resources such as users, groups, and computers according to the group and security policies that need to be applied to them and simplify the administration of like objects.
- Facilitate the application of duplicate permissions for multiple shared resources by associating them with an OU and assigning the permissions once to the OU.

The Active Directory installation process creates a default structure that consists of six default containers and one default OU that can be viewed using the Active Directory Users and Computers administrative console, as shown in Figure 3-8. Each of these items holds various default objects such as users, groups, and computers. Table 3-2 describes the function of each of the default containers and the OU.

TABLE 3.2   Function of Default Containers and OU

Default Container/OU	Function
Builtin	This container holds the default built-in local security groups, such as administrators, users, guests, backup operators, print operators, server operators, and replicators.
Computers	This container holds computer accounts created as Windows 2000 servers and clients join the domain.
Domain Controllers	This OU holds the computer accounts for domain controllers in the domain.
ForeignSecurityPrincipals	This container holds security identifiers (SIDs) of trusted domains external to this domain, such as the Everyone group.

(Continued)

TABLE 3.2 *CONTINUED*	
Default Container/OU	**Function**
Users	This container holds domain-specific user and group accounts created in the domain by the administrator.
LostAndFound	This additional container holds objects that are orphaned when a parent container is deleted—for example, a child OU of a parent OU.
System	This container holds built-in system settings such as DNS SRV record objects and IP Security objects.

Travel Advisory

The last two objects listed in Table 3-2 cannot be viewed by default through the Active Directory Users and Computers tool. You can display them, however, by selecting View | Advanced Features on the Tool's menu bar.

It should be stressed that creating OUs is relatively easy, assuming you are a member of the Domain Admins and Enterprise Admins groups in the domain and forest, respectively. In the administrative console Active Directory Users and Computers, you simply right-click the domain or existing OU where you want to create the new OU, choose New from the context menu, and then choose Organizational Unit. Enter the name of the new OU, click OK, and you're done. That's the easy part. Figure 3-8 displays an example of a simple OU structure along with the default structure implemented during Active Directory installation.

The hard part involves planning an effective organizational unit structure that can provide your company with an easy, efficient way to manage and administer network resources within the domain. This takes more work and more time and

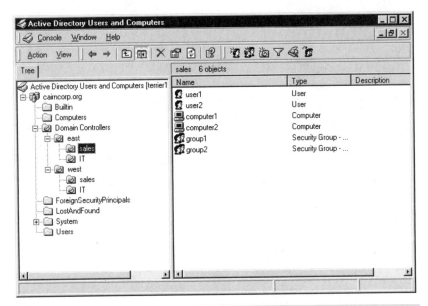

FIGURE 3-8   Sample organizational unit structure

may involve not only the ultimate creation of OUs but also the creation of sites, the modification of server roles (such as the global catalog server), and the implementation of effective group policies. These actions will be discussed in Part III.

Exam Tip

You can also create a child OU in a parent OU if you have been given the following permissions on the parent OU: Read, Create Child (OU), and, optionally, List Contents (so you can see the new child OU after you create it).

Travel Advisory

You cannot create an OU in a container. You can only create an OU in another OU. Therefore, you would build your OU structure off the Domain Controllers OU in Active Directory Users and Computers.

CHECKPOINT

✔ **Objective 3.01: Install Forests, Trees, and Domains**   The Active Directory Installation Wizard, initiated by running the **dcpromo** command, can install a domain controller in four ways: as the first domain controller in a new forest, as the first domain controller for a new tree in an existing forest, as a child domain in an existing domain in a forest, or as an additional domain controller within a domain. All domains within a forest share a common schema—a set of objects and attributes. All domains in a tree share a common namespace. All domain controllers within a domain share a common Active Directory database consisting of users, groups, computers, resources, and group and security policies. Finally, what Dcpromo giveth, it also taketh away. A domain controller—and therefore Active Directory—can be removed by rerunning Dcpromo on that server.

✔ **Objective 3.02: Automate Domain Controller Installation**   The dcpromo command accepts the use of an answer file to automate the installation of Active Directory on a domain controller. The parameter values you use in the answer file match those you would input if you were manually running Dcpromo at the server. The answer file can either be invoked by running Dcpromo after the installation of Windows 2000 Server, Advanced Server, or Datacenter Server, or as part of a larger Windows 2000 automated server installation. However, regardless of how you run Dcpromo, you must have the appropriate level of permissions to install Active Directory—either by logging on as the appropriate user or by specifying the credentials of an appropriate user through the answer file.

✔ **Objective 3.03: Verify and Troubleshoot Active Directory Installation**   Remember that throughout the execution of the Active Directory Installation Wizard, the process itself is verifying your input. Problems usually fall into three categories: permissions, naming conventions, and disk space. If you are not allowed to create a domain controller or if you receive an "access denied" message, you have not supplied the appropriate account credentials. You must be a local administrator to create the first domain controller in a new forest, a member of the Domain Admins group to add a domain controller to an existing domain, and a member of Enterprise Admins in the forest to add a new domain tree in the forest. Use naming conventions that result in unique NetBIOS names as well as unique DNS names and remember that Active Directory requires a minimum of 200MB disk space for its database and 50MB for its transaction log, plus room for expansion.

✔ **Objective 3.04: Implement an Organizational Unit Structure**   Active Directory creates a default management structure for your domain that consists of containers and OUs for users, groups, computers, and other resource objects. However, you should create your own OU structure to supplement this basic design to further organize and structure your domain, to facilitate the management of users, groups, and other resources by grouping them together into logical administrative units, and to make the application of access permissions and other types of security more effective by grouping resources with similar security needs.

REVIEW QUESTIONS

1. You have just created a new domain for your company and you want to add two additional domain controllers for load balancing and fault tolerance. However, when you attempt to add the additional domain controller while running Dcpromo, you receive an error message that the domain you are trying to join cannot be contacted. What two steps should you take so you can successfully add domain controllers to this domain?

   A. Check the DNS server for SRV records for the domain.

   B. Run Dcpromo with an answer file that provides the correct domain name and credentials.

   C. Start and stop the Net Logon service to reregister the SRV records for the domain.

   D. Install DNS on the server before you make it a domain controller and configure it for dynamic updates.

2. As the network administrator for your company, you have created a new domain in a new forest called xyz.com. As part of your Active Directory implementation plan, you would like to allow for the following goals:

   • Provide for load balancing of authentication and Active Directory requests within xyz.com.

   • Provide for fault tolerance of the Active Directory database within xyz.com.

   • Create a directory structure that meets the administrative needs of your company's departments and regions.

   • Create an effective way to assign permissions to resources that have similar security requirements.

You decide to perform the following actions: You create two additional domain controllers in the xyz.com domain. You create organizational units within xyz.com that match the administrative needs of your company. You assign permissions to each resource as is necessary for that resource. Which of the goals have you accomplished?

A. Provide for load balancing of authentication and Active Directory requests within xyz.com.

B. Provide for fault tolerance of the Active Directory database within xyz.com.

C. Create a directory structure that meets the administrative needs of your company's departments and regions.

D. Create an effective way to assign permissions to resources that have similar security requirements.

3. Your company recently acquired another company and you need to assimilate it into the forest you created for your company. You need to retain the acquired company's identity and its domain name, but you want it to share the same schema used within the forest and remain self-administered. What step would you take to accomplish this?

A. Create a new forest for the new company and connect it to your forest with a two-way transitive trust relationship.

B. Create a child domain to your company's domain in the existing domain tree.

C. Create a new domain tree for the new company in the existing forest.

D. Create an organizational unit structure for the new company within your existing domain.

4. You are planning to roll out Windows 2000 Active Directory and want to create a new domain in a new forest as well as three additional domain controllers in that domain for load balancing and fault tolerance. You want to automate the installation process. Which of the following steps would you need to take?

A. Create one answer file with two [DCInstall] sections—one for the first domain controller installation and one for the additional domain controller installation.

B. Create one answer file with four [DCInstall] sections—one for the first domain controller installation and one for each of the additional domain controller installations.

C. Create two answer files—one for the first domain controller installation and one with three [DCInstall] sections for each of the additional domain controller installations.

D. Create four answer files—one for each domain controller installation.

5. You are the network administrator for xyz.com, which has a corporate office in Chicago, a western regional office in San Francisco, and an eastern regional office in New York City. As you implement your Active Directory domain and forest structure you would like to accomplish the following goals.

- Administer each of the three locations in its own domain.
- Provide for load balancing and fault tolerance within each domain.
- Optimize server performance and Active Directory performance within each domain.
- Identify the west and east regions as west.xyz.com and east.xyz.com, respectively.

You decide to create a new domain tree for each location within the same forest. You create two additional domain controllers in each domain. You install Active Directory using all the Dcpromo defaults for the location of files. Which of your goals will you accomplish?

A. Administer each of the three locations in its own domain.

B. Provide for load balancing and fault tolerance within each domain.

C. Optimize server performance and Active Directory performance within each domain.

D. Identify the west and east regions as west.xyz.com and east.xyz.com, respectively.

6. Before you can run Dcpromo for the first time to create a new domain controller in a new forest, you must have the appropriate permissions on the Windows 2000 server. How should you be logged in?

A. You should log in with an account that is a member of the local Administrators group on the Windows 2000 server.

B. You should log in with an account that is a member of the Domain Admins group.

C. You should log in with an account that is a member of the Enterprise Admins group.

D. Any of the above.

7. When you run Dcpromo to create a new domain tree in an existing forest, you must supply the network credentials of an account that has the appropriate level of permissions. What group or groups should the account be a member of?

A. The account should be a member of the local Administrators group on the Windows 2000 server.

B. The account should be a member of the Domain Admins group.

C. The account should be a member of the Enterprise Admins group.

D. Any of the above.

8. Because of an organizational restructuring taking place within your company, you need to demote some domain controllers and remove Active Directory. What is the most efficient way to remove Active Directory?

A. Launch the Server Configuration tool from the Administrative Tools program group and select Remove Active Directory from the Installed Services program list.

B. Launch the Add/Remove Programs utility from the Control Panel, select Active Directory Services in the Installed Services list, and then click Remove.

C. Run the **dcpromo** command and confirm the removal of Active Directory.

D. You cannot demote a domain controller once Active Directory has been installed.

9. You are the network administrator for xyz.com. You have configured one Active Directory domain for your organization and have created several OUs within the domain that correspond to various departments and regional locations. You want to allow certain department heads to be able to create child OUs within their specific OUs so that they can manage their own resources. You do not want them to be able to have administration rights outside their OUs. Which of the following will let the department heads create child OUs without compromising domain security?

A. Give the department heads Read, List Contents, and Create Child (OU) permissions to their respective domain OUs.

B. Make the department heads members of the local Administrators group on their domain controllers.

C. Make the department heads members of the Domain Admins group for the domain.

D. Make the department heads members of the Enterprise Admins group for the forest.

10. Which of the following default container objects holds the domain user and group accounts that you as the administrator can create?

A. Builtin

B. Domain Controllers

C. Users

D. Groups

11. You are preparing to install Active Directory on a server running Windows 2000 Advanced Server. The server has three drives. Drive C is the system drive and has 300MB of free space. Drive D is formatted with NTFS and has 1GB of free space. Drive E is on a second hard drive, has 1GB of free space, but is not formatted with NTFS. You want to choose the location for the Active Directory database, transaction log, and Sysvol files to provide room for growth and optimize server performance. Which of the following combinations will accomplish your goal?

A. Place the Active Directory database file on C, the transaction log on D, and the Sysvol folder on E.

B. Place the Active Directory database file on E, the transaction log on C, and the Sysvol folder on D.

C. Place the Active Directory database file on C, the transaction log on E, and the Sysvol folder on D.

D. Do nothing. The default paths will accomplish your goals.

REVIEW ANSWERS

1. **A** and **C** The Active Directory Installation Wizard assumes that a DNS server is already available when you are adding an additional domain controller to a domain and it looks for SRV records for that domain. Therefore, you'd want to be sure that the SRV records exist. If they don't, you can force the domain controller to register its SRV records by stopping and starting the Net Logon service. B is incorrect because you would have the same problem whether you used an answer file or ran Dcpromo manually. D is incorrect because the Active Directory Installation Wizard assumes that a DNS server is already available when you are adding an additional domain controller to a domain. There is no need to install another DNS.

2. **A B C** Creating two additional domain controllers provides both fault tolerance and load balancing within the domain. Creating an effective organizational unit structure facilitates the administration of network resources. However, assigning permissions to each resource is not the most efficient way to handle security, so D will not be accomplished. A more effective way to handle resource permissions would be to organize resources with similar

security needs into organizational units and then assign the permissions once to the OU.

3. **C** A new tree in the existing forest will establish a new administrative and security boundary for the new company while retaining the Active Directory schema of the existing forest. A is incorrect because creating a new forest will also create a new schema for that forest. B is incorrect because although creating a child domain does establish a new security and administrative boundary, the child domain shares the same namespace as the parent. Therefore, the identity of the new company would not be maintained. D is incorrect because although organizational units certainly simplify administration, they would not necessarily result in a separate administrative and security boundary for the new company nor result in it maintaining its own identity.

4. **D** A, B, and C are incorrect for the same reason. A Dcpromo answer file can have only one [DCInstall] section in it. Because each domain controller installation will be different if for no other reason that each must have a unique DNS and NetBIOS name, you will need to create four answer files—one for each domain controller you are installing.

5. **A** and **B** are the only goals you will accomplish. By creating a separate domain for each location and installing additional domain controllers in each, you set up separate administrative boundaries for each location and provide for fault tolerance and load balancing. However, by creating the new domains as separate trees in the same forest, you give each its own distinct domain name rather than sharing the same contiguous namespace, as required for goal D. The default path for the location of the Active Directory database and transaction log files is the same directory. Microsoft recommends placing the two files on different hard disks if you want to increase server and Active Directory performance. Therefore, goal C will not be accomplished.

6. **A** is the only correct answer because when you run Dcpromo for the first time to create a new domain in a new forest, you need only be a member of the local Administrators group on the server. Since no domain or forest yet exists, there is no Domain Admins or Enterprise Admins group.

7. **C** is the only correct answer because when you create a new domain tree in an existing forest, you are in effect asking that new domain to join the existing forest. Although you need to be a member of the local Administrators group to launch Dcpromo, you will need to supply the network account name and password for an account that is a member of the Enterprise Admins group for the forest.

8. **C** Active Directory—and the domain controller—are installed by running Dcpromo. What Dcpromo gives it can also take away. If you run Dcpromo again on a domain controller, it assumes that you want to remove Active Directory and demote the domain controller to a member server or standalone server. Active Directory cannot be installed or removed through the server setup utility or through Add/Remove Programs.

9. **A** Giving the department heads Read and Create Child (OU) permissions is enough to allow them to create child OUs within their respective domain OUs, although List Contents allows them the ability to see the child OU after they create it. B is incorrect because OUs are domain entities rather than local entities and making them members of local Administrators also gives them more administrative rights on the domain controller than you intended. C and D, although certainly giving them the appropriate level of permission to create child OUs, nevertheless also gives them far more authority within the domain than you intended and certainly compromises domain security.

10. **C** The default Users container holds user and group accounts that you create. A is incorrect as the Builtin container holds the default local account groups. B is incorrect because the Domain Controllers OU contains computer accounts for the domain controllers created for the domain. D is incorrect because there is no default container called "Group."

11. **B** Placing the Active Directory database and transaction logs on separate hard drives will improve server performance, and the Sysvol folder must be placed on an NTFS partition. The only NTFS partition is D. A is incorrect because Sysvol must be placed on an NTFS partition (D) and because leaving the database and transaction logs on the same hard drive does not improve server performance. C can be argued to be correct. However, one goal is to provide for growth. The C drive only has 300MB of free space, whereas the E drive has 1GB of free space. Because the transaction log requires far less disk space than the database file and because you want to place these on separate hard drives to increase server performance, you would want to place the transaction log on C rather than the database file. D is incorrect because the default would automatically place all three on the C drive.

Configuring
Server Objects

	NEWBIE	SOME EXPERIENCE	EXPERT
ETA	3 hours	2 hours	1 hour

In Chapter 3, you explored the installation process for Active Directory. You looked at the different roles domain controllers could play within an Active Directory forest and studied the default database structure created during the installation process. You were also introduced to the concept of organizational units (OUs) and the benefits they can bring regarding the administration and security of your domain.

This chapter continues your exploration of the Active Directory implementation process. Whereas OUs can be used within a domain to facilitate the management of users, groups, and other network resources, other server objects can be used to control how information is replicated among domain controllers in a domain.

The Active Directory structure can be further refined through the use of site objects, subnets, site links, and connection objects. You will also study the operations master roles that are assumed by domain controllers within the Active Directory and see how your implementation of various server objects may depend on the assignment of those operations master roles.

Objective 4.01 Transfer Operations Master Roles

Because some of your decisions regarding the creation and configuration of additional server objects may depend on the operations master roles assigned to various domain controllers, your tour begins with an exploration of those roles as well as to what extent you can—or should—modify those roles.

As you have learned already, a copy of the Active Directory database is maintained on all domain controllers within a domain. Changes to Active Directory that occur on any one domain controller will be automatically replicated to all the other domain controllers.

However, some Active Directory maintenance activities are assigned to specific servers within the domain to minimize the amount of replication traffic that can be generated and to ensure that certain conflicts do not occur through changes made to the same objects on two different servers. These activities are

---

Exam Tip

The process of maintaining a copy of Active Directory on all domain controllers and allowing changes on any domain controller to be replicated to all others is known as *multimaster replication.*

known as single master operations as they are performed on only one domain controller in the domain.

Although the assignment of single master operations roles does indeed help to control network traffic generated by the replication process, if a server performing a needed task is unavailable, that task might not get carried out. For example, in a mixed-mode environment in which Windows NT 4 *backup domain controllers* (BDCs) coexist with Windows 2000 domain controllers, the BDCs need to periodically synchronize their account databases with a *primary domain controller* (PDC).

In a Windows 2000 domain, one domain controller assumes the role of PDC emulator. If this server is unavailable when the BDCs need to synchronize, their account data will not be updated and users whose accounts have been modified (password changes, and so on) might not be able to log on to the network.

There are five single master operations roles. Two of these roles, schema master and domain naming master, are specific to the forest. The other three roles are specific to each domain and are known as the infrastructure master, PDC emulator, and RID master.

Forest-Specific Roles

The schema master is responsible for maintaining and managing updates and changes to the forest-wide schema (object classes and attributes) as well as for replicating the schema to all domain controllers in the forest. You must be a member of the Schema Admins group in order to modify the Active Directory schema. The domain naming master controls the addition or deletion of domains in the forest, ensuring that their names and naming conventions are unique within the forest. Any domain controller in the forest may be assigned one or both of these roles, but the forest must have these roles assigned to some domain controller in it.

Travel Advisory

If the domain controller assigned the domain naming master role is unavailable, you will not be able to add or delete domains in the forest. Furthermore, the domain controller assigned the domain naming master role must also be identified as a global catalog server.

Infrastructure Master Role

Within each domain, users, groups, and other accounts are referenced by their unique identifiers—their GUIDs (globally unique identifiers across domains) or SIDs (security identifiers unique within a given domain). Recall that two-way transitive trust relationships exist among the domains within a tree in a forest as well as among domain trees in the forest. Because of these trust relationships, it is possible to allow users and groups in one domain permission to use resources in another domain. This is done by assigning user or group accounts in one domain membership to specific group accounts in another domain. Objects other than users and groups (such as printers) can also be referenced across domains.

In reality, it is the object GUID or SID that is referenced in the group membership. Subsequently, if changes occur to objects in one domain that are referenced in groups in another domain, the account references will need to be updated across the domains.

For example, if an account—or any object—is moved within a domain from one OU to another, its DN obviously changes. If an object moves across domains, its domain SID changes. It should be clear that changes of this kind need to be propagated wherever the object is referenced; otherwise, the object will no longer have access or be accessible across the domains.

It is the responsibility of the infrastructure master within each domain to update its references to accounts in other domains and then replicate those changes to all the other domain controllers within its domain.

Travel Advisory

Unlike the domain naming master, which requires the presence of the global catalog, the infrastructure master and global catalog cannot both reside on the same domain controller. Similarly, if the forest consists of one single domain, the infrastructure master role will have no meaning because there wouldn't be any other outside domain objects to reference.

PDC Emulator Role

As mentioned earlier in this chapter, the PDC emulator functions like a Windows NT 4 PDC for NT BDCs that coexist in the domain with Windows 2000 domain controllers. Whereas Windows 2000 domain controllers replicate account changes to all other Windows 2000 domain controllers within the domain using a multi-master replication model, BDCs periodically query a PDC for account changes. In a mixed-mode Active Directory environment, an NT BDC will query a Windows 2000 domain controller that is assigned the PDC emulator role.

Ordinarily, when a Windows 2000 client changes a password, the change is recorded on any available domain controller and then replicated to the other domain controllers in the domain, including the PDC emulator. Down-level clients such as Windows NT, Windows 98, and Windows 95 make these changes on the PDC only in a Windows NT network environment. In a Windows 2000 environment, the PDC emulator is responsible for handling such changes from down-level clients and then replicating the changes to the other domain controllers within the domain. Furthermore, in the event that a logon fails due to an incorrect password, rather than lock out the user, the other domain controllers will first forward the password authentication request to the PDC emulator to ensure that the failure to authenticate was not the result of a password update that had not yet been replicated to all the domain controllers.

Travel Advisory

Microsoft has an Active Directory client service that can be installed on some down-level clients. This client service will allow down-level clients to modify passwords on any Windows 2000 domain controller.

In addition, some other network applications, while capable of running on a Windows 2000 platform, still need to contact a PDC in order to carry out a task. For example, Systems Management Server (SMS) 2.0 has the capability to enumerate the users and groups in a domain for the purposes of defining collections for package distribution. SMS does this by contacting the PDC for a list of the users and groups stored in its account database. In a Windows 2000 Active Directory environment, it would be the PDC emulator that responds to this request.

Finally, the PDC emulator in each domain becomes the time server for its domain, each one synchronizing with the time server of the forest root domain to ensure that all Windows 2000 clients' system clocks are closely synchronized. The PDC emulator also assumes the role of domain master browser in a mixed-mode domain.

RID Master Role

New objects created within a domain are assigned a GUID that is unique within the forest as well as a SID, which must be unique within its domain. The SID itself has two main pieces—one that is the same for all objects created within the domain and represents that domain, and one that is unique for the object. The unique component of the SID is called the *relative identifier* (RID). Because every domain controller within a domain has the potential for creating new objects in the domain—such as users, groups, computers, and so on—it is essential that the objects' SIDs remain unique. Therefore, each domain controller must ensure that the RID portion of an object's SID is unique within the domain.

The domain controller functioning in the RID master role is responsible for delegating unique blocks of RIDs to each domain controller in the domain. As each domain controller uses up its quota of RIDs, it requests an additional block or blocks from the RID master. If the RID master is unavailable to provide a new block of RIDs, object creation cannot proceed on the domain controller that needs the RIDs.

The RID master is also responsible for managing the disposition of an object when it is moved from one domain to another. It keeps track of the fact that an object has moved, and it removes that object from the current domain after the move takes place.

Exam Tip

By default, the first domain controller in the forest root assumes the two forest-wide roles (schema master and domain naming master) and the three domain-based roles (infrastructure master, PDC emulator, and RID master) as well as the global catalog server. The first domain controller implemented in each successive domain in the forest assumes the three domain-based operations master roles.

Determining Roles

As you implement your domain structure and install domain controllers, the single operations master roles are assigned by default to the first domain controllers created in each domain. However, for various reasons, you may choose to reassign one or more of those roles within the forest or domain.

The first thing you'll need to do, of course, is determine which domain controllers have been assigned which single operations master roles. Recall that the single operations master roles are divided into forest-specific (schema master and domain naming master) and domain-specific (infrastructure master, PDC emulator, and RID master) roles. Subsequently, you will use different tools to determine which domain controllers have been assigned which roles. In fact, you will use three different tools.

To determine which domain controller has been assigned the infrastructure master, PDC emulator, or RID master role, you will use the Active Directory Users and Computers administrative tool in each domain. When you have launched the tool, you should right-click the entry Active Directory Users and Computers and then choose Operations Masters from the pop-up menu. Click the tab relating to the operations master role you are interested in—RID, PDC, or Infrastructure—to view the name of the domain controller that has been assigned that role. Figure 4-1 shows the PDC tab.

You use the Active Directory Domains and Trusts administrative tool to determine which domain controller has been assigned the domain naming master operations role. After you launch the tool, you should right-click the entry Active Directory Domains and Trusts and then choose Operations Master from the pop-up menu to display the Change Operations Master dialog box. You can view the name of the domain controller currently assigned the domain naming master role in this dialog box, as shown in Figure 4-2.

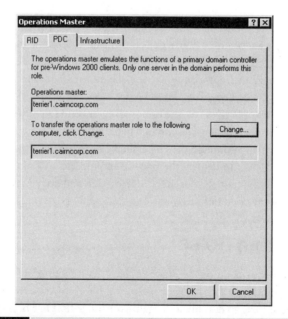

FIGURE 4-1   The PDC emulator tab in the Operations Master dialog box

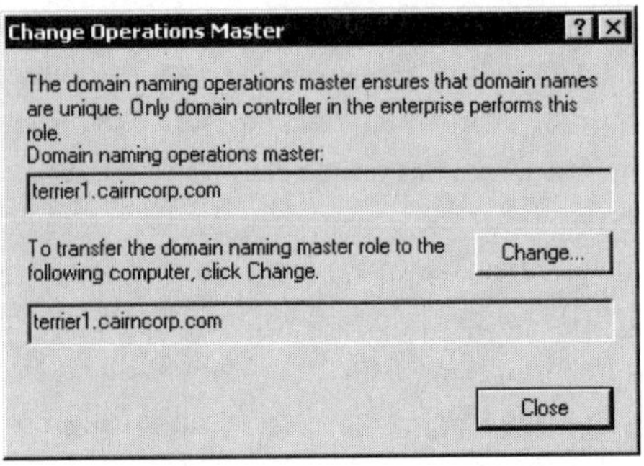

Change Operations Master ? X

The domain naming operations master ensures that domain names are unique. Only domain controller in the enterprise performs this role.
Domain naming operations master:

terrier1.cairncorp.com

To transfer the domain naming master role to the following computer, click Change.   Change...

terrier1.cairncorp.com

Close

FIGURE 4-2   The Change Operations Master dialog box for the domain naming master role

Before you can determine which domain controller has been assigned the schema master operations role, you must first enable a tool that is not operational by default—the Active Directory Schema snap-in. You must register this tool by typing the following command in a Windows 2000 command prompt on a domain controller: **regsvr32.exe %systemroot%\system32\schmmgmt.dll**. You will be prompted when the process completes. This makes the snap-in available to use, but you'll still have to add it to a Microsoft Management Console (MMC).

Once you have done that, you can launch the MMC containing the Active Directory Schema tool. You'll then right-click the entry Active Directory Schema, choose Operations Master from the pop-up menu, and view the name of the domain controller currently assigned the schema master role in the Change Schema Master dialog box, as shown in Figure 4-3.

Each of these tools gives you the option of connecting to other domains first before using the tool to manage resources. Therefore, you can run these tools in any domain to view which domain controllers have been assigned the various roles. When you right-click to display the pop-up menu, select Connect To Domain Controller first to change the focus of the tool to a different domain controller. Then proceed to view the operations master role assignments as previously discussed.

Transferring Roles

Generally, once the operations master roles have been assigned, you will not need to monkey around with them as your network grows. However, the occasion may arise when you have to demote a domain controller that has been assigned an operations master role back to member server status, or you might need to bring

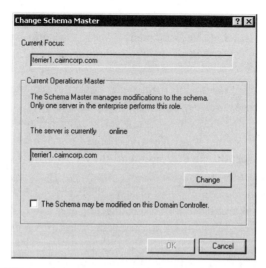

FIGURE 4-3   The Change Schema Master dialog box for the schema
master role

online a new server better suited for the role or modify the placement of global catalog servers (which can effect the domain naming master and infrastructure master roles).

In each of these cases, you can control how the operations master roles are reassigned by transferring the roles yourself prior to making any change. For example, when you demote a domain controller to the role of member server, any operations master roles that it was performing will automatically be reassigned to another domain controller—perhaps not a domain controller that you would have chosen yourself. Transferring the role(s) first eliminates the possibility of inappropriate server selection. Both domain controllers must be available and able to communicate with each other for the transfer to complete successfully.

Exam Tip

Changing the schema master role requires you to be a member of the Schema Admins group in the forest. Changing the domain naming master role requires you to be a member of the Enterprise Admins group in the forest. Changing the three domain-specific roles requires you to be a member of the Domain Admins group in the designated domain.

Also, a server performing one or more of these roles may crash, thus preventing the orderly transfer of role assignments. This last scenario involves seizing an operations master role and thrusting it upon another server. This is discussed in detail in Chapter 9.

To transfer any of the three domain-specific operations master roles, begin by launching the Active Directory Users and Computers tool and connecting to the domain controller that will assume the role you are transferring. Then, right-click the entry for that domain controller and choose Operations Masters from the pop-up menu. Select the tab that represents the role you are transferring (RID, PDC, or Infrastructure) and click Change.

To transfer the domain naming master role, begin by launching the Active Directory Domains and Trusts tool and connecting to the domain controller that will assume that role. Right-click the entry Active Directory Domains and Trusts and choose Operations Master from the pop-up menu. Click Change on the Change Operations Master dialog box to transfer the role.

To transfer the schema master role, begin by launching the Active Directory Schema MMC and connecting to the domain controller that will assume that role. Right-click the entry Active Directory Schema and choose Operations Master from the pop-up menu. Click Change on the Change Schema Master dialog box to transfer the role.

Global Catalog Server

Another server function that can be assigned to a domain controller and that plays a significant role in Active Directory is the global catalog server. The global catalog maintains a subset of the Active Directory database. It contains attributes of objects in the database that are most frequently looked for, such as a user's logon name or a printer's location, and performs two main roles in Active Directory:

- Allows users to log on to the network
- Allows users to locate Active Directory objects anywhere within the forest

The first domain controller in the forest becomes the global catalog server by default. However, unlike the single operations master roles, you can designate additional domain controllers to be global catalog servers.

The Active Directory itself is composed of three logical directory components called *partitions*. They are the schema, configuration, and domain partitions.

The schema partition stores the definitions of all the objects that can be created in the forest along with their attributes as well as how they can be managed.

The configuration partition defines the Active Directory structure as characterized by its domains, sites, and server object configurations. There can only be one schema and configuration partition within the forest, and a copy is replicated to all domain controllers in a forest.

The domain partition identifies and defines objects (such as users, groups, printers, and OUs) specific to the domain in which they were created. A copy of the domain partition is replicated to all domain controllers in a given domain.

Here is how the global catalog fits into this partition structure. The global catalog represents a read-only subset of the objects in the domain partition and is replicated to all the domain controllers in the domain. This ensures that users will be able to log on to their domain anywhere in the forest and be able to locate and access Active Directory objects and resources anywhere in the forest.

When a user attempts to locate an object in the forest, such as a printer, that query is sent to a global catalog server for resolution. Without the global catalog server, the query would have to be processed against all the domain controllers within a forest. Indeed, if your forest consisted of only one domain, you wouldn't even need the global catalog, because each domain controller would already have a copy of the Active Directory and know where all the domain objects were located. Obviously the same is not true in a forest consisting of multiple domains or domain trees, because domain objects are unique to the domain.

However, perhaps the greater significance of the global catalog server is to assist in the authentication process when a user logs on to the network. Among the object attributes maintained in the global catalog are the universal group memberships of each user account. When a user logs on, the logon account's universal group membership is passed to the domain controller authenticating the user. If the user logs on using a *user principal name* (UPN), such as steve@xyz.com, the name is resolved against the global catalog before the user is authenticated.

Exam Tip

If a global catalog server is unavailable and the user had logged on to the network earlier, the user can be authenticated using cached credentials, similar to the way Windows NT functions. However, if cached credentials are not available, the user will only be able to log on to the computer locally—without access to network resources.

For example, if the user logs on as steve@xyz.com on a computer in the domain north.xyz.com, the domain controllers in the domain would not have that user in their Active Directory database. However, they can query a global catalog server for xyz.com to find the user name, authenticate the user, and provide the user an access token for accessing network resources.

Because global catalog servers play such a significant role in the authentication and lookup processes in Active Directory, it makes sense that you would want to do some load balancing and optimum server placement to facilitate these functions. You can create as many global catalog servers as you feel are necessary. However, Microsoft recommends implementing at least one global catalog server per site. You'll see why this recommendation makes sense when you read about sites in the next section of this chapter.

You can assign the role of global catalog server to a domain controller through the Active Directory Sites and Services administrative tool. After you have launched the Active Directory Sites and Services tool, find and expand the entry that represents the domain controller that will become a global catalog server. Among the subfolders, beneath the domain controller entry, right-click the folder NTDS Settings an choose Properties from the pop-up menu. Select the option Global Catalog to assign the role to—or clear it to remove the role from—the domain controller, as shown in Figure 4-4.

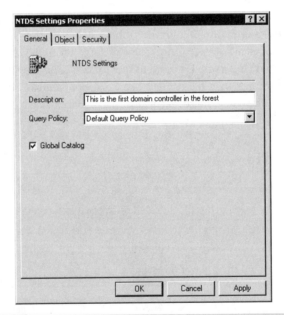

FIGURE 4-4   Assigning the global catalog server role to a domain controller

Create Sites, Subnets, Site Links, and Connection Objects

Sites, subnets, site links, and connection objects are all Active Directory objects that are used to control how the replication of data takes place among domain controllers within a domain as well as between domains. Before you can appreciate the significance of planning and configuring these objects, a discussion of replication in Active Directory is in order.

Active Directory Replication

As you have seen several times now, domain controllers are responsible for replicating changes made to the Active Directory database to all other domain controllers within a domain, and sometimes to domain controllers in other domains. Sometimes changes can occur at any domain controller, such as a password update performed on a Windows 2000 client. Other times, changes are managed by domain controllers that have been assigned a specific operations master role. In either case, it is an essential element of Active Directory that all domain controllers that host Active Directory be kept synchronized.

As mentioned earlier, Active Directory employs a multimaster replication model. This ensures that, with the exception of those domain controllers assigned a single operations master role, there is no single point of failure among the domain controllers as each maintains an "up-to-date" copy of the Active Directory database. The multimaster replication model also allows you to implement as many domain controllers as you deem necessary to provide fault tolerance and load balancing within the physical as well as bandwidth boundaries of your network.

Any change to Active Directory can trigger a replication event. For example, creating a new object (such as a computer account), modifying an existing object attribute (such as the location of a printer), moving an object from one OU to

---

Local Lingo

Originating Update An originating update reflects a change that occurs at a domain controller that initiates a replication event. A replicated update reflects a change made to the Active Directory database on a domain controller as a result of a replication event initiated at another domain controller.

another within a domain (or from one domain to another), and deleting an object all necessitate a change to the Active Directory database, and that change must be synchronized on all copies of the Active Directory database.

Because any available domain controller can potentially manage a change to an Active Directory object, it is possible that the same object might be modified on two different domain controllers. The question then becomes, Which change takes effect? This is not as messy as it may at first appear. In fact, Active Directory has a built-in way of handling potential update conflicts of this nature.

Most changes to objects occur and are replicated at the attribute level. An attribute includes items such as user name, password, e-mail address, phone number, and so on. If a change is made to one attribute of an object at one domain controller and to another attribute of the same object at another domain controller, there really is no conflict. Even though the same object has been modified, it was modified in two different attributes, thus no conflict.

However, Active Directory also maintains an update identifier for each attribute that contains a version number that is incremented as each successive change takes place, a timestamp representing the time and date of the originating update, and the GUID of the domain controller on which the originating update took place.

Therefore, if a conflict occurs due to updates made to the same attribute of an object on two or more different domain controllers, there is a mechanism to resolve the update conflict. Typically the originating update with the higher update identifier takes precedence over those with lower values.

When a change to the Active Directory database occurs, the change is generally not replicated immediately. The exception to this rule involves changes of security-related updates, such as the enabling of an account lockout. This type of change triggers an immediate replication event and is sometimes called *urgent replication*. In most other cases, however, after a configurable period of time, change notifications are generated by the domain controller originating the update and sent to other domain controllers that, in turn, copy the changes from the domain controller that sent the notifications.

As you install additional domain controllers for your domain, Active Directory automatically sets up a replication topology that ensures that an Active Directory update travels no further than three domain controllers (replication hops) to propagate a change among all the domain controllers. Although you can configure which domain controllers are replication partners with each other to achieve a custom replication topology, you must maintain the three-hop limit.

Also, although it's a configurable value, the default delay before a domain controller initiates a notification event to its replication partners is 5 minutes. Therefore, the maximum amount of time it should take before the update is replicated to all domain controllers should be, by default, no more than 15 minutes (a 5-minute delay at each domain controller, with a three-hop limit).

Travel Advisory

Even if no change notifications were issued, by default, each domain controller will initiate a replication event with its replication partners once an hour to make sure it didn't miss anything.

The default replication topology is generated by an Active Directory process called the *Knowledge Consistency Checker* (KCC)—not to be confused with a fast food outlet with a similar acronym. The KCC runs on each domain controller and determines replication partnerships that preserve the three-hop limit. Pertinent, finally, to the discussion at hand, the KCC uses connection information as configured by you through sites, subnets, site links, and custom connection objects to determine the optimum configuration of replication partners. The priorities or costs you associate with connection objects may affect the replication topology that the KCC will implement. Figure 4-5 shows what one replication topology might look like. Notice that updates never have to travel through more than three domain controllers to update all domain controllers.

Each line between two domain controllers in Figure 4-5 connects two replication partners. Notice that without the connections between DC1 and DC5, and DC1 and DC8, you could not replicate an update to DC5, DC6, DC7, or DC8 within three replication hops.

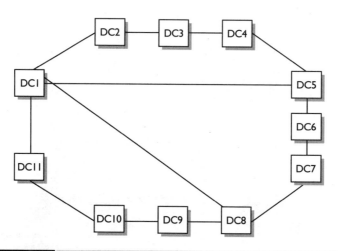

FIGURE 4-5 Example of a replication topology

When you let the KCC determine the replication topology, it will create all the appropriate connection objects required. Connection objects identify which domain controllers are replication partners. Every set of replication partners requires two connection objects: one that defines replication from domain 1 to domain 2, and another that defines replication from domain 2 to domain 1.

You can customize the replication topology by creating your own connection objects through the Active Directory Sites and Services administrative tool. You simply find each domain controller that will participate as a replication partner in the console tree, right-click the NTDS folder for each domain, and choose New Active Directory Connection from the pop-up menu.

In the mini-wizard that launches, you'll need to select the domain controller's replication partner from the list provided and give the connection a name. The new connection object appears in the NTDS folder for the domain controller, and you can view or modify its properties as you see in Figure 4-6.

If you click the Change Schedule button in the connection object's Properties dialog box, you can see that, by default, replication takes place four times an hour—every 15 minutes (see Figure 4-7).

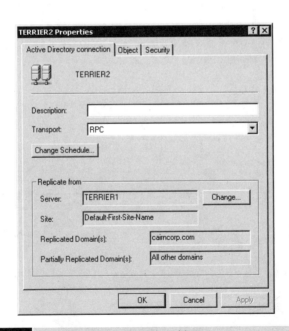

FIGURE 4-6 Creating a new connection object

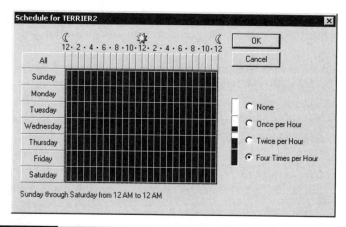

FIGURE 4-7   The default replication schedule for a connection object

Travel Advisory

You can force replication to take place from one domain controller to another by selecting the appropriate connection object in the Active Directory Sites and Services console, right-clicking it, and choosing Replicate Now from the pop-up menu.

Site, Subnet, and Site Link Objects

All that replication can really take a toll on your network bandwidth. However, you can help to control and manage how and when replication takes place by creating sites. Sites define for Active Directory the physical layout of the network by organizing domain controllers by their subnet addresses. In fact, a site is defined by the subnet addresses assigned to it and may consist of zero or more subnets.

Furthermore, a site can include domain controllers from any domains in a forest. You see, what you are doing here is defining a physical relationship among the domain controllers in the forest to facilitate and optimize replication and authentication traffic. Therefore, a key element in creating and configuring sites is to understand the network infrastructure of your organization.

Replication information is propagated uncompressed when initiated within a site. Replication between sites can be scheduled, throttled, and compressed. In both cases, the amount of replication traffic can be substantial, as you have already seen. In addition, clients generate their own Active Directory traffic when looking for network resources in the forest or when authenticating a user logging on to the network.

Given these revelations about replication, it should come as no surprise to you that sites should represent domain controllers in subnets connected by reliable, high-speed network communications. You can define what the acceptable thresholds are for "reliable" and "high-speed." All kidding aside, though, because the replication traffic within the site is uncompressed and cannot really be scheduled, you want to make sure the network connections within the defined site will have enough available bandwidth to support replication and logon traffic. Your clients' operating systems and applications will use the subnet information associated with a site to locate servers "closest" to them as well as domain controllers in the same site as users logging on.

The replication process within and across sites can use two communication protocols: RPC and SMTP. Within a site, Active Directory will always use RPC over IP, an industry-standard high-speed connection protocol. SMTP is a network communication protocol that uses a store-and-forward method to replicate schema and global catalog information to a domain controller in another site. It cannot be used to replicate domain partition information to domain controllers within the same site or within the same domain. You can choose to use SMTP when setting up replication between sites if you are replicating to a bridgehead server that is a domain controller in another domain. However, it is far more likely that you will choose RPC over IP as the communication protocol between sites largely because of the limitations in replication data posed by SMTP and the potential latency in the delivery of the data.

When you install your first domain controller for a forest, a default site is created called "Default-First-Site." All subsequent domains and domain controllers are added to this default site. When you implement your own site structures, you'll need to perform three main tasks, which are all done in the console of the Active Directory Sites and Services tool.

The first task you'll perform is to create and name the site. In the Active Directory Sites and Services console, right-click the Sites entry, choose New Site from the pop-up menu, and type the name of the new site in the New Object—Site dialog box, as shown in Figure 4-8. You will be asked to associate the new site with a site link. Choose the appropriate site link or the default if no other is available. Site links will be discussed shortly.

After you create the new site, the Active Directory message shown at the top of the next page appears reminding you of the tasks you need to perform. Note that a site can be empty—that is, you don't have to install all your domain controllers before you create your sites.

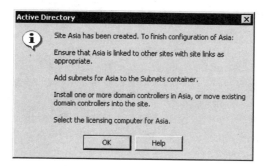

Exam Tip

You should be very familiar with the tasks required to successfully create and configure sites.

The next task you will perform is to create and associate one or more subnets with your new site. In the Active Directory Sites and Services console, expand the Sites entry, right-click the Subnets entry, and choose New Subnet from the pop-up menu. Enter the subnet's address and subnet mask in the appropriate text boxes and then choose the site that the subnet should be associated with, as demonstrated in Figure 4-9.

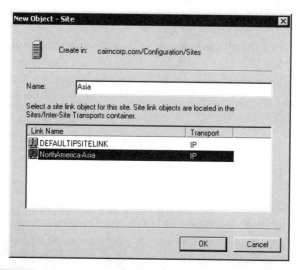

FIGURE 4-8   The New Object – Site dialog box

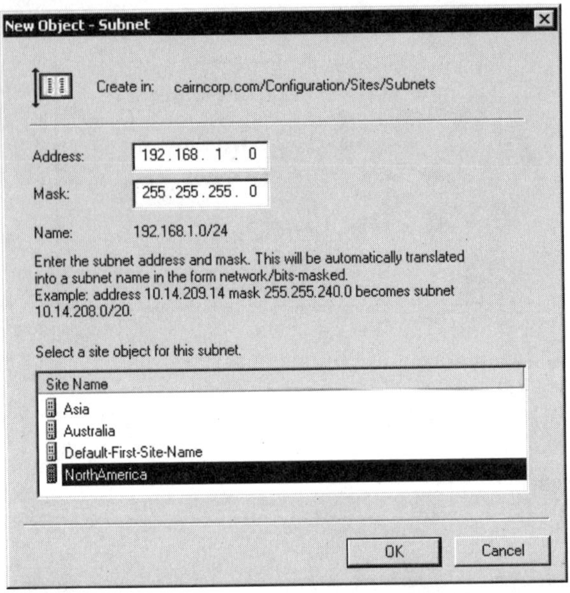

FIGURE 4-9   The New Object - Subnet dialog box

Your final task is to create a site link. Site links control and manage how replication takes place between sites. In particular, you can assign a cost value as well as configure a replication schedule and a replication interval for each site link. Table 4-1 outlines the five configuration values you can set for the site link.

In the Active Directory Sites and Services console, expand the Inter-Site Transport entry and right-click the communications transport that you want to use. Choose New | Site Link from the pop-up menu. Enter a name for the site link, select two or more sites from the Sites list, and then click Add. You can then configure the cost, replication interval, schedule values, and site link members on the General tab of the new site link's Properties dialog box, as you see in Figure 4-10.

Site Link Bridges

Replication within a site is uncompressed between domain controllers in the site. Replication across sites is compressed and can be scheduled to occur at optimum times and through selected domain controllers called *bridgehead servers*. Bridgehead servers are so named because they act as the communication "bridge" between sites. A bridgehead server is selected automatically within a site and uses the *Intersite Topology Generator* (ISTG) to make the connection to a bridgehead server in another site. The connection relationship between two bridgehead

TABLE 4.1	Site Link Configuration Parameters
Parameter	**Description**
Cost	A priority value that reflects the speed and eliability reliability of the physical network connection associated with the site link relative to that of other available site links. The default value is 100.
Member Sites	The sites that are associated with and will use the site link.
Replication Interval	The frequency with which replication will take place within the schedule you define. The default value is 180 minutes (3 hours).
Schedule	The time range within which replication can occur. The default value is 24/7.
Transport	The network connection protocol (RPC or SMTP) to be used by Active Directory when initiating a replication event.

servers is called a *site link*. However, you can also select your own preferred bridge-head server much as you can customize your own replication topology.

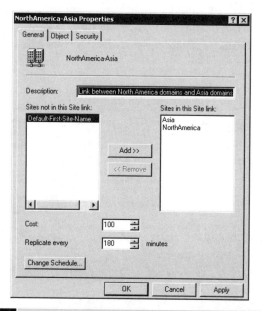

FIGURE 4-10   Site link configuration parameters

Travel Advisory

You can identify which domain controller is the bridgehead server for a given site by selecting a site through the Active Directory Sites and Services tool, right-clicking its NTDS Site Settings folder, and choosing Properties from the pop-up menu. Look for the role ISTG.

You can further affect how replication occurs through the creation of site link bridges. A site link bridge defines a path, or route, that Active Directory can take as it replicates information from one site to another. Site link bridges act somewhat like transitive trusts do between domains in a forest. Suppose you have three sites defined: North America, Asia, and Australia. You have defined a site link between North America and Asia called "NorthAmerica-Asia" and a site link between Asia and Australia called "Asia-Australia," as shown in Figure 4-11.

Perhaps you do not have a high-speed connection between North America and Australia, or the connection is not reliable. You can create a site link bridge between site North America and Australia by associating the two existing site links with the site link bridge. This defines a path that Active Directory can take to replicate data from North America to Australia by passing "through" Asia. Any costs associated with the existing site links are added up and reflect the cost of the site link bridge, as

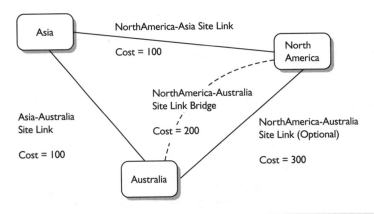

FIGURE 4-11   Diagram of a site link bridge

you see in Figure 4-11. If there is a network connection between North America and Australia, but it isn't fast or reliable, you might still create a site link for North America and Australia but set its cost higher than that for the site link bridge. In this way, the site link bridge would be used as the preferred connection route, but the site link would be available as a backup route if the site link bridge is unavailable.

Like transitive trusts, by default, all site links are bridged to ensure that there are many options for Active Directory—and many paths it can take depending on the cost values configured for the various site links—to take when initiating replication of data. However, you may decide or need to disable the default and create your own site link bridges if your sites exist in an IP subnet infrastructure that is not fully routed or is constrained in some other way, such as through the use of firewalls. In this case, all domain controllers may not be able to communicate directly or easily with other domain controllers in which the KCC and ISTG automatic configuration choices may not be appropriate or accurate.

You might also decide to create your own site link bridges if the number of sites proves to be too many for the KCC and ISTG processes to actually calculate the topology and bridgehead servers consistently or in a reasonable amount of time. The KCC reconfigures the topology periodically based on cost updates, new or deleted domain controllers, and so on. On the other hand, the KCC might create too many replication paths—more than is actually needed or efficient. In either case, you would probably want to create your own site link bridges.

You create a site link bridge similar to the way you created a site link. In the Active Directory Sites and Services console, expand the Inter-Site Transport entry and right-click the communications transport you want to use. Choose New Site Link Bridge from the pop-up menu. Enter a name for the site link bridge, select two or more site links from the Site Links list, and then click Add, as you see in Figure 4-12.

Objective 4.03 Configure Server Objects

Server objects are created for each domain controller when you promote a Windows 2000 server and are used to define connection objects for replication. However, you can also create server objects yourself that represent existing or new domain controllers or member servers and then associate them with your sites. Indeed, Active Directory will not be able to create an effective—or working—replication topology without you first having identified the servers that belong to each site. In Figure 4-12, you can see the server objects created for each site. These server objects can be used to identify which servers should act as bridgehead servers for the site. Figure 4-13 shows an example of this kind of configuration.

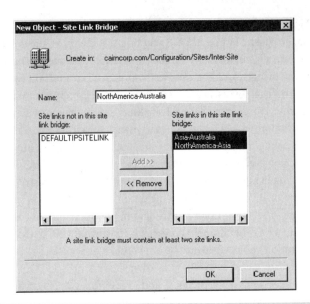

FIGURE 4-12   New Object – Site Link Bridge dialog box

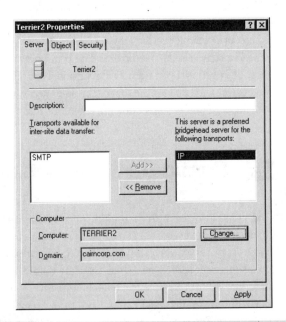

FIGURE 4-13   Server object configuration for a bridgehead server

You can create a new server object for a site by right-clicking the site entry in the Active Directory Sites and Servers console and choosing New Server from the pop-up menu. You'll give the object a name and associate it with an existing computer. The object name does not have to be the same as the computer name, although it would probably be easier for you to manage if the names match.

Creating these server objects will also help you to more easily visualize and plan your site-building strategy and identify which domain controllers have been assigned which roles (for example, global catalog server).

Exam Tip

All sites must have at least one server object associated with a domain controller in it or else Active Directory cannot generate a replication topology that includes that site.

CHECKPOINT

✔ **Objective 4.01:** **Transfer Operations Master Roles**   A copy of the Active Directory database is maintained on all domain controllers in a forest. Most objects that are added or modified in Active Directory are replicated to all domain controllers within a domain using a multimaster model. However, certain domain controllers are assigned one or more single operations masters roles to control the replication of specific Active Directory objects, such as the directory schema, or to provide services to down-level clients, servers, or applications, such as the role of PDC emulator, which provides the services of a Windows NT PDC.

There are five single operations master roles: schema and domain naming master, which are forest specific, and PDC emulator, RID master, and infrastructure master, which are domain specific. These roles are automatically assigned to the first domain controller in the forest and to the first domain controller in each successive domain in the forest. Before you replace, remove, or demote a domain controller currently assigned one of these roles, you should transfer the role to another appropriate domain controller.

The role of global catalog server is significant in that it provides lookup services and logon services for all users in the forest. Indeed, a user may not be able to log on at all if a global catalog server is not available. There can be multiple global catalog servers within the forest or domain, and it is recommended that you assign at least one in each site.

✔ **Objective 4.02: Create Sites, Subnets, Site Links, and Connection Objects**
Active Directory uses sites, subnets, site links, site link bridges, and connection objects to control how and what kind of replication takes place among domain controllers. Sites generally define computers installed on subnets that are connected by high-speed, reliable network connections and because of that may contain domain controllers from different domains. Sites use site links, site link bridges, and connection objects to determine a replication topology between sites in a forest. Once you have created your sites and site links, Active Directory can use the KCC to generate a replication topology. However, you can customize or create your own replication topology to optimize network traffic or create alternate routes by creating your own connection objects, site link bridges, and designated bridgehead servers.

✔ **Objective 4.03: Configure Server Objects**   Every domain controller you install will have a server object created for it by default. You can move these server objects into appropriate sites as you configure your Active Directory replication structure or create your own for the purpose of identifying bridgehead servers. All sites must have at least one server object associated with a domain controller in it or else Active Directory cannot generate a replication topology that includes that site.

REVIEW QUESTIONS

1. You have configured three sites for your company: West, Central, and East. All three sites are connected by reliable network connections. However, the connection between West and East is not as fast as the other connections. You want to make use of the network connection between West and East but would prefer that replication events pass through Central, making use of the high-speed connection and extra bandwidth. You have already created site links between East and Central, West and Central, and East and West. What two additional steps should you take?

    A. Set the cost of the East-West site link to be lower than the cost of the other two site link costs combined.

    B. Create a site link bridge between East and West.

    C. Set the cost of the East-West site link bridge to be higher than the cost of the East-West site link.

    D. Set the cost of the East-West site link bridge to be lower than the cost of the East-West site link.

2. Your company consists of three regional offices—East, West, and Central— each with its own domain in the forest. Domain controllers for each domain exist in each of the regional offices. The operation master roles and global catalog all reside on domain controllers in the Central regional office. Each office has a high-speed, reliable network. Each office is connected to the other offices by a T1 connection. You want to accomplish the following goals: optimize replication traffic between the regional offices, ensure that users can access resources anywhere in the forest, and ensure that users can easily and quickly log on from anywhere in the forest.

You decide to make each regional office a site in Active Directory and create site links between each site. Which of your goals have you accomplished?

    A. Optimize replication traffic between the regional offices.

    B. Ensure that users can most efficiently access resources anywhere in the forest.

    C. Ensure that users can easily and quickly log on from anywhere in the forest.

    D. None of these goals.

3. You are the network administrator for your company. A colleague in another office is having difficulty creating a new child domain for her domain. Active Directory will not accept the new domain name. What two things would you check to troubleshoot the problem?

    A. Is she logged on as a member of Domain Admins?

    B. Is she logged on as a member of Enterprise Admins?

    C. Is the domain naming master available?

    D. Is the PDC emulator available?

4. You have been experiencing intermittent problems with your network, making some of your servers, at times, unavailable. You support a mixed client base consisting of Windows 2000 clients and Windows 98 clients. The help desk is fielding a number of calls from users running as Windows 98 clients, complaining that logon requests are slow and that password changes are not being affected. What would you check to troubleshoot this problem? Choose the best answer.

A. Check for the availability of the global catalog server.
B. Check for the availability of the PDC emulator.
C. Check for the availability of the domain naming server.
D. Check for the availability of the infrastructure master.
E. Check for the availability of the RID master.

5. You are planning to replace some of your domain controllers with more powerful computers. One of the domain controllers that you are replacing has been assigned the schema master role. How would you go about replacing the server and preserving the role?

A. Demote the current domain controller and install the new domain controller. After you install the new domain controller, assign the schema master role to it.
B. Install the domain controller and assign it the schema master role. Then demote the current domain controller.
C. Install the domain controller and transfer the schema master role to it. Then demote the current domain controller.
D. You cannot transfer the schema master role from the first domain controller in the forest without re-creating the forest.

6. What is the significance of the global catalog server in a single-domain forest?

A. The global catalog server allows users to log on from any domain controller in the domain.
B. The global catalog server allows users to easily find Active Directory resources located on any domain controller in the domain.
C. The global catalog resides on each domain controller in the domain.
D. The global catalog server has no significance.

7. Which of the following objects must you create in Active Directory in order for the KCC to successfully build a replication topology? Select all that apply.

A. Site
B. Site link
C. Subnet
D. Site link bridge
E. All of the above

8. You let the KCC build a replication topology for your Active Directory network. As you review the topology, you decide that you would like to customize the

replication paths that will be used to take better advantage of high-speed connections that you know are available between certain sites. Which of the following objects should you create to customize the replication topology? Choose two.

A. Site
B. Site link
C. Connection object
D. Site link bridge

9. You are in the process of creating a replication topology. One of your site links will connect two domain controllers in the same domain. Which communication protocol will you select when you create the site link object?

A. RPC
B. SMTP
C. TCP/IP
D. KCC

10. You have created five sites for your Active Directory structure, in addition to the default site, and have installed domain controllers in domains in the forest. However, you notice that no replication topology has been generated. How would you troubleshoot this? Choose two.

A. Create server objects for each site object and associate them with existing servers.
B. Move domain controller server objects from the Default-First-Site site into the appropriate site objects.
C. Enable full-site bridging.
D. Enable the Knowledge Consistency Checker and force a topology rebuild.

REVIEW ANSWERS

1. **B** and **D** Because the East-West site link uses a lower-speed connection, you want to pass replication through Central using the high-speed connection. Creating a site link bridge that uses the site links between East and Central and West and Central accomplishes that goal. The cost of the East-West site link bridge is the sum of the costs of the two site links it is composed of. Therefore, you want to be sure that the cost of the East-West site

link is higher than the overall cost of the site link bridge to ensure that replication takes place across the site link bridge, but can still use the site link if necessary. You would not want the East-West site link cost to be lower, as would be the case with A and C. That would cause replication to take place over the slower connection.

2. **A** is correct (which automatically makes D incorrect). Creating sites and site links certainly accomplished the goal of optimizing replication traffic between the sites. Also, certainly users will be able to log on and locate resources successfully. However, what makes B and C incorrect is that the global catalog server resides in Central. This means that when users need to look up a resource or log on to the network, they would have to find the global catalog server in Central or check all the domain controllers, and this is not the easiest or most efficient way to operate. Microsoft recommends placing a global catalog server in each site.

3. **B** and **C** When adding a domain controller to an existing domain, you need to be a member of the Domain Admins group within that domain. However, when you are creating a new domain, you must be a member of Enterprise Admins in the forest. Also, the domain naming master server must be available to create a new domain. If it is not, you will not be able to create a new domain in the forest. For these same reasons, A and D are incorrect.

4. **B** Although you could argue that without the global catalog server (A), you may not be able to log on (you could log on with cached credentials), that is not the primary complaint. Users complain that logging on is slow and that password changes are not taking effect. It is the PDC emulator that supports down-level clients for this kind of function. C, D, and E are incorrect because they refer to single operation master roles that do not play a part in the logon or password-update process for down-level clients.

5. **C** You can easily transfer any operations master role from one domain controller to another as long as both are available and communicating. There is no restriction in this matter for the schema master, which makes D incorrect. You cannot assign the schema master role to more than one domain controller in the forest, as would be the case with B, nor can you assign any operations master role to a domain controller easily if the original domain controller is unavailable, as would be the case with A.

6. **D** Although A and B are certainly correct in a multidomain forest, in a single domain forest, each domain controller has a copy of Active Directory

(not the global catalog, as stated incorrectly in C). Therefore, the goals of A and B are accomplished without the aid of a global catalog server.

7. **A** **B** and **C**   The KCC uses sites, site links, and subnet objects that you create to build its replication topology. A site link bridge (**D**) is an additional object that you can create when you do not have a fully routed network or have a slower or unreliable connection between two sites and want to route replication traffic through two other site links. However, the KCC does not need site link bridge objects to generate a topology.

8. **C** and **D**   If you create new sites or site links (A and B), you will cause the KCC to reevaluate the topology automatically and rebuild it. However, the KCC may still not take best advantage of the connections that are available. By creating connection objects that utilize the high-speed connections and associating lower costs with these connections, you will provide a preferred path for replication using the connections. Site link bridges, too, provide a way for you to route replication between sites over a preferred network connection.

9. **A**   The only two choices you can make are RPC (displayed as IP in the Active Directory Sites and Servers console) and SMTP (making answers C and D incorrect). SMTP (B) cannot be used to replicate data between domain controllers in the same site or domain controllers that are in the same domain in different sites.

10. **A** and **B**   Although a site can be empty, each site must have a server object associated with a domain controller in order for the Knowledge Consistency Checker (KCC) to work. Therefore, you either need to create server objects yourself and associate them with appropriate servers, move the existing domain controller server objects into the appropriate sites, or some combination of both. Full-site bridging (C) does not really play a role in this; however, it too, like D (the Knowledge Consistency Checker) could not take place if no server objects existed in the site objects.

Configuring, Managing, Monitoring, Optimizing, and Troubleshooting Change and Configuration Management

Creating Group Policies

ETA	NEWBIE	SOME EXPERIENCE	EXPERT
	8 hours	5 hours	3 hours

The first two parts of this book, and of the certification exam, dealt with the planning, implementation, and configuration of an Active Directory domain structure. This section focuses on one of the primary purposes of Active Directory—change and configuration management of user and computer environments through the use of group policies.

This chapter, in particular, reviews the basic concepts of group policy and discusses how to implement and configure an effective group policy structure. Chapter 6 takes this discussion to the next level and explores how to use group policy to manage network configurations, software availability, and desktop environments. Chapter 7 looks at a different aspect of change and configuration management as it relates to computer setup by discussing the Remote Installation Service feature of Active Directory.

Objective 5.01

Implement and Troubleshoot Group Policy

One of the organizational issues facing many network administrators is the high cost of managing what seems to be exploding numbers of computers and computing environments. This is generally referred to as the *total cost of ownership* (TCO) and includes not only your time as an administrator but downtime experienced by the user due to inadvertent (or intentional) changes that occur in the user's computing environment.

Group Policy can be viewed as a means of lowering the total cost of ownership of the computing environment through the use of rules or templates that are applied to the user or the user's computer as part of their participation in an Active

Directory–enabled network. Group Policy provides a flexible means of affecting the computing environment of a single user or computer or groups of users or computers, within a specific location or OU, or even across the network, without you having to "travel" to the specific user's or computer's location.

Once you have defined the environment through Group Policy, Active Directory proceeds to continually enforce it throughout the network. To sum up, then, Group Policy gives you four main benefits:

- It lowers the total cost of ownership of your network environment.
- It ensures that user and computer environments are consistent, standard, and conform to the business needs of your organization.
- It centralizes control of user and computer environments.
- It provides a secure environment.

Exam Tip

Windows 2000 computers natively support the application of Group Policies. However, down-level versions of Windows operating systems such as Windows 98 and Windows NT 4.0 do not. Microsoft does provide an Active Directory client for down-level operating systems. This client, however, gives the clients the benefit of logging in to any domain controller and the ability to search Active Directory objects.

Several settings can be configured in Group Policy to effect a specific environment for a user or computer. For example, administrative templates provide Registry configuration settings, limit access to the Control Panel, and control how services load and run. Also, security settings can control how and what a user can access on the network, audit resource access, and enable account policies such as mandatory password changes and lockout policies.

Four types of scripts are supported through Group Policy. In addition to the traditional logon script that you are used to, you can implement scripts that execute when a user logs off the network or when a computer starts or shuts down. Also, settings can be used to customize and manage Internet Explorer on Windows 2000 clients. Indeed, applications can be published or assigned to users and computers based on the application of Group Policies (explored in Chapter 6).

Group Policy is one cog in a gear mesh of technologies offered in Windows 2000 that provide effective and efficient change and configuration management of computing environments. Other key elements you will read about in other books (and study for other exams) include Synchronization Manager, Microsoft Intellimirror, Offline Files, and Remote Installation Services (which you will review in Chapter 7).

As you can see, Group Policy is a powerful tool aimed at minimizing administrative overhead and lowering the total cost of ownership in the computing environments while maximizing and centralizing change and configuration management in those same environments. Like Active Directory implementation, it is important that you plan your Group Policy structure before rolling it out. Indeed, a significant part of your Group Policy implementation plan will include the effective implementation of an OU structure for the domains in your forest, as reviewed in Chapter 3.

You need to identify the business, security, and user computing needs within your organization before you start creating and assigning Group Policy objects. Of course, you also need to test your policies to ensure that they are applied as you intended. The better part of troubleshooting lies in the post-production testing of your policies.

You can monitor Group Policy activity through the Event Viewer by enabling its diagnostic logging feature. This must be done in the Windows 2000 Registry by taking the following steps:

1. In the Registry, locate the key HKEY_LOCAL_MACHINE\Software\ Microsoft\WindowsNT\CurrentVersion and add a new key to it called Diagnostics.
2. To this new key, add the DWORD parameter RunDiagnosticLoggingGlobal with a value of 1.

Group Policy events will be added to the Application log. It is likely that a very large number of events will be generated, so you should monitor or perhaps change the Application log file size and perhaps only use this feature for troubleshooting purposes.

Windows 2000 also provides a couple command-line tools that can assist you when troubleshooting Group Policy. Both are part of the Windows 2000 Support Tools add-on included with the source CD. Netdiag.exe can help to locate and troubleshoot Group Policy issues that may be related to network issues by testing the status and functionality of the client experiencing a problem. The results of its tests are written to a log file called netdiag.log on the computer on which it is run. Sometimes Group Policy problems can arise when Group Policy objects are not fully replicated or synchronized among domain controllers. Replmon.exe allows you to monitor the status of replication events involving Group Policy in a graphic interface, view the replication topology, and force synchronization among domain controllers.

Travel Assistance

The Windows 2000 Resource Kit also provides a set of tools that can help you troubleshoot Group Policy issues. In particular, gpresult .exe displays the effect of a Group Policy on a given computer or logged-on user.

Other problems that you may encounter with Group Policy will be attributed to the inheritance of policy settings (including blocked inheritance and disabled Group Policy objects), incorrect permissions for creating, modifying, or applying a Group Policy object, or simply inadequate testing of the policy before and after rolling it out. The remainder of this chapter focuses on specific aspects of implementing and configuring Group Policy objects, including inheritance and security.

Objective 5.02 Create and Modify a Group Policy Object

The Group Policy object (GPO) is the primary mechanism for implementing Group Policy. The GPO itself actually consists of two parts stored in different places: the Group Policy container (GPC) and the Group Policy template (GPT).

The GPC is stored as an object in Active Directory and can be viewed as a container object through the Active Directory Users and Computers console tool. The GPC stores the attributes and extensions of the Group Policy, including the location of the GPTs. It also contains version information used by domain controllers to control the replication of GPOs. As you can see in Figure 5-1, each GPC container is maintained under System\Policies and is named after the GUID assigned to the GPO by Active Directory.

The GPT information for each domain is stored in a folder structure under *systemroot*\SYSVOL\sysvol*domainname*\Policies on each domain controller, as you can see in Figure 5-2. Like the GPC container, the folder name is the GUID of the GPO you created.

GPOs are generally associated with sites, domains, and/or OUs, giving you added flexibility and control over how much or how little of the network you will manage. So, if you want to apply a specific desktop policy GPO to users in the Accounting OU, you can associate, or *link*, that GPO to the Accounting OU. If you

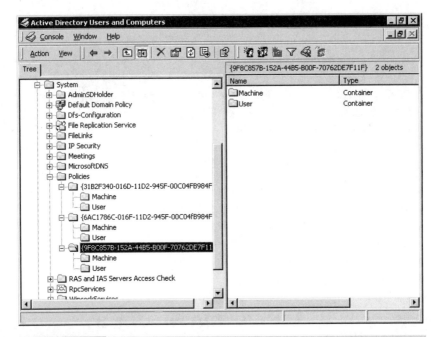

FIGURE 5-1   An example of the GPC for a domain

want to apply an account-lockout policy to all accounts in a domain, you can link a GPO that affects that policy with the domain in question. However, you can only link GPOs with an OU. This means that you cannot apply a Group Policy to the Users, Computers, or Builtin default containers.

Travel Advisory

You can view the GPC in Active Directory Users and Computers by enabling the Advanced Features View option and then expanding the domain, System, and Policies containers.

Local Lingo

GUID   All objects in Active Directory are assigned a GUID, or *globally unique identifier.* The GUID is a 128-bit value that an object is assigned when it is created to ensure that it is unique within the forest, domain tree, and domain in which is was created.

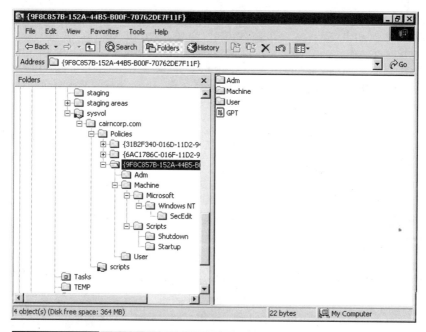

FIGURE 5-2 An example of the GPT for a domain

As you have seen, Group Policy can be applied to users and computers at the site, domain, or OU level. In any case, Windows 2000 takes a "top-down" approach, as it were, in evaluating and applying any GPO by always starting with the GPO "furthest away" from the affected user or computer.

GPOs assigned to a site are always processed first, then those assigned to a domain, and then finally those assigned to an OU, child OU, and so on. Policy settings are cumulative, and the process is known as *inheritance*. You'll read more about inheritance later in this chapter.

Exam Tip

Many exam questions incorporate the way policy settings are applied to a user or computer. Remember the order: sites, domains, and OUs. Polices are always applied in this order and are cumulative. Also, in general, when there is a conflict, the setting "nearer" the user or computer will be applied.

When the computer starts, any computer policy settings and startup scripts are applied such as service settings, security settings (such as who can log on at the computer), computer-specific Registry settings, application settings, and so on. User-specific policy settings are next applied at the time the user logs on and include desktop settings, user security (such as access to Control Panel applications) assigned and published applications, folder redirection, and logon (or logoff) scripts.

Travel Advisory

All GPOs assigned to a computer must finish processing before the logon screen will be displayed for a user. Also, by default, each successive GPO that must be applied to a computer and user must complete before the next one is applied. This is known as *synchronous processing,* and it ensures that if there are any dependencies or conflicts among the GPOs, they will be appropriately resolved. However, if you know that the GPOs do not need to be processed in a particular order or have any settings that might need conflict resolution, you could set each GPO to process asynchronously to speed up processing by using multiple threads. Asynchronous processing, nevertheless, is not recommended.

Sometimes computer and user settings can conflict with each other. When this happens, the computer-based policy settings will win out over the user settings. Besides being applied when the computer starts or a user logs on, Group Policy settings are refreshed on a specific, although configurable, default interval: every 90 minutes on client computers and every 5 minutes on domain controllers.

You'll use the Active Directory Users and Computers console to create and associate GPOs with a domain or OU, and you'll use the Active Directory Sites and Services console to do the same with sites. To create and link a GPO to a site, you must be a member of the Enterprise Admins group. To create and link a site to a domain or OU, you must be a member of the Domain Admins group or have been delegated control to do so.

The steps are straightforward. Using the appropriate console, you right-click the site, domain, or OU for which you are creating or linking the GPO, choose Properties from the pop-up menu, and switch to the Group Policy tab. Click New and enter the name of the new GPO you want to create, as you see in Figure 5-3.

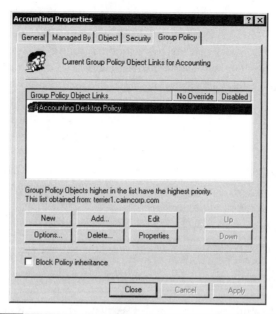

FIGURE 5-3   Creating a new Group Policy

You can then proceed to edit the policy settings as you need to. If you need to modify the GPO later, you can do so by returning to the Group Policy tab, selecting the GPO you want to modify from the Group Policy Object Links list box, and clicking Edit.

Recall from Chapter 4's discussion of operations master roles that certain Active Directory objects are managed by domain controllers that have assumed specific operations master roles in order to control replication and the updating of objects in Active Directory. GPOs are a fine example of this use of roles. GPO management is always handled by the PDC emulator. This ensures that only one version of the GPO is being created, edited, and so on and that the edits take place on one specific server. In this way, Active Directory can be sure that there are no update conflicts in the event that the same GPO is being modified by more than one administrator.

If the PDC emulator is not available, you receive a message advising you of this and asking whether you want to override GPO settings on an alternative domain controller. If you answer Yes, whichever administrator makes the final changes will win out. It is best to use the override option only if no one else is working with the same GPO and if you are sure that any previous changes to the GPO have already been replicated throughout the site or domain.

You could alternatively specify a domain controller other than the PDC emulator to manage GPO changes by using the DC Options command from the View menu of the Group Policy snap-in console or by creating a GPO to identify which domain controller should be used to manage GPOs.

When you create a GPO, its settings are based on a standard administrative template. By default, the policy itself does nothing outside the defaults of the operating system—that is, no additional restriction or security is added. However, you can edit the policy and thus customize the working environments for users and computers.

You edit a GPO by selecting the GPO you want to modify from the Group Policy Object Links list, as shown in Figure 5-3, and then clicking Edit. Figure 5-4 displays a sample GPO-editing console. Note that GPO settings are divided into computer and user settings. Each of these folders are further divided into software settings, used for publishing and assigning applications (Chapter 6), Windows settings, such as account policies, services, and so on, and administrative templates, used for desktop management, Registry entries, and so on.

In Figure 5-4, in the Tree window, you can see that the name of the policy is Accounting Desktop Policy. You can also see that this policy modifies the user's desktop so that the My Network Places icon will not be displayed. Each policy has

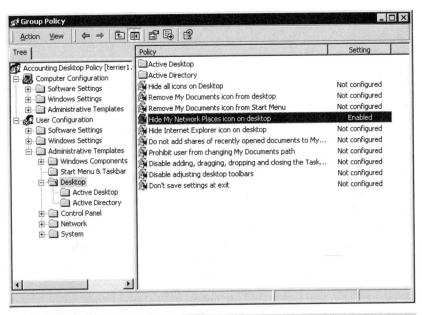

FIGURE 5-4   Group Policy–editing console

three options that can be set: Not Configured, Enabled, and Disabled. The Not Configured option means that this policy setting has not been configured and therefore should be ignored when evaluating which settings to apply. The Enabled option means that this policy should be considered and applied as the whole policy is evaluated. The Disabled option means that this policy should not be applied as the whole policy is evaluated.

For example, if a higher policy disables this setting, a value of Enabled for the same setting evaluated in a GPO "closer" to the user or computer would take precedence, and a value of Not Configured would mean that the previous value (Disabled, in this case) would stand. Similarly, if a higher policy enables this setting, a value of Disabled for the same setting evaluated in a GPO "closer" to the user or computer would take precedence.

In general, you should try to limit the number of GPOs that need to be processed if for no other reason than to preserve your own sanity and facilitate troubleshooting why some settings are being processed and some settings are not. Another way to make your management life easier is to group related policy settings in a single GPO, much like the Cairncorp Default Desktop Policy example, which holds the most common desktop standard settings for the company. Try to avoid linking GPOs to sites that contain multiple domains because those GPOs will be applied to all computers in that site and therefore in the various domains.

Travel Assistance

Chapter 6 explores more Group Policy settings relating to user environments, software configuration, and network management. Chapter 10 will focus specifically on security policies.

 **Objective 5.03** | # Link to an Existing Group Policy Object

When you create a new GPO, you are actually linking it with a particular site, domain, or OU. However, existing GPOs can be linked to other sites, domains, or OUs as is necessary. You can link multiple GPOs to one site, domain, or OU, for example, if you have separate GPOs for desktop settings, application assignment, and security. You can also link one GPO to many different sites, domains, and OUs to take advantage of policy settings that are more global in scope.

For example, say you create a standard user desktop policy for a site. It would be inefficient—if not downright silly—for you to re-create the same GPO for every existing or new OU that you create, particularly because if you need to modify the GPO at all, you might need to modify all the other GPOs as well.

It is possible to create GPOs that are not linked to any site, domain, or OU initially. This could be particularly useful in situations where you have not had time to test the GPOs or are in the process of planning a larger implementation of Group Policy within an organization—or simply when creating and testing GPOs is the responsibility of a specific group within your organization.

In order to create an unlinked GPO, you need to create a new Microsoft Management Console (MMC) with the Group Policy snap-in. When you choose the Add Snap-In option for the MMC and select Group Policy, you launch the Select Group Policy Object Wizard, as shown in Figure 5-5.

By default, you will create a local policy for use on the computer you are using. However, if you want this policy to be available through Active Directory, in the Select Group Policy Object dialog box, click Browse to display the Browse for a Group Policy Object dialog box. On the All tab, right-click anywhere in the All Group Policy Objects Stored in This Domain list box and choose New from the

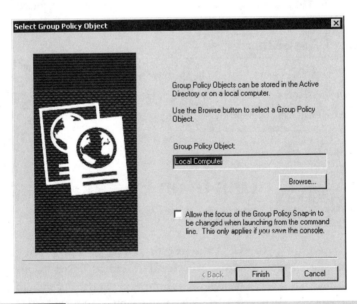

FIGURE 5-5   Launching the Group Policy snap-in

pop-up menu. Enter a name for the GPO (Figure 5-6), click OK, and then click Finish. Exit out to the MMC, where you will be able to edit the new GPO. The new GPO will be available to be linked to other sites, domains, or OUs.

You can link a GPO to a domain or OU through the Active Directory Users and Computers console similarly to the way you created a new GPO. You right-click the domain or OU for which you are linking the GPO, choose Properties from the pop-up menu, switch to the Group Policy tab, and click Add. Select the Domain/OUs, Sites, or All tab, depending on where the existing GPO resides. Then select the name of the specific domain, OU, or site that the GPO is linked to currently from the Look In list box. Then select the GPO you want to link to from the Group Policy Objects Linked to This Container list. For example, if you want to link the unlinked GPO you created earlier (Figure 5-6), you would look for it in the All tab list box, as you see in Figure 5-7.

Linking an existing GPO to a site is done through the Active Directory Sites and Services console. As in the previous steps, you right-click the site for which you are linking the GPO, choose Properties from the pop-up menu, switch to the Group Policy tab, and click Add. Select the Domain/OUs, Sites, or All tab, depending on where the existing GPO resides. Then select the name of the specific domain, OU, or site that the GPO is linked to currently from the Look In list box. Then select the GPO you want to link to from the Group Policy Objects Linked to This Container list.

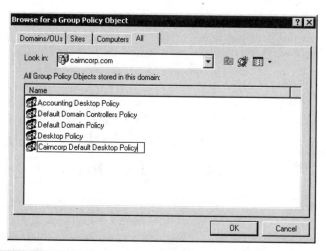

FIGURE 5-6 Creating an unlinked GPO using the Group Policy snap-in

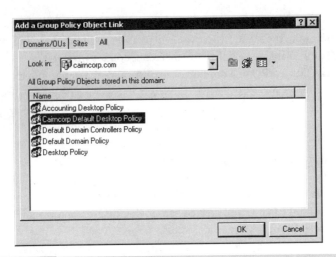

FIGURE 5-7   Linking an existing GPO to a container object

Travel Advisory

You are generally discouraged from linking an existing GPO to a site rather than creating a new GPO for the site. Anyone who has read and write permissions to the GPO can make changes. If the GPO is linked to a site, those changes are propagated throughout the site, which may very well compromise the policy settings you intended to apply.

Objective 5.04

Delegate Administrative Control of Group Policy

Remember that, by default, members of the Enterprise Admins group can create and link GPOs to sites, and the members of Domain Admins (and Enterprise Admins) can create or link GPOs to domains or OUs. However, in many organizations, it may be desirable or necessary to delegate the management of various aspects of GPOs to specific users or groups. For example, perhaps each domain might have an administrator responsible for creating and modifying GPOs for that domain. Perhaps all GPOs are maintained by a specific IT group, but delegation of control for linking GPOs to domains and OUs is assigned to a specific administrator or group within each domain. You can delegate control over the creation, editing, and linking of GPOs.

Each site, domain, and OU includes two attributes in Active Directory that are specific to Group Policy: gPLINK and gPOptions. These attributes store information about the GPOs that are linked to the containers and what the GPO option settings are. In order for someone other than the designated default group members to manage links or modify GPO options, they must be given at least read and write permissions to these two attributes.

The easiest, and preferred, method of giving users the ability to manage GPO links is to run the Delegation of Control Wizard (right-click the site, domain, or OU in question and choose Delegate Control from the pop-up menu) and assign the user the Manage Group Policy Links task, as demonstrated in Figure 5-8. Assigning the task in this way automatically assigns the user read and write permissions to the gPLINK and gPOptions attributes for the site, domain, or OU.

To give a user the ability to modify the GPO settings and options, they must be given explicit read and write permissions to the GPO. This is done by selecting the specific GPO from the Group Policy's Properties dialog box and then displaying the Security tab in the GPO's Properties dialog box, as shown in Figure 5-9.

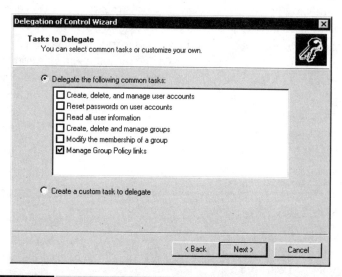

FIGURE 5-8   Delegation of control for managing GPO links

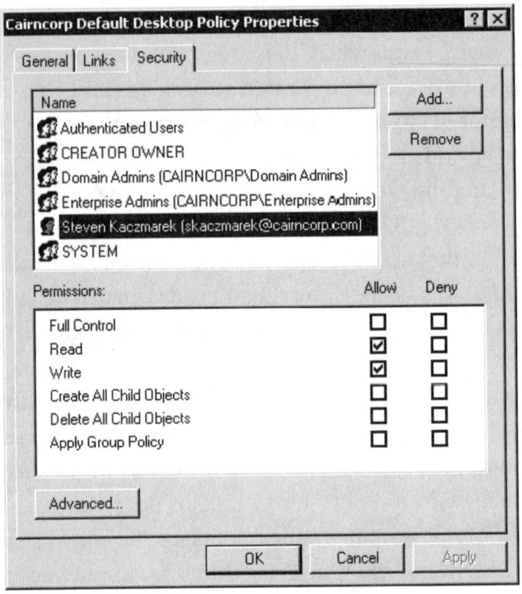

FIGURE 5-9   Giving Edit control over a GPO

GPO security can be set by any member of the Enterprise Admins or Domain Admins groups or by the Group Policy Creator Owner of the GPO in question.

To give a user the ability to create new GPOs, you need only make the user a member of the Group Policy Creator Owners security group in the appropriate domains. The user can then create new GPOs and edit them. However, the user cannot edit any GPOs that they did not explicitly create or were not given permission to edit. Furthermore, if you do not also use the Delegation of Control Wizard to assign the GPO link task to the user, the user will not be able to link the GPO to any site, domain, or OU.

Travel Advisory

As always, you should try to limit the number of persons who can control your GPOs. Remember the old saying about too many cooks spoiling the broth. The more persons involved in "seasoning" the GPO settings, the more difficult it will be to troubleshoot and control Group Policy issues.

Modify Group Policy Prioritization and Configure Group Policy Options

Objective 5.05

As you have seen, you can link one GPO to multiple sites, domains, or OUs, and you can link multiple GPOs to any one site, domain, or OU. The ultimate Group Policy that is applied to a user or computer is the cumulative application of GPOs assigned to the site, domain, and OU that the user or computer belongs to. This process is known as *inheritance*. GPOs closer to the user or computer take precedence over GPOs further away. As each GPO is evaluated and a cumulative policy is compiled, whenever there is a conflict, the settings of the GPO closer to the user or computer will be applied. The only exception as noted earlier is when computer and user settings conflict. In this case, the computer settings will take precedence.

Because multiple GPOs can be linked to the same container object, conflicts among settings in these GPOs can certainly occur. For example, suppose the Accounting OU has two GPOs linked to it: Cairncorp Default Desktop Policy and Accounting Desktop Policy. Cairncorp Default Desktop Policy has the setting Hide My Network Places Icon on Desktop enabled, but Accounting Desktop Policy has the same setting disabled. Which GPO should be applied?

As it turns out, when multiple GPOs are linked to the same container, as you see in Figure 5-10, they are evaluated in a bottom-up fashion. The settings for the GPO at the top of the list will take precedence and settle any conflicts. You can change the order of these GPOs by selecting each GPO and clicking the Up or Down button, as appropriate.

You can also alter the way that the final cumulative policy is generated by blocking the inheritance of GPO settings from a domain's or OU's parent container. By selecting the Block Policy Inheritance option you see at the bottom of Figure 5-10, you essentially will restart the policy setting evaluation process beginning at this point in the hierarchy.

For example, suppose that you have created a standard desktop policy called Cairncorp Default Desktop Policy that can be applied to the majority of the users in the Central domain and which you have linked to the Central domain. However, users in the Accounting OU require a customized desktop environment that identifies specific security and application settings. You can create a custom desktop for the Accounting OU users called Accounting Desktop Policy and link

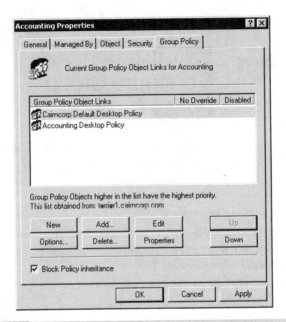

FIGURE 5-10   Modifying policy priority and blocking inheritance

Exam Tip

When you select the Block Policy Inheritance option, you will be blocking the inheritance of policy settings for all GPOs in the parent containers. You cannot choose to block inheritance for only selected GPOs. Therefore, in the preceding example, if there were other policies linked to the Central domain that needed to be applied to the Accounting OU, they would also be ignored.

it to the Accounting OU in the Central domain. Then, you can select the Block Policy Inheritance option to ensure that the Cairncorp Default Desktop Policy settings are not evaluated or applied.

There are two additional GPO options you can set that further define just how GPO settings will or will not be evaluated by the time they reach the user or computer. Selecting an appropriate GPO from the list and clicking the Options button on the GPO tab of a container's Properties dialog box displays these two options, as you see in Figure 5-11.

The first option is the No Override option. When you select this option, you say that regardless of whether or not the Block Policy Inheritance option has been selected

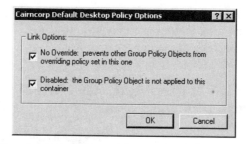

FIGURE 5-11 GPO policy options

in a lower container, the settings for this particular GPO cannot be ignored. In other words, nothing can block these settings. Because the No Override option is set for the specific GPO, and that GPO can be linked to other containers, the No Override option only applies to that specific container and its child containers for inheritance.

Exam Tip

Here's where inheritance gets tricky. Generally, GPO settings are evaluated from highest to lowest, with the lowest ultimately taking precedence. However, when more than one GPO has the No Override option enabled, and there are conflicts among these GPOs, the conflicting setting in the *highest* GPO will win out. Although this is not immediately intuitive, it should make sense. If you are overriding settings, presumably you want the initial settings to take precedence over subsequent settings, right? Hence, the highest settings win.

The second option is the Disabled option. When you select this option, you are in effect ignoring any settings for that GPO in this container only. Child containers will continue to inherit the settings for the GPO—unless, of course, you choose to block policy inheritance further down the line.

Travel Advisory

GPOs set with the No Override option enabled should only contain critical settings such as security settings. Because these settings will always be applied, it's possible that you can inadvertently override other settings that are equally—or more—important.

Try not to overuse the blocking and disabling options. The more you introduce these twists and turns in the way your polices are to be applied, the more difficult it will be to troubleshoot a Group Policy problem.

Objective 5.06

Filter Group Policy Settings by Using Security Policies

When you assign GPOs to sites, domains, and containers (OU), the policy settings are evaluated as we've discussed and applied to all users and computers in their respective containers. This is the default, and by and large, this is the way you'll want the policies to be processed. However, you may not always want all GPOs in a container to apply to all users or computers in a container. For example, you may not want a standard user desktop policy to apply to the manager of a department or to the IT help desk users who are members of that particular container.

Active Directory gives you the ability to identify which users and computers should not have a policy applied to them by setting GPO permissions appropriately. This is known as *filtering* the GPO settings. By default, all authenticated users (and computers) are given the Allow·Read and Allow Apply Group Policy permissions in the DACL for each GPO you create.

Local Lingo

DACL   The Discretionary Access Control List is similar to the Access Control Lists in Windows NT 4.0. The DACL is an attribute of an object in Active Directory and is really nothing more than a list of permissions that can be granted or restricted for users and computers that affects to what degree the users and computers can access that object.

Also, by default, members of the Domain Admins group, Enterprise Admins group, and the System account are given the permissions Allow Read, Allow Write, Allow Create All Child Objects, and Allow Delete All Child Objects. Because members of these groups are also members of Authenticated Users, their effective rights will also include Allow Apply Group Policy. You might consider giving administrators Deny Allow Group Policy because some GPO settings might restrict the administrators in undesirable ways.

Therefore, if you do not want the GPO to be applied, you must set both the Read and Apply Group Policy permissions to Deny for the appropriate user or users. You can explicitly add the user to the DACL and then set those two permissions to Deny (not recommended), or you can add the users to an Active Directory security group, add the security group to the DACL, and set the two permissions to Deny.

Exam Tip

It's always recommended by Microsoft to add users to groups and set permissions based on group membership. It's more efficient in the long run. Whenever you have the option to use groups in an exam question, use groups. It's always the best answer.

Another more precise way to apply the GPO would be to remove Authenticated Users altogether from the GPO's DACL and add in the users based on their group memberships. Recall the block inheritance example from Objective 5.05 earlier. If you block inheritance at the Accounting OU, you block inheritance of all GPOs from all parent containers. That could mean that some settings from parent containers that should be applied actually won't be applied.

However, you could create and then add a security group called Accounting Users to the DACL for the Cairncorp Default Desktop Policy GPO and give that security group Deny Read and Deny Apply Group Policy permissions, as shown in Figure 5-12. This means that if a user is a member of the Accounting Users group and the Cairncorp Default Desktop Policy GPO is being evaluated for a container that they are a member of, the Cairncorp Default Desktop Policy GPO would not be applied. Any other GPOs, however, would be applied, as long as the users are not explicitly denied Read and Apply Group Policy permissions.

Exam Tip

Deny permissions act like No Access permissions did in Windows NT 4.0. A user could be a member of multiple groups. Each group can be represented in the DACL for a GPO with a different set of permissions. Usually a user's effective permissions are cumulative of the permissions granted via the user's group memberships. However, if even one group has been explicitly denied Read and Apply Group Policy permissions, that user will not have the GPO applied.

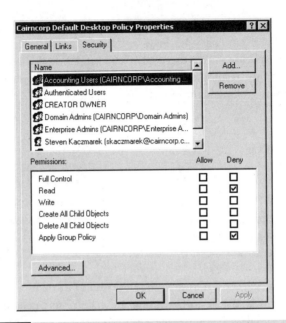

FIGURE 5-12   The DACL for a Group Policy

✔ **Objective 5.01: Implement and Troubleshoot Group Policy**   Implementing an effective Group Policy strategy can result in four main benefits:

- Lower total cost of ownership
- Consistency and standardization of computer, user, and network settings
- Centralization of control over the working environment
- Increased security

Group Policy can be used to modify Registry entries, standardize desktop and computer environments, publish and configure applications, and secure network resource access. Group Policy is one element of a group of Windows 2000 features that provides a suite of change and configuration management tools, including Intellimirror, Remote Installation Service, offline file and folder redirection, and synchronization management.

Successful implementation of Group Policy implies having a well-thoughtout implementation plan and the tools available to help you monitor and troubleshoot Group Policy events.

✓ **Objective 5.02: Create and Modify a Group Policy Object**   GPOs can be associated or linked to site, domain, and OU containers. They are evaluated in a top-down fashion and are generally cumulative in nature. If settings conflict, the settings in the GPO closest to the affected user or computer always takes precedence, except when the settings conflict between the computer and the user. In this case, the computer settings will take precedence.

GPOs that are associated with sites are created, linked, and modified using the Active Directory Sites and Services console (Enterprise Admins only). GPOs that are associated with domain or OU containers are created, linked, and modified using the Active Directory Users and Computers console (Domain Admins or Enterprise Admins).

✓ **Objective 5.03: Link to an Existing Group Policy Object**   A GPO may be linked to many different containers, and likewise many GPOs can be linked to any one container. Usually, you create the GPO as you link it to a site, domain, or OU. However, using the Group Policy snap-in, you can create an unlinked GPO and then link it later as you plan and implement your site, domain, and OU structure. Although this gives you much flexibility in creating and linking GPOs, you should try to avoid having to evaluate too many GPOs for each user and computer. That makes it harder for you to manage and requires more processing resource.

✓ **Objective 5.04: Delegate Administrative Control of Group Policy** Although Enterprise Admins and Domain Admins by default can create, manage, and link GPOs, you can delegate these functions to other users if necessary. The Delegation of Control Wizard lets you identify who can manage GPO links. Any user made a member of the Group Policy Creator Owner group will have the ability to create new GPOs and manage them. Any user given Read and Write permission in the DACL of the GPO will be able to modify that GPO. As per Microsoft's best practices, permissions like these should always be given via a user's group membership rather than explicitly to the user's account.

✓ **Objective 5.05: Modify Group Policy Prioritization and Configure Group Policy Options**   Although most GPO processing is performed in a top-down fashion from site to domain to OU, other rules may also be applied. When two or more GPOs are linked to the same container, they are processed in a bottom-up fashion, with the top GPO resolving any final conflicts. You can also choose to block inheritance of all GPO settings from parent containers using the Block Policy Inheritance option in the Group Policy properties of any given container. Setting this option effectively restarts GPO processing at the container level. However, this option can itself be ignored if you set the No Override option for that GPO in the parent container. You can also choose to disable a GPO from being applied within a given container.

✔ **Objective 5.06: Filter Group Policy Settings by Using Security Policies**
You can determine which users or computers should or should not have a GPO applied to them through permission changes made in the GPO's DACL. By default, all users have Read and Apply Group Policy permissions on all GPOs. However, if you deny these permissions on a GPO, that GPO's settings will not be considered when the user's or computer's effective Group Policy settings are evaluated. Once again, the most effective—and recommended—way to grant permissions is through the use of security groups.

REVIEW QUESTIONS

1. After implementing a Group Policy structure within your organization, you are experiencing problems in the way the policies are being evaluated and applied to some computers and users. Connectivity does not appear to be the issue. What two steps could you take to help troubleshoot the problem?

   A. Enable diagnostic logging in the Event Viewer.
   B. Run the netdiag.exe command-line tool.
   C. Run the replmon.exe command-line tool.
   D. Run the gpresult.exe command-line tool.

2. Your Active Directory structure consists of a single site, three domains—East, West and Central—and an Accounting, IT, and HR OU in each domain. Users and computers are distributed among the OUs. A GPO for the site hides the My Network Places icon on the desktop and disables the Start | Run menu. A GPO for the East domain blocks inheritance from the site but disables the Start | Run menu. A GPO for the Accounting OU in East enables the Start | Run menu. What will be the effective settings for users and computers in the East Accounting OU?

   A. Start | Run is enabled; My Network Places is enabled.
   B. Start | Run is disabled; My Network Places is hidden.

    C. Start | Run is disabled; My Network Places is enabled.

    D. Start | Run is enabled; My Network Places is hidden.

3. You are in the process of creating a GPO structure for your organization. You have one large Active Directory domain with locations in three major cities in the United States represented as OUs in the domain. You are intermittently receiving error messages when you try to create a GPO in one of the OUs asking you whether you want to store the GPO on a specific domain controller. What might be causing this problem?

    A. The global catalog server for the domain is unavailable.

    B. The PDC emulator is for the OU unavailable.

    C. The PDC emulator is for the domain unavailable.

    D. The global catalog server for the OU is unavailable.

4. You are in the process of creating a new GPO to control the desktop settings for users in a particular OU. You want to control settings such as desktop wallpaper, access to the Control Panel, and so on. When you open the edit console for the GPO, where should you make these setting changes?

    A. Under Computer Configuration | Administrative Templates.

    B. Under User Configuration | Administrative Templates.

    C. Under Computer Configuration | Software Settings.

    D. Under User Configuration | Software Settings.

5. As you plan your GPO structure, you begin to see common threads in the way policies can be applied throughout your organization. In particular, there are three main policies relating to network configuration, software configuration, and desktop management that can be applied to most of the users and computers in the domains in your site. You have not yet implemented all your domains and OUs, but you want to have these main GPOs available to link when you do implement them. What is the most efficient way to accomplish this?

    A. Create the three GPOs in the site. As you add each domain, it will inherit the GPO settings.

    B. Create the three GPOs as unlinked GPOs. Link them to the site after you add the domains so that the domains will inherit the GPO settings.

    C. Create the three GPOs as unlinked GPOs. Link them to each domain when and as appropriate.

    D. Create a new GPO for each domain when you add the domain.

6. The Accounting department has an IT resource administrator who needs to be able to link and modify GPOs in the Accounting OU but should not be able to control GPO settings in any other OU. Which two steps can accomplish this?

   A. Use the Delegate Control Wizard on the Accounting OU to assign Group Policy link control to the administrator.

   B. Give the administrator Allow Read an Allow Write permissions to the appropriate GPOs.

   C. Use the Delegate Control Wizard on the site containing the Accounting OU to assign Group Policy link control to the administrator.

   D. Give the administrator Allow Read and Allow Apply Group Policy permission to the appropriate GPOs.

7. You have delegated control over the GPOs in the Human Resources OU to the local resource administrator by using the Delegate Control wizard and granting her Allow Read and Allow Write permissions to the GPOs, however, she tells you that she is still unable to modify the GPOs. How can you fix the problem?

   A. Grant her Deny Apply Group Policy permission on the GPOs in her OU.

   B. Make her a member of the Group Policy Creator Owner group.

   C. Block policy inheritance at the Human Resources OU.

   D. Make her a member of the local Administrators group.

8. You are delegating control over GPOs at the OU level to local administrators who are members of each OU. You want the local administrators to be able to create new GPOs, link existing GPOs to their respective OUs, and modify the GPO settings. You use the Delegate Control Wizard at each OU level and make each local administrator a member of the Group Policy Creator Owners group. Which of your goals have you accomplished?

   A. Local administrators can create new GPOs.

   B. Local administrators can link existing GPOs to their respective OUs.

   C. Local administrators can modify GPO settings.

   D. All of the above.

   E. None of the above.

9. You have created and linked two GPOs at the site level. One GPO defines a standard desktop environment for the users throughout all domains in the site. The other GPO defines security settings for the network. Each of your domains includes an IT OU that should be exempt from all desktop setting

changes other than those defined in its own GPO linked to its respective OU, but not the security settings. How should you alter inheritance on the IT OUs so that settings are applied as required?

A. Do nothing. Default inheritance will apply the settings as required.

B. Block inheritance at the IT OUs for any GPOs that alter the desktop settings but not for the security GPO.

C. Block inheritance at the IT OUs for any GPOs that alter the desktop settings and set the No Override option at the site level for the security GPO.

D. Block inheritance at the IT OUs for all parent GPOs and set the No Override option at the site level for the security GPO.

10. You have created and linked two GPOs at the site level. One GPO defines a standard desktop environment for the users throughout all domains in the site. The other GPO defines security settings for the network. Each of your domains include IT users who should be exempt from all desktop setting changes other than those defined in their own GPO linked to their respective domains, but not the security settings. How should you alter inheritance on the domains so that settings are applied as required to all users?

A. Create a security group that contains the IT users and set the Disabled option for the desktop settings GPO.

B. Create a security group that contains the IT users and grant them the Deny Read and Deny Write permissions in the DACL of the desktop setting GPO.

C. Create a security group that contains the IT users and grant them the Deny Read and Deny Apply Group Policy permissions in the DACL of the desktop setting GPO.

D. Create a security group that contains the IT users and grant them the Deny Read and Deny Apply Group Policy permissions in the DACL of the desktop setting GPO. Set the No Override option for the security GPO at the site level.

REVIEW ANSWERS

1. **A** and **D** Diagnostic logging will record GPO events such as the processing of settings for computers and users in the Application log of the Event Viewer. B evaluates connectivity, which was not the issue in this question. C evaluates replication issues.

2. **A** Because the East domain is blocking inheritance from the site, the site's GPO does not have to be considered. The GPO for East disables the Start | Run menu. However, because the GPO for Accounting enables the same option and is closer to the user or computer, it takes precedence.

3. **C** In order to maintain the integrity of a GPO, Active Directory always places the focus for creating GPOs on the PDC emulator. Only one domain controller in a domain can be the PDC emulator. It is not an OU-specific role, which makes B incorrect. The availability of the global catalog server does not affect your ability to create GPOs, thus making A and D incorrect.

4. **B** The question indicates that you are modifying settings for the users in the OU, so answers A and C are automatically wrong. The choice is between Administrative Templates (B) and Software Settings (D). However, items such as wallpaper settings and Control Panel access fall under administrative stuff rather than application-related configuration, thus making D incorrect.

5. **C** When you create an unlinked GPO, it is available to be linked when and as it should be used. In this case, because the GPO settings can apply to most of the domains (not all), it is most efficient to link the GPO to each domain when it does apply to the domain, rather than linking it to the site and letting the domains inherit the settings. B does give you more control, but by linking the GPOs to the site, all the domains will inherit the settings, including some domains for which the settings should not apply. The problem with A is that creating the GPO up front in the site automatically implies inheritance to all domains—again, including some that perhaps should not inherit the settings. The main issue with inheriting in this question lies in the efficiency part. Yes, letting the domains inherit is an automatic part, but you then have to do something about the domains that should not inherit— block inheritance, disable the GPO—another task. Creating new GPOs as suggested in D is simply not efficient nor recommended as a best practice.

6. **A** and **B** The Delegate Control wizard has the ability to grant the link GPO task to an administrator. However, you must execute the wizard in the container in which you want to delegate control, in this case at the Accounting OU. Giving the administrators Read and Write permission gives them the ability to modify existing GPOs. Answer C is incorrect because control is being delegated at the site level effectively giving the administrators the ability to link GPOs anywhere in the site rather than just at the Accounting OU level. Answer D is incorrect because the Read and Apply Group Policy

permission only allow the GPO to be processed and applied to the users. These permissions do not give change control over the GPO.

7. **A** Very likely the problem is that one or more security settings in the existing GPOs are preventing her from administering the GPOs themselves. By granting her Deny Apply Group Policy permission on all the GPOs, none of the GPOs will be applied to her. Of course, it would be better if you discovered which GPO was the culprit and just deny that one, especially if there are other settings that should be applied to her as well. B only serves to give her the added ability to create new GPOs, and she might still be restricted from doing that due to some other GPO setting. Blocking inheritance (C) would certainly stop her from getting the GPO settings applied, but it would also prevent everyone else in the OU as well. Membership in the local Administrators group (D) will give her local administrative access on the server in question but not change how GPO settings are applied to her.

8. **A** and **B** Making the users members of the Group Policy Creator Owner group gives them the ability to create new GPOs, and executing the Delegate Control Wizard at each OU level ensures that they can link GPOs in their respective OUs. In order to allow them to modify existing GPO settings, you must also give them Allow Read and Allow Write permissions to the GPOs, which makes the remaining answers incorrect.

9. **D** When you set the Block Inheritance option at an OU, you effectively block all GPOs from all parent containers. You cannot selectively block GPOs, as is implied in B and C. Yes, we are playing with words, but the wording in an exam question very often does have a significant role in whether one answer or another is correct. Setting the No Override option is also necessary to ensure that the security GPO is always enforced, no matter how the blocking option is set. Default inheritance (A) means that all GPO settings will always trickle down to the users or computers unless restricted in some way on the way "down."

10. **C** Because you do not want that specific GPO to be applied to a specific set of users, you need to grant those users Deny Read and Deny Apply Group Policy permissions. Placing users in a security group first and then applying permission to the group is a Microsoft best practice. A starts out good; however, you cannot set the Disabled option for only one group of users. The Disabled option disables processing of that GPO for all users and computers in the container in which it was disabled. B also starts out good,

but the Deny Write permission does not stop the GPO from being applied. Answer D is actually overkill. The first part is correct, because it's the same as C and will implicitly allow the security settings to be applied. You don't also have to set the No Override option in this case because the Deny permissions are assigned only to the desktop settings GPO. Remember that No Override overrides any other inheritance blocking in any child container, and you may have a case in which you do need to block that GPO for other users in other containers.

Managing Environments Using Group Policy

	NEWBIE	SOME EXPERIENCE	EXPERT
ETA	4 hours	3 hours	2 hours

In Chapter 5, you explored how to implement Group Policies and associate (or *link*) them to sites, domains, and OUs. You also saw different ways that inheritance of policy settings could be controlled and managed. In this chapter, you will examine some practical ways to use Group Policy to manage your users' computing environment, application configuration, and network configuration.

Manage and Troubleshoot User Environments by Using Group Policy

The process of managing a user's computing environment entails identifying what that environment should look like, how they connect to the network, what resources they have access to, and how their computer should run. In Windows NT, this kind of user management involved what's known as a *roaming profile* as a means to ensure that a user's settings "followed" them wherever they logged on. Group Policy settings can assist you in this endeavor by providing a more effective method of standardizing and enforcing computer configurations and users' desktops, such as network connections, account policies, wallpaper, desktop shortcuts, user profiles, security, and so on. The combination of Group Policy, software configuration (Intellimirror), and folder redirection provide an alternative means of reproducing the user's environment wherever the user logs on.

The most common way to manage the user environment is through the use of existing policy settings know as *administrative templates*. The Administrative Template policy settings effect changes in the computer and user environment by modifying Registry settings in HKEY_LOCAL_MACHINE (for the computer-oriented settings) and HKEY_CURRENT_USER (for the user-oriented settings). These settings may be applied at the site, domain, and OU levels, and they vary somewhat from level to level. For example, a setting that might be appropriate at the OU level, such as Internet Explorer program settings, may not be appropriate to apply at the domain level or a site level.

Policy settings are applied as described in Chapter 5, with those settings closest to the user or computer taking precedence. Many of the policy settings for the computer and user environments are the same. Recall from Chapter 5 that when a computer setting conflicts with a user setting, the computer setting will take precedence. When a computer starts up, all computer-oriented settings will be applied before the user settings. In fact, the user logon screen will not even be displayed until the computer settings have been applied.

The Administrative Template settings for each Group Policy object (GPO) you create are stored in a file called registry.pol on each domain controller. There is a registry.pol file for user and computer settings stored, respectively, in the \User and \Machine folders beneath the Group Policy template (GPT) folder for each GPO.

Exam Tip

Recall from Chapter 5 that each GPO you create is assigned a GUID and is stored in a folder named after the GUID in the following default location on each domain controller: *systemroot*\SYSVOL\Sysvol*domain-name*\Policies\.

Group Policy settings are divided into those affecting the computer environment, such as Windows 2000 operating system settings, hardware, services, and so on, and those affecting user environments, such as color schemes, shortcuts, access to Control Panel applications, and other desktop settings. As you can see in Figure 6-1, within these two groupings are several categories of settings you can configure. Table 6-1 outlines these categories.

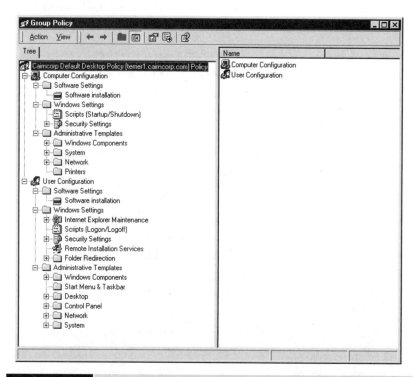

FIGURE 6-1   Group Policy categories for computer and user settings

TABLE 6.1	Categories for Group Policy Settings
Category	**Description**
Control Panel	Available for User Configuration only. Allows you to restrict access to Control Panel applications such as Add/Remove Programs, Display, System, Administration Tools, and so on.
Desktop	Available for User Configuration only. Allows you to modify the way the user's desktop looks. For example, you could hide all the desktop icons or specific icons such as My Network Places, remove the Run command on the Start menu, and disable or remove the Shut Down option.
Network	Available for both User and Computer Configuration. Allows you to control how network connections are established and used, including the network connection sharing feature of Windows 2000.
Printers	Available for computer configuration only. Allows you to control how printers are published to Active Directory.
Start Menu & Taskbar	Available for User Configuration only. Allows you to control which menu items are available to the user, such as access to the Run option, as well as what icons appear in the menu and whether the user can save changes. You can also remove the user's ability to search, and you can hide common program groups.
System	Available for User and Computer Configuration. Allows you to establish logon\logoff policies, set disk quotas, and define how the policies should be executed—for example, whether policy settings should be applied synchronously (each GPO must complete before the next one runs) or whether loopback processing is enabled, which ensures that computer-oriented settings are applied in preference to user-oriented settings.

(Continued)

TABLE 6.1	*CONTINUED*
Category	**Description**
Windows Components	Available for User and Computer Configuration. Allows you to restrict access to Windows 2000 tools such as the Map Network Drive and Disconnect Network Drive functions, restricts the capability to create new tasks in the Task Scheduler, or, for users, prevents users from altering Internet Explorer options and hides specific drives and drive mappings in My Computer.

Travel Advisory

A note about loopback processing. Computer-oriented policy settings and user-oriented policy settings will both affect the computer that the user is logging in to. User settings are applied last, and if there is a setting conflict, the computer setting wins. However, in some cases, such as kiosk computers, dedicated work-stations, or perhaps even servers, it may not be appropriate or advisable for user settings to be applied at all, or it may be necessary that computer settings always be applied last. If this scenario is true, you should enable one of two loopback-processing modes. Enable Replace Mode to ensure that user settings are effectively ignored or Merge Mode to ensure that computer settings are always processed last—and always take precedence.

You configure GPO settings by editing the properties of the GPO in question. For example, if you want to modify the User/System settings for a GPO called Accounting Desktop Policy linked to the Accounting OU, you would select that GPO from the Group Policy tab of the Account OU's Properties dialog box and click Edit. You would then locate the setting you want to modify under Computer Configuration or User Configuration and view that setting's properties. For example, if you want to prevent users in the Accounting OU from modifying their display settings, you could enable the Disable Display in Control Panel policy setting located in User Configuration\Administrative Templates\Control Panel\Display, as shown in Figure 6-2.

Each policy has three options that can be set: Not Configured, Enabled, and Disabled. The Not Configured option means that this policy setting has not been configured, so it should be ignored when evaluating which settings to apply. The Enabled option means that this policy should be considered and applied as the whole policy is evaluated and, as such, is added to the registry.pol file for the user or the computer. The Disabled option means that this policy should not be applied as the whole policy is evaluated, and it's also added to the appropriate registry.pol file.

For example, if a domain policy disables a setting, a value of Enabled for the same setting evaluated in a GPO linked to an OU "closer" to the user or computer would take precedence, whereas a value of Not Configured at the OU level would mean that the previous value (Disabled, in this case) would stand. Similarly, if a domain policy enables this setting, a value of Disabled for the same setting evaluated in a GPO linked to an OU would take precedence.

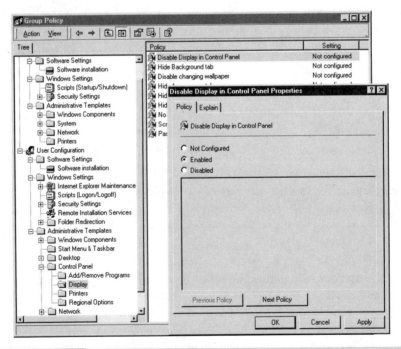

FIGURE 6-2   Enabling the Disable Display in Control Panel policy setting

Exam Tip

If the Administrative Template settings do not appear to be applied, you should check the usual suspects, as outlined in Chapter 5. For example, do all the users and computers in question have both the Read and Apply Group Policy permissions, or has inheritance been blocked at some point? You can run the Windows 2000 Resource Kit tool Gpresult.exe in verbose mode to determine whether the settings have been applied. If Administrative Template settings have been applied, you will see the following text in the result window: "The user (or computer) received 'Registry' settings from these GPOs." Check whether the GPOs in question contain your settings.

Install, Configure, Manage, and Troubleshoot Software by Using Group Policy

Objective 6.02

Group Policy provides an easy way to deploy and manage software applications throughout your network without having to visit each computer to configure the applications manually. Windows 2000 uses two components to offer this functionality: the Windows Installer Service and the Windows Installer Package. The Windows Installer Service is a Windows 2000 service that runs on Windows 2000 clients and is concerned with the installation, configuration, and repair of software applications on the client.

The Windows Installer Service uses Windows Installer Packages as its instruction set. Windows Installer Packages are self-executing script files that contain all the instructions necessary to successfully carry out the installation, configuration, or repair of an application on the client. Windows Installer Package files have the extension .MSI.

Two immediate benefits of using these Windows Installer components are the ability to completely and cleanly remove an application when it is no longer required and the ability to automatically reinstall the application or replace corrupted application files if application files are found to be missing or corrupt. In other words, the Windows Installer Service, using the Windows Installer Package files, keeps track of the state of the application. This makes it easy for you to upgrade, patch, and make other modifications to the application as well as install it or remove it.

Unlike Microsoft Systems Management Server 2.0, which gives you much more flexibility in advertising and deploying applications and tasks based on schedules throughout a forest, Windows 2000 provides two ways to deploy applications: They may be assigned or published to users or computers through a Group Policy.

The main difference between assigning and publishing an application lies in the requirements for that application. When you assign an application to a user, the application is basically available to the user and appears, or is advertised, on the user's Start menu or desktop. It also appears as a shortcut. When the user executes the shortcut or opens a file associated with that application, an installation routine is initiated. When you assign an application to a computer, the application is installed on that computer as part of the startup process.

Travel Advisory

You cannot assign a software application to a domain controller.

When you publish an application, you essentially make it available for the users to install at their leisure. It appears as an option in Add/Remove Programs, as shown in Figure 6-3, and will also be installed on demand if a user opens a file associated with the application, although you could disable this method of deployment.

Local Lingo

On-demand installation Installation of an application by clicking a shortcut or opening an associated file.

Before you configure your Group Policy to deploy an application, you must have already created (and tested) the MSI file and copied it to a shared network location that you will reference when you create the Group Policy. As added security, you can set permissions on the application folders to ensure that specific users or groups have access to specific folders, and you can also make the share point a hidden share so that users cannot casually browse for the folders.

Travel Advisory

Windows Installer packages may not be published to a computer.

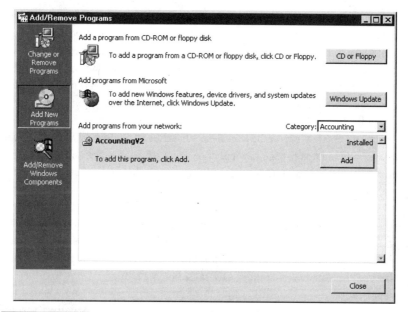

FIGURE 6-3   A published program available through Add/Remove Programs

---

Travel Assistance

For more information about using Windows Installer, visit Microsoft's Windows 2000 Web site at www.microsoft.com/windows2000 and search for Windows Installer.

Defining Deployment Options

As with administrative templates, you need to create or select an appropriate GPO to configure for application deployment and then edit it. Select Software Installation under User Configuration | Software Settings or Computer Configuration | Software Settings, depending on how you intend to install the application. Then right-click and choose New Package from the pop-up menu. A brief wizard will walk you through the deployment steps. Begin by selecting the MSI file in the File Open dialog box. Next, select a deployment method—assigned or published—in the Deploy Software dialog box.

You can also specify default deployment options for all new applications through the Properties dialog box for the Software Installation folder. As you can see in Figure 6-4, you can define how the application is deployed, what options the user has during deployment, and whether the application should be uninstalled if the GPO no longer applies. Active Directory stores a list of filename extensions and the applications associated with them. Although you cannot modify this list at all, you can alter the priority of applications to use when opening a file on the File Extensions tab. Finally, you can create, modify, or delete categories for sorting your applications (on the Categories tab).

You can further define how each application is deployed by opening the Properties dialog box for the new package. Here, you can refine the deployment options, specify how upgrades and modifications to the applications should take place, and categorize the applications as well.

On the Deployment tab, shown in Figure 6-5, you can change the deployment method if necessary. You can disable installation on demand when the user opens a file associated with the application, flag the application to be uninstalled when the user or computer falls out of the "jurisdiction" of the GPO (as might happen if the user or computer changes OU membership), and opt not to advertise the application through Add\Remove Programs. You can also affect whether the application installs with default values or gives the user an opportunity to alter the installation under Installation User Interface Options.

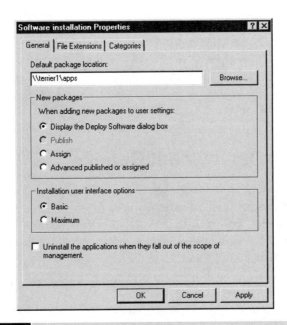

FIGURE 6-4   Software installation properties

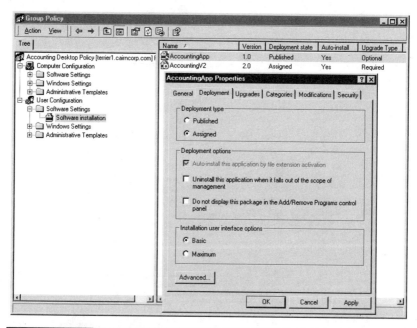

FIGURE 6-5 Deployment options for a software application

A powerful function available to you when you deploy an application through Group Policy is the ability to also deploy and manage upgrades to that application. Upgrades can be designated as *mandatory*, meaning that an application is automatically upgraded the next time a computer starts up or a user opens the application or an associated file. Upgrades can also be designated as *optional*, meaning that users can apply the upgrade through Add/Remove Programs at their leisure. You can only upgrade packages that have been already been deployed.

You begin by creating a package for the upgraded version of the application. In this new package's Properties dialog box, on the Upgrades tab (see Figure 6-6), click the Add button and select the older version of the package. If the upgrade will be mandatory, leave the Required Upgrade for Existing Packages option enabled. If the upgrade will be optional, deselect the option.

The Categories tab gives you the option of sorting your applications according to category. For example, you might group applications by OU, department, user group, or application type—for example, graphics, database, Microsoft, non-Microsoft, and so on. You first create your categories in the Software Installation Properties dialog box; then you can assign a specific application to a specific category on the Categories tab.

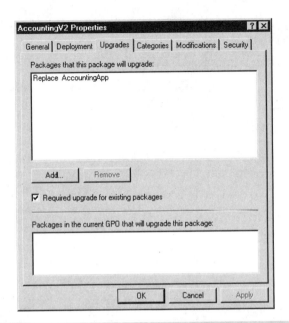

FIGURE 6-6   The Upgrades tab's options for a software application

Another option is to deploy different configurations of the same application by creating custom instruction files called *software modification files*, which have an .MST extension. These files control how the MSI package executes. On the Modifications tab, you would click the Add button and then locate the appropriate MST file. You can select as many MST files as you want. They will be read and executed in the order they are listed.

Applying Service Packs and Patches

Another type of application deployment is the application of service packs or patches. This process is generally referred to as *redeployment* because it involves reinstalling the application at worst, and deploying new or updated files at best. Because of this, you must have new MSI files for the application that contain the updated data files.

You redeploy applications in much the same way that you publish them. You first make the redeployment MSI file available in the original applications' installation folders. Then find the appropriate package(s) in the appropriate GPOs, right-click each, choose All Tasks from the pop-up menu, and then choose Redeploy Application. Select Yes in the Redeployment dialog box.

The service pack or patch will be applied depending on how the application was installed in the first place. If the application was assigned or published to a user, the application's shortcuts and Registry settings will be updated at the next user logon. The updates will be applied when the application is started through a short-cut or when an associated file is opened. If the application was initially assigned to a computer, the patch or service pack will be applied at the next startup.

Removing Applications

Just as you use Group Policy to giveth, you can also use it to take away applications when they are no longer required. You already saw that you can determine how a deployed application is handled if a user or computer is no longer affected by the GPO that deployed it initially. However, you can also choose to delete the application from a given GPO. This is simple enough to do. You find the application in the affected GPO, right-click it, and select All Tasks | Remove from the pop-up menu.

You will have two options regarding removing the application. You can choose to automatically delete the application from all computers affected by this GPO by enabling the Immediately Uninstall Software from Users and Computers option. The next time the computer starts up or the user logs in—depending on the orig-inal deployment policy—the application will be removed. You could, however, choose to allow existing deployments to remain installed by enabling the Allow Users to Continue to Use the Software but Prevent New Installations option.

Exam Tip

Besides the obvious troubleshooting step of testing your packages before deploy-ing them, you should keep in mind the same guidelines you would use when troubleshooting the application of any Group Policies. For example, is the policy really being applied or is inheritance being blocked?

Travel Advisory

You can set up your share points using Distributed File System (DFS). Because the DFS structure is replicated to all domain controllers, share points will be accessed within users' own sites, thus reducing network traffic, facilitating load balancing, and taking advantage of DFS redundancy.

Objective 6.03

Manage Network Configuration by Using Group Policy

The topic of network configuration and management is quite broad because most everything the user does regarding Active Directory requires a network connection. You have already seen earlier in this chapter how you can manage a user's access to the network through the use of administrative templates, which define which network mappings a user can see, whether the user can map or disconnect drives, and whether they can even access the My Network Places icon to browse the network or read or change network property settings.

Through Group Policy you can also manage users' network access through the use of scripts, folder redirection settings, dial-up settings, and security templates. Security templates will be discussed as a separate exam topic in Chapter 10.

Using Scripts

If you have been a network administrator for any length of time, you will already be familiar with the concept of *logon scripts*. Logon scripts typically range from those that perform simple tasks, such as mapping network drives, to those that determining network access based on group membership or based on dial-in versus LAN connections. Active Directory takes this concept to a new level by providing you with the ability to execute a script for a user or a computer based on a GPO assigned to it.

You can still assign a logon script to a user by identifying the script filename in the user's account profile. However, a more elegant and efficient way to do this is through a GPO setting. You'll find the script settings under Computer or User Configuration | Windows Settings | Scripts. As you see in Figure 6-7, there are four different kinds of scripts you can execute—two each for users and computers.

You have, of course, the logon script you are familiar with. However, you now—and only through Group Policy—have the option of executing a logoff script. This could be used to disconnect drive mappings, clean the desktop, or perform any other post-session maintenance that needs to be done when the user logs off.

In addition to logon and logoff scripts, you also have startup and shutdown scripts that can be assigned at the computer level. Startup and shutdown scripts are run based on whether the computer is starting up or shutting down and might include such actions as setting or resetting service options, launching background applications, and making network connections to specific resources, such as shared folders, printers, and so on.

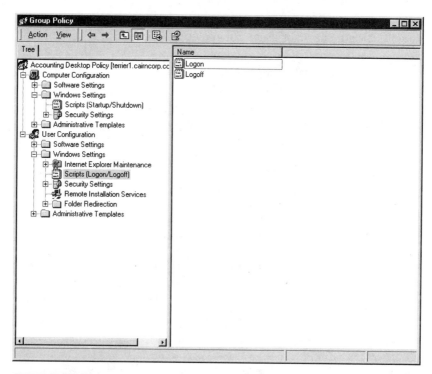

FIGURE 6-7   User and computer-oriented scripts

A script can take the form of the traditional command-based batch file, but it can also be an executable file or any script file supported by the Windows Script Host. The Windows Scrip Host executes scripts written in most languages and includes the Visual Basic and Java script engines. When a computer is started, the startup script runs first, and then the user logon script runs when the user logs on. When a user logs off and the computer shuts down, the logoff script is executed first, and then the shutdown script is executed.

All scripts are allotted a 10-minute window for processing. However, you can modify how long the scripts have to run with a—you guessed it—Group Policy setting. You'll find a policy setting that controls this processing window under Computer Configuration\Administrative Templates\System\Logon. You can change the value in the setting Maximum Wait Time for Group Policy Scripts, but this value affects the processing time window for all scripts.

You identify which script you want to use for logon, logoff, startup, or shutdown by adding it into the appropriate GPO. For example, let's say you create a user logon script called AccountingLogon.vbs, which should be executed for all users who are members of the Accounting OU. Select the GPO for the Accounting

OU that will apply the script and edit it. Because this is a user logon script, you would locate and highlight User Configuration\Windows Settings\Scripts and then double-click Logon. Click the Add button. Browse the list for the script, click Open, add any additional parameters (such as command-line switches) that may be necessary, and then click OK (see Figure 6-8).

Alternatively, you can locate the script file using the Windows Explorer. You then create or select an appropriate GPO and edit it. Locate the Logon folder and display its properties. Click the Show Files button (Figure 6-8), and then copy the script from the Windows Explorer to the Show Files window . This action actually imports the script into the GPT of the GPO you are working with. Then you can use the Add button to reference the script.

Folder Redirection

Windows 2000 introduces an additional means to manage user profiles and ensure that a user's desktop settings "follow" that user no matter where they log on. This feature is called *folder redirection*. Five folders are considered part of a

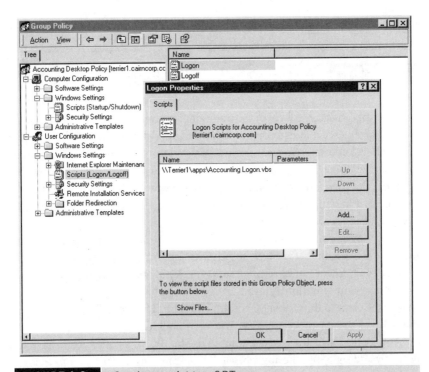

FIGURE 6-8   Copying a script to a GPT

user's profile and can be redirected to a network location: Application Data | Desktop | My Documents | My Pictures and Start Menu.

With a regular roaming profile, the data in the folders is copied back and forth from the local computer to the network each time the user logs on and off. However, when you redirect a folder, you are actually identifying an alternate network location for storing the folder data. From the user's point of view, the data appears to reside locally.

There are several advantages in using folder redirection:

- Folder data is always available to the users no matter where they log on.
- Users always receive their standard, personal folder settings no matter where they log on.
- Because the folder data is stored on a network location, it is easier to include in regular server backup routines.
- Because the folder data does not have to be copied back and forth between the network location and the computer, network traffic is reduced, the logon process for the users is made faster, and less local storage space is consumed.

Exam Tip

When you redirect a folder, the user has read and write access to the contents of that folder. This means that a user could make changes to their Start Menu or Desktop settings if you have not restricted them through a Group Policy. As a way to ensure that a user cannot modify the Start Menu or Desktop folders, redirect them to a partition formatted with NTFS and then restrict the user to read-only access.

Folder redirection is itself an extension of Group Policy and is configured much like you configure other GPO settings. You begin by creating or selecting the appropriate GPO and editing it. You'll find Folder Redirection under the User Configuration\Windows Settings policy folder. Select and display the properties for the folder you want to redirect.

On the Target tab (see Figure 6-9), by default, no location is specified. You can choose to redirect all users' folders to the same network location by selecting Basic, or you can identify specific locations for users based on their security group membership by selecting Advanced.

On the Settings tab, shown in Figure 6-10, four options are enabled by default. The option Grant the User Exclusive Rights to *Foldername* ensures that users and

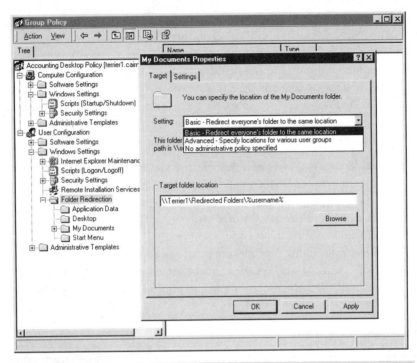

FIGURE 6-9   The Target tab for folder redirection properties

---

Travel Advisory

You can direct the policy to create a separate folder for each user when you specify the target location by using the environmental variable %username%. For example, if you are redirecting folders to a shared network location called Folders on a server called Terrier1, as shown in Figure 6-9, you would enter the target path \\Terrier1\Folders\%username%.

---

the system (but not the administrator) have permissions to access the folder. The option Move the Contents of *Foldername* to the New Location ensures that the contents of the folder are moved to the network folder location. If you disable this option, the folder will be redirected but not its contents. The option Policy Removal dictates that once the folder has been redirected, it will remain in the network location even if the Group Policy itself is removed. However, you can choose

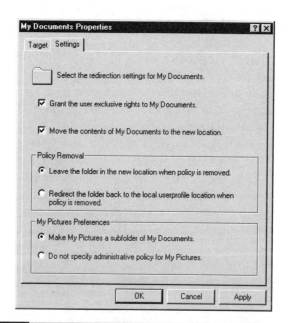

FIGURE 6-10   The Settings tab for folder redirection properties

to have the folder directed back to the user's local profile in the event that the Group Policy is removed.

My Pictures is generally stored as a subfolder of My Documents and will be redirected that way by default. However, you could choose to not specify a policy for My Pictures when redirecting My Documents. This action allows you to set redirection properties of My Pictures independently of My Documents.

Sometimes you may encounter problems when trying to redirect a folder to a network location. For example, if the user does not have sufficient permissions to the target share point or folder location (especially if the folder already exists), you may not be able to redirect the folder, or the user may not be able to access or save data there. Also, if disk quotas have been enabled, it is possible that the process of redirecting a folder may inadvertently exceed the quota limits for the user. Both of these situations are relatively easy to correct.

Exam Tip

A Microsoft best practice recommends that the My Documents folder at least be redirected to ensure that users will always have access to their documents.

Other Network Settings

Group Policy also provides a number of policy settings related to dial-up connections and security that can be applied both as computer-oriented and user-oriented settings. Figure 6-11 displays the settings that can be configured for Network and Dial-up Connections under User Configuration. These are enabled much like you enabled settings under other administrative templates.

Like administrative templates, security templates allow you to standardize and enforce security settings, such as account policies, by importing them into appropriate GPOs in Active Directory or by configuring them individually for each computer. Like folder redirection, once a security setting has been applied, by default, it remains in place even if the Group Policy itself is removed. Security policies as they apply to the exam will be covered in detail in Chapter 10.

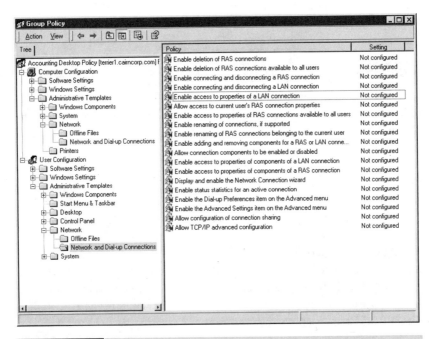

FIGURE 6-11   Network and dial-up Administrative Template settings

CHECKPOINT

✔ **Objective 6.01:** **Manage and Troubleshoot User Environments by Using Group Policy**   Group Policy settings can assist you in managing your users' and computers' working environments by providing a more effective method of standardizing and enforcing computer configurations and users' desktops, including network connections, account policies, wallpaper, desktop shortcuts, user profiles, security, and so on. The primary components of Group Policy you'll use are the administrative templates. These templates represent Registry changes that affect how the user and computer environments are configured and presented. The settings are maintained in registry.pol files stored as part of the Group Policy template data on domain controllers. These policy settings are evaluated according to the same rules governing inheritance.

✔ **Objective 6.02:** **Install, Configure, Manage, and Troubleshoot Software by Using Group Policy**   Software applications can also be configured and maintained through Group Policy. Applications can be assigned to computers and users, indicating that the applications must be installed upon startup or on demand or published and installed through Add/Remove Programs. Applications that are deployed through Group Policy use Windows Installer Package files (MSI files) and the Windows Installer Service to affect configuration and maintenance of applications on Windows 2000 clients. Through Group Policy, deployed applications can be upgraded (with service packs, patches, and newer versions), categorized, and automatically "repaired" by the Windows Installer Service if a file is found to be missing or corrupt. Deployed applications can also be configured to be removed when the GPO no longer applies to the user or computer in question.

✔ **Objective 6.03:** **Manage Network Configuration by Using Group Policy**   Users' and computers' network environments can be modified through the use of logon and logoff scripts and startup and shutdown scripts, respectively. Scripts of these types are applied through a Group Policy and give you more flexibility and control over configuration options. You can also redirect user profile folders such as My Documents, Desktop, Start Menu, My Pictures, and Application Data to a shared network location. This will ensure that the user's data files, particularly significant for My Documents, are always available no matter where the user logs on. This will also result in reduced network traffic, faster logon, and better management of local disk storage. Other network options, such as dial-up options, and security settings can also be applied to further control the computing environment.

REVIEW QUESTIONS

1. Settings that you enable through an administrative template in Group Policy are stored in which location?

    A. A GPO container in Active Directory
    B. A registry.pol file in the GPT folder
    C. A Group Policy GUID folder
    D. The HKEY_Local_Machine Registry hive

2. You want to prevent users from using My Network Places to map drives to network servers, and you want this desktop setting to be applied to all computers in your organization. What GPO setting should you configure?

    A. Set the Hide My Network Places setting to Disabled under User Configuration.
    B. Set the Hide My Network Places setting to Enabled under User Configuration.
    C. Set the Hide My Network Places setting to Disabled under Computer Configuration.
    D. Set the Hide My Network Places setting to Enabled under Computer Configuration

3. You want to prevent users from using Control Panel to modify their desktop settings, and you want this setting to be applied to all computers in your organization. However, you want administrators to be able to use Control Panel. What two GPO settings should you configure?

    A. Set the Disable Control Panel setting to Enabled under User Configuration.
    B. Set the Disable Control Panel setting to Enabled under Computer Configuration.
    C. Block inheritance of the GPO for the Administrators group.
    D. Set permissions on the GPO so that it is not applied to the Administrators group.

4. You are configuring a GPO for the users in the Accounting OU that accomplishes the following tasks:

- Adds a custom shortcut for a proprietary accounting application to everyone's desktop
- Automatically installs the accounting application on each computer in the Accounting OU
- Ensures that each user has access to their data files regardless of where they log in
- Ensures that each user's data files are stored in a network folder specific to that user

To accomplish these tasks, you perform the following actions:

- Assign the accounting application to all users in the Accounting OU.
- Create and assign a user logon script that creates the shortcut.
- Redirect each user's My Documents folder to a shared network location.

Which of your tasks have you accomplished?

A. Adds a custom shortcut for a proprietary accounting application to everyone's desktop

B. Automatically installs the accounting application on each computer in the Accounting OU

C. Ensures that each user has access to their data files regardless of where they log in

D. Ensures that each user's data files are stored in a network folder specific to that user

5. You are planning to redirect the My Documents and Application Data folders for each user in the Accounting OU to a shared network location, and you want each user's data to be stored in a folder specific to that user. How can you accomplish this?

A. Redirect the folder to a shared network location.

B. Redirect the folder to a shared network location using the Advanced setting and specifying a path for each user.

C. Redirect the folder to a shared network location using the Basic setting and the variable %username%.

D. Create a folder for each user at a shared network location and then redirect the folders using the Basic setting.

6. You are in the process of reconfiguring several GPOs in the Central Region OU, and you have found certain settings that you would like to remove from users' desktops. How should you remove these settings?

    A. Delete the settings from the GPO.

    B. Create a new GPO that removes the settings and make it the primary GPO.

    C. Configure the settings so that they are set to Disabled.

    D. Configure the settings so that they are set to Not Configured.

7. You are deploying several applications to users in the Central domain. You want to minimize network traffic as well as load-balance users' access to the applications when they are installed. Which of the following actions can accomplish your goal?

    A. Set up a domain-based Distributed File System and place the application packages on share points there.

    B. Sort the applications by category.

    C. Assign the applications to computers rather than users.

    D. Publish the applications rather than assigning them.

8. You have several applications that you want to deploy to domain users based on the OUs the users are members of. You want to be sure that users install the correct applications for their OUs and can do so on demand. Which steps will accomplish your goals?

    A. Categorize the applications by OU and then publish them to all users in the domain.

    B. Create and link a GPO to each OU that assigns the appropriate applications to the users in that OU.

    C. Categorize the applications by OU and then assign them to all users in the domain.

    D. Create and link a GPO to each OU that publishes the appropriate applications to the users in that OU.

9. You recently deployed version 1.0 of a virus-protection application to all the users in the domain. The developer of the application has now released version 2.0 of the application. You want to deploy the new release to all existing computers as well as to any new computers that are installed in the domain. Which of the following actions should you take to accomplish your goal?

    A. Deploy the new release as a mandatory upgrade to all existing computers.

    B. Redeploy the new release to all computers in the domain.

    C. Assign the new release to all computers in the domain.

    D. Publish the new release to all computers in the domain.

10. Which of the following Windows 2000 client components manages application configuration through Group Policy?

    A. MSI

    B. Windows Installer Service

    C. Windows Management Service

    D. Active Directory Client Service

REVIEW ANSWERS

1. **B** Administrative Template settings represent modifications made to user and computer Registry values and are stored, respectively, in the \User and \Machine folders beneath the Group Policy template (GPT) folder for each GPO. The GPT folder is named after the GUID for the GPO. The GPO container (A) stores the attributes and extensions of the Group Policy, including the location of the GPTs. Therefore, A is incorrect. Although C is close, B is the better answer because it mentions the registry.pol file. Therefore, C is incorrect. HKEY_Local_Machine (D) is one part of the Registry that a setting can modify, but it does not hold the settings to be modified, thus making D incorrect.

2. **B** Configuring any policy setting to Enabled means that it will be applied to users and/or computers, thus making A and C incorrect. D is incorrect because the question directs you to apply the desktop setting to all computers, and desktop settings can only be set under User Configuration, not Computer Configuration. This is a subtle difference, but once again, in certification exams, the words used are significant.

3. **B** and **D** This is a setting to be applied to all computers and will therefore affect the users logged on at them. A applies the setting to all users, which would also have the same effect but is not how the question was worded. You learned in Chapter 5 that you can control who the GPO is applied to through the use of the Read and Apply Policy permissions. Blocking inheritance would effectively keep the policy from being applied at all, which is contrary to your intention. Therefore, C is incorrect.

4. **A** and **C** The logon script will create the shortcut, and folder redirection ensures that users can always access their data through the network. Assigning an application to users means the application be installed when a

user clicks a shortcut or opens an associated file. You would need to assign the application to the computers to affect an automatic installation, which makes B wrong. Redirection only places the data files on a shared network point. If you want the files for each user stored in their own location, you need to do that by specifying the path using the %username% variable, which makes D incorrect.

5. **C**   The %username% variable creates a folder for each user at the shared location using the user's account name. Just redirecting the folder (A) will not accomplish this. Therefore, A is incorrect. You could redirect each user based on group membership to a specified path, as stated in B, but this is not very efficient. Therefore, B is incorrect. You could create the users folders ahead of time, as stated in D, but, again, this is not very efficient, and you can't use the Basic setting to distinguish between different paths. Therefore, D is incorrect.

6. **D**   The Not Configured option removes the setting from the registry.pol file so that the next time the policy is evaluated, the setting is removed. The Disabled option (C) actually sets the value to off but doesn't remove it. Therefore, C is incorrect. You cannot delete settings (A) from a GPO. Therefore, A is incorrect. You could create a new GPO with settings that override the original (B), but that is not very efficient. Therefore, B is incorrect.

7. **A**   Using DFS will allow users to look for applications first in their sites, thus minimizing traffic. Because Dfs is domain based, it is replicated to all domain controllers, thus providing load balancing. Sorting the application (B) doesn't affect traffic or load. Neither does assigning (C) or publishing (D) the application. Therefore, B, C, and D are incorrect.

8. **B**   Assigning an application to users makes the application available on demand—when the user clicks a shortcut or opens an associated file. Publishing an application (A and D) lets the user install the application when they want to through Add\Remove Programs. The way to ensure that the right applications are deployed to the right OUs is to create a GPO for each OU that deploys the right applications. Therefore, A and D are incorrect. Categorizing the applications (C) doesn't have the same effect. Therefore, C is incorrect.

9. **A**   You would create a GPO to deploy the new version and configure it to be deployed as a mandatory upgrade through its properties. Redeployments (B) are used to apply patches and service packs. Therefore, B is incorrect.

Assigning and publishing the new version (C and D) would make the application available as a separate package, which would result in two versions installed on the same computer rather than an upgrade of an older version. Therefore, C and D are incorrect.

10. **B** The Windows Installer Service manages application configuration through Group Policy. MSI (A) is the file extension for Windows Installer Packages and is used as an instruction file by the Windows Installer Service. Therefore, A is incorrect. The Windows Management Service (C) is a core service of the Windows 2000 operating system. Therefore, C is incorrect. There is no Active Directory Client Service, thus making D incorrect.

Remote Installation Services

ETA	NEWBIE	SOME EXPERIENCE	EXPERT
	4+ hours	3+ hours	2+ hours

The focus of this section of the book has been on change and configuration management of computers in your network. The methods of configuration have included managing the Registry, desktop environment, network environment, and software configurations of existing computers through the use of Active Directory Group Policy. However, another aspect of change and configuration management is the initial setup and installation of the computer itself—in particular, the installation of the operating system.

This chapter focuses on the use of Remote Installation Services to implement Windows 2000 Professional on new computer installations within an Active Directory–enabled network environment.

Configure Active Directory to Support Remote Installation Services

Objective 7.01

Along with the other Microsoft Intellimirror features designed to assist in lowering the overall total cost of ownership (TCO) of computers in your organization, Windows 2000 provides the Remote Installation Services (RIS) feature. RIS lets you deploy the Windows 2000 Professional operating system to new computer installations within your network to create and implement a standard workstation without having to be physically present to do so.

In order for remote installation to be successful, you must configure a RIS server or servers to host the process. The RIS server runs the Remote Installation Services and stores the Windows 2000 image to be deployed. You must have a valid RIS client identified as well. The RIS client is a computer that has the ability to connect to a RIS server and access the Windows 2000 image. And, of course, you must prepare the Windows 2000 Professional image, itself, that represents the workstation configuration you intend to deploy to RIS clients.

In order for Windows 2000 to support RIS for the network, you must have identified and registered a valid Dynamic Host Configuration Protocol (DHCP) server in Active Directory. You must also have enabled Active Directory for the network, which means you have configured a valid DNS server that supports SRV records as well. These, then, are the three service requirements for RIS: the DHCP Server service to assign IP address information to all clients, including the new client, the DNS Server service to locate Active Directory's directory service, and the Active Directory service, itself, to locate RIS servers, manage RIS settings, and include new clients.

Exam Tip

This certification exam does focus on the requirements needed to support RIS deployment methods. RIS requires that the new client have an IP address. It is not necessary for an operating system to have been installed first. DHCP hands out IP address information during the boot-up process of the computer. The new computer therefore needs to be able to access a DHCP server either directly, through a router that is RFC 1542-compliant (supports routing of DHCP requests), or through a DHCP proxy agent. Once it obtains its IP information, the new computer can locate the RIS server in the network.

Configuring the RIS Server

The RIS server is set up using two utilities. First, you install Remote Installation Services through the Add/Remove Programs, Add/Remove Windows Components application in Control Panel on the designated server. Then, at the Start | Run command, you'll enter **risetup** to launch the RIS Setup Wizard. As you see in Figure 7-1,

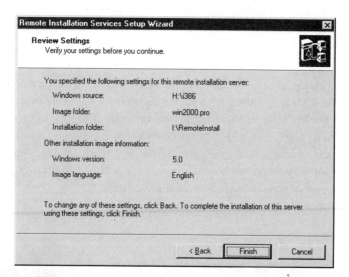

FIGURE 7-1   The Remote Installation Services Setup Wizard

the wizard will prompt you for several related pieces of information. For example, you'll need to supply the location of the NTFS partition, other than the boot or system partition, the image folder name in which the initial CD image will be created, the location of the Windows 2000 Professional source files, and how you want the Remote Installation Services to respond to clients when they access the image files.

Travel Advisory

Install RIS servers in the same Active Directory sites that the clients will belong to in order to reduce network traffic associated with RIS installations. Remember: We are talking about a full Windows 2000 Professional installation over the network that may include application setup as well.

Exam Tip

The default client response is not to respond. It is generally recommended by Microsoft that you leave the default selected until you have created and tested the image and all supporting answer files and application files before making the RIS server available to respond to client requests.

The next step is to create and configure the image that the RIS server will host. This will be discussed in more detail next in this chapter. After the image has been prepared, the RIS server must be authorized in Active Directory. RIS servers are authorized through a valid DHCP server. As you see in Figure 7-2, in the DHCP management console, you right-click DHCP and select Manage Authorized Servers from the pop-up menu and then click the Authorize button. Supply the name or the IP address of the RIS server and then click OK.

Exam Tip

As always, understanding who can do what in Active Directory is a big part of any certification exam. Only members of the Enterprise Admins group can authorize a RIS server.

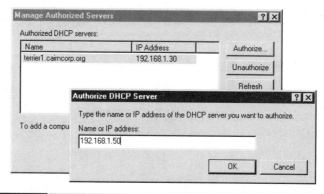

FIGURE 7-2 Authorizing the RIS server through DHCP

Configuring the RIS Image

The RIS image represents the way you want the new computer to be configured. The standard installation of RIS on a server includes a standard Windows 2000 Professional operating system image only and is referred to as the *CD-based image*. The image can also include applications that need to be installed and other desktop settings. This kind of image involves setting up a default source computer that exactly mirrors what you want the standard installation to look like and then copying that image to the RIS server using the RIPrep tool.

Every image requires an associated answer file, which is used primarily to assign a name for the new computer and a location for creating the computer account in Active Directory. Answer files can also be used to more fully automate an installation, providing answers to several setup questions that the users would otherwise have to answer themselves—for example, the location of the system files, the name of the computer, time zone settings, network settings, and display settings.

RIS images cannot be maintained on the same partition as the boot or system partition on the RIS server, so they will require their own NTFS partition. This partition must have at least 2GB of free space to store the RIS images, which consist of the Windows 2000 Professional source files and other RIS support files. The partition cannot be part of a Distributed File System (DFS) structure or use the Encrypting File System (EFS).

There are two types of images you can create. The default image is simply the Windows 2000 Professional CD source files image that is created when you install the Remote Installation Services. This image can be modified through the use of an answer file. You can either modify the standard answer file, called RIStndrd.sif, or create your own using the Setup Manager utility. A portion of the RIStndrd.sif answer file is shown in Figure 7-3.

```
ristndrd.sif - Notepad                                                    _ □ X
File  Edit  Format  Help
[data]
floppyless = "1"
msdosinitiated = "1"
oriSrc = "\\%SERVERNAME%\RemInst\%INSTALLPATH%\%MACHINETYPE%"
oriTyp = "4"
LocalSourceOnCD = 1

[SetupData]
OsLoadOptions = "/noguiboot /fastdetect"
SetupSourceDevice = "\Device\LanmanRedirector\%SERVERNAME%\RemInst\%INSTALLPATH%"

[Unattended]
OemPreinstall = no
NoWaitAfterTextMode = 0
FileSystem = LeaveAlone
ExtendOEMPartition = 0
ConfirmHardware = no
NtUpgrade = no
Win31Upgrade = no
TargetPath = \WINNT
OverwriteOemFilesOnUpgrade = no
OemSkipEula = yes
InstallFilesPath = "\\%SERVERNAME%\RemInst\%INSTALLPATH%\%MACHINETYPE%"

[UserData]
FullName = "%USERFIRSTNAME% %USERLASTNAME%"
OrgName = "%ORGNAME%"
ComputerName = %MACHINENAME%

[RemoteInstall]
Repartition = Yes
```

FIGURE 7-3   A portion of the RIStndrd.sif answer file

Travel Advisory

The Setup Manager utility can be found in the file deploy.cab on the Windows 2000 CD-ROM.

Exam Tip

A new section called [RemoteInstall] is available for answer files that you create, and it exists in the default answer file RIStndrd.sif. This section specifies whether the hard disk on the computer being installed should be repartitioned. If the Repartition parameter value in this section is set to Yes, or is not specified at all, the remote installation will begin by deleting all existing partitions (except OEM-created partitions), create one large partition, and format it with NTFS. The default value for the Repartition parameter is Yes.

The other type of image you can create involves setting up a source computer and using the Remote Installation Preparation (RIPrep) tool to generate the image. Creating an image using this method can offer three benefits:

- Flexibility in customizing the operating system environment
- Potentially faster overall installation of the operating system, because only necessary files will be copied based on your configuration of the source computer
- The ability to include applications and other components as part of the installation

The source computer, basically, is a representative client computer that you have configured with all the components, Registry settings, applications, and so on that you want all other new computers to have. For example, if all computers will be running Windows 2000 Professional with a company logo as the desktop wallpaper, an access restriction to Control Panel, and Microsoft Office installed, you can set up your source computer to "look" like that. If some computers will require Microsoft Office Professional and others Microsoft Office Small Business Edition, you will require two source computers, each with the appropriate version of Microsoft Office installed. Of course, you can accomplish many of the same environment and software settings through the use of Group Policies. In many cases, Group Policy may be the more efficient method. RIPrep images are best suited for deploying the most standard and basic computer environments.

Travel Advisory

It is very important that you confirm and test your configuration before you generate the image. Once the image has been generated, you cannot alter it. The image can only be modified later by replacing it with a new image.

In order for you to install Windows 2000 Professional on the source computer and modify operating system and other settings, you will have to be logged in as an administrator. This means, however, that customized user settings will be stored on the source computer as part of the administrator's profile and not made available by default to users. After you complete the customization of the source computer, you should copy the administrator's profile to the default user profile on the source computer so that after a user initiates and completes a remote installation on a new computer, she will receive those settings as part of her new profile on the new computer.

You can copy the administrator's profile on the User Profiles tab of the System Properties dialog box for the source computer. Select the administrator's profile from the list and click Copy To; then enter the path to the Default User profile folder, usually C:\Documents and Settings\Default User, as shown in Figure 7-4. Make sure that the Everyone group appears in the Permitted to Use area of the dialog box.

Now you can run the RIPrep tool and generate an image based on the configuration of the source computer. You can find RIPrep.exe in the Reminst\Admin\ i386 folder on the RIS server. From the source computer, execute RIPrep.exe through the Start | Run menu. You'll provide the name of the RIS server and the folder where you want to store the image, as well as some descriptive text about the image. RIPrep will create the image on the RIS server as well as the associated answer file.

Exam Tip

RIPrep images can only be copied to a RIS server if that server has an existing copy of the original CD image created when the RIS server was installed.

Travel Advisory

RIPrep can generate an image on only one RIS server. If you want the same image to be available, you'll need to copy that image to the other RIS servers.

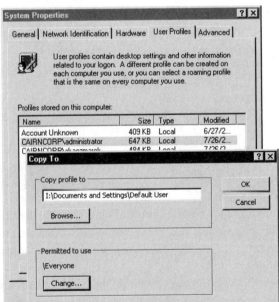

FIGURE 7-4   The Copy To dialog box for the default user profile

RIS Client Requirements

Client computers access a RIS server during boot up and therefore must be configured with a network adapter that supports the Pre-Boot Execution (PXE) boot ROM, version .99c. Alternatively, you can create a RIS startup disk that simulates the PXE boot process, provided that the network adapter is supported. A RIS startup disk can be created on any Windows 2000 computer by entering the following command at the Start | Run prompt: *RISserver*\reminst\admin\i386\ rbfg.exe. This command will launch the Remote Boot Disk Generator, where you'll select the Create Disk option.

Initiating a Remote Installation

When a user boots up the new client computer that conforms to the PXE standard, he will press the F12 key to request a network startup. If the computer does not conform to the PXE standard, but you have provided a RIS startup disk, the user can boot the computer using that disk.

At this point, the computer will obtain an IP address from a DHCP server and establish a connection with a RIS server. The user will be prompted to press the F12 key once again to launch the Client Installation Wizard from the RIS server and then must log in to the appropriate domain. As you see in Figure 7-5, a list of

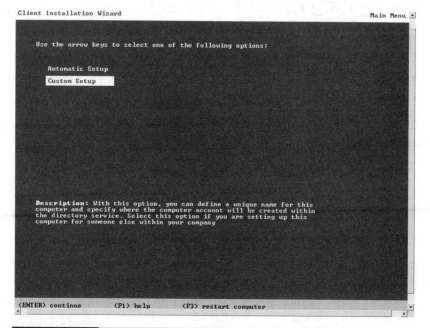

FIGURE 7-5   The Client Installation Wizard's Installation Options screen

installation options is now presented to the user that can include any or all of the following choices: Automated Setup, Custom Setup, Restart a Previous Setup Attempt, Maintenance, and Troubleshooting.

The actual list that is presented to the user depends on how much control you want to give your users over the installation process. For example, in Figure 7-5, the user has only been given the Automatic and Custom Setup options. These options can be modified by you through the use of a Group Policy and will be covered in the next section of this chapter.

Objective 7.02

Configure RIS Options to Support Remote Installations

There are, of course, many ways to configure RIS support for remote installations. Some options are configured through the RIS server itself, and others are configured through Group Policy settings.

Configuring Options Through RIS Server Settings

You can configure RIS server settings through its Properties dialog box. Three components can be configured there: providing the new computer's name information, associating answer files with images on the server, and identifying third-party management tools to distribute as part of the installation.

Using the Active Directory Users and Computers console, right-click the RIS server entry and choose Properties from the pop-up menu. Next, click the Remote Install tab and then click Advanced Settings to display the Remote Installation Services Properties dialog box.

As you know, all Windows 2000 computers must have computer accounts created for them in Active Directory. As part of the remote installation process, you need to identify how the new computer account should be named. On the New Clients tab, shown in Figure 7-6, you'll specify a naming option for the new clients by choosing from a predefined list or by customizing a naming convention and then choosing the location in Active Directory where the computer account should be created. The default names generally represent some combination of the user's

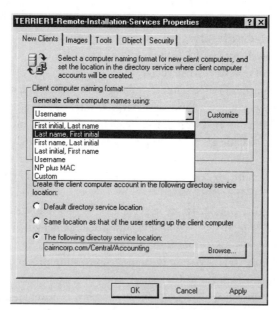

FIGURE 7-6 The New Clients tab of the Remote Installation Services
Properties dialog box

account name—for example, first initial/last name, first name/last initial, username, and so on. Custom names can consist of any combination of alphanumeric text and/or one of the five variables outlined in Table 7-1, up to a total of 64 characters.

TABLE 7.1 Custom Client Naming Variables

Variable	Returns the Value
%#	An incremental number
%First	User's first name
%Last	User's last name
%Mac	Network interface card (NIC) address
%Username	User's logon account name

By default, new computers are added to the Computers container for the domain in which the RIS server resides; however, you could create the new computer account in the same OU as the user who owns the computer (and is presumably setting it up), or you can specify the OU.

As you saw earlier in this chapter, you may have created one or more answer files for the images you are hosting on the RIS server. Each image may have a different answer file associated with it. You create this association on the Images tab of the Remote Installation Services Properties dialog box (see Figure 7-7). On this tab, click the Add button to start a wizard and then follow the screens to associate a new answer file with an existing image. The steps are very straightforward and need not be reviewed in detail here.

More and more third-party developers are creating management and troubleshooting tools you can use to maintain hardware components that can be installed on users' computers as part of the remote installation process. You can make these utilities available to users as part of the remote installation process by running the appropriate setup program provided by the vendor. This setup copies the utilities' files to the RIS server's image folder along with any necessary answer files. The tools that have been installed in this manner can be viewed on the Tools tab.

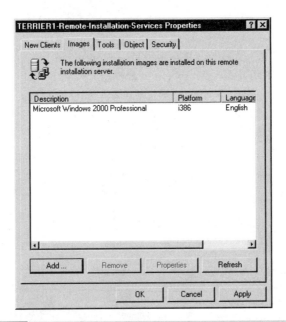

FIGURE 7-7   The Images tab of the Remote Installation Services Properties dialog box

Through Group Policy and NTFS permissions, you can then make the tools available to users and secure access to them. Once the tools have been made available to users, they can access these tools through the Maintenance and Troubleshooting option displayed during a network service startup on their computer.

Configuring Options Through Group Policy

When users initiate a remote installation on a new computer, they are presented with a menu of options from which they can choose. You can configure the manner and extent to which these options are presented through a Group Policy.

Just as you might create and link Group Policies at a domain level to apply more global administrative settings to all users and computers and then further define those settings for specific users and computers in specific OUs, you can similarly configure RIS settings.

RIS policy settings are considered user-oriented settings and can be found under User Configuration | Windows Settings | Remote Installation Services when you edit or create a Group Policy object (GPO). Figure 7-8 shows the Choice Options available for you to configure. As you can see, there are four options you can configure, each with three possible settings.

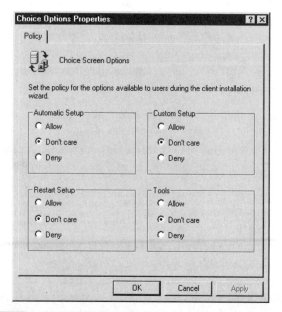

RIS policy settings

Automatic Setup, allowed by default, means that the installation will proceed using information for the computer name and location that you configured through an answer file or a pre-staged client. The Custom Setup option gives the user the ability to override the computer name and account location in Active Directory. The Restart Setup setting gives the user the option to restart an installation that may have failed for some reason, retaining any data entered up to the point of failure. The Tools option gives the user access to any third-party maintenance tools you have included as part of the installation, as discussed earlier in this chapter.

For each of these options, Allow makes the option available as a choice for the users when they initiate a remote installation. Don't Care means that the setting for the option can be inherited from a parent GPO. Deny, of course, means that the option is explicitly prevented when remote installation is initiated, regardless of any parent GPO setting. The options presented to the user in Figure 7-5 would have been affected by selecting Allow for both the Automatic Setup and Custom Setup options in Group Policy.

Pre-staging Clients

As a point of security, you might want to ensure that only authorized computers in your company will have the ability to access a RIS server and initiate a remote installation of Windows 2000 Professional. You can do this by *pre-staging* the computer. When you pre-stage a computer, you are providing a computer account for the new computer and, if you choose, even assigning it to a specific RIS service for installation. Pre-staging provides two key benefits:

- It prevents unauthorized RIS client computers from joining a domain and illegally installing Windows 2000 Professional.
- It offers a way to load-balance server resource handling and network traffic related to remote installations by assigning clients to RIS servers.

There are two ways to pre-stage a client, and both require that you obtain the GUID of the computer you are pre-staging. The first method involves obtaining the GUID ahead of time.

If the computer has a network card that is PXE compliant, as mentioned earlier, its GUID will be available probably on a label affixed to the computer itself or through the computer BIOS. As you saw, however, you can initiate a remote installation using an RIS startup disk if the network card is supported by RIS. In this case, you should use the MAC address of the network card.

Once you have the GUID, you use Active Directory Users and Computers to locate and select the OU where the new computer account will reside. Right-click the OU, select New from the pop-up menu, and then select Computer to launch the Create New Object Wizard. Enter a name for the computer and then, as shown in Figure 7-9, enable the This is a Managed Computer option and enter the GUID. If you like, especially if you want to load-balance your remote installations, identify the RIS server that will perform the remote installation and then conclude the wizard.

If you don't know the GUID, you can still pre-stage the computer. In order to do this, you'll have to have access to the computer itself. Basically, you'll need to boot the computer and initiate a remote installation, selecting an installation option and an image. During the process, a Warning screen will be displayed. At that point, press ENTER. The GUID assigned to the computer will be displayed on the screen. Simply turn off the computer. The computer account will have been created in Active Directory, just as though you had pre-staged it as described in the previous paragraph. In fact, you can access the new computer's properties through Active Directory Users and Computers and assign it to a specific RIS server if you like.

In both pre-staging scenarios, when the remote installation process is initiated, the client will locate the appropriate RIS server hosting its GUID and proceed with the installation.

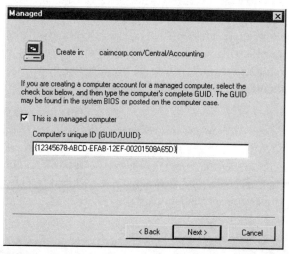

FIGURE 7-9   Pre-staging a computer with a known GUID

Objective 7.03   Configure RIS Security

In addition to the security you can create by configuring installation options through Group Policy and the fact that you must be a member of the Enterprise Admins group to install the Remote Installation Services in the first place, you can set security for RIS in two other locations.

When a computer is installed using RIS, a computer account is created for the new computer in the OU specified during the installation process. If you pre-staged the client, you will have already created the computer account. If not, the user performing the remote installation must be able to create the computer account during installation.

By default, Active Directory allows each user account to create a maximum of ten computer accounts. This was done to ensure that users could install Windows 2000 Professional and join a domain with a minimum of hassle. However, if a user needs to create more than ten user accounts, or if user permissions were restricted through Group Policy so as to alter the default permission, it may be necessary to grant users the right to create a user account in the domain when performing a remote installation.

If you need to give users the permission to create computer accounts, you can do so by running the Delegation of Control Wizard. In Chapter 5, you saw how to use the Delegation of Control Wizard to designate which users could have administrative control over GPOs in an OU. Another task that you can delegate is the creation of new objects in a folder. This is a custom task and can be created in the following manner. After launching the Delegation of Control Wizard for the OU in which the computer accounts will reside and selecting the name of the users or groups who should have the ability to create computer accounts, simply follow these steps:

1. Select Create a Custom Task to Delegate on the Tasks to Delegate Page and click Next to display the Active Directory Object Type page.
2. In the section Delegate Control Of, select the option This Folder, Existing Objects In This Folder, and Creation of New Objects in This Folder. Click Next to display the Permissions page.

3. In the section Show These Permissions, select the option Creation/Deletion of Specific Child Objects.

4. In the section Permissions, select the option Create Computer Objects and click Next and then Finish.

You can also affect security by restricting access to available images. There is really nothing special involved in doing this. You are simply using NTFS security to identify which users or groups have Read and Read & Execute permissions on the answer files associated with the images. By default, unless you have already modified NTFS permissions on the image folders, the Everyone group will have access to the answer files. You would, of course, remove the Everyone group and add in the users or groups that require access to each answer file. For example, in Figure 7-10, the Accounting group has been given Read and Read & Execute permissions to the default CD image answer file RIStndrd.sif.

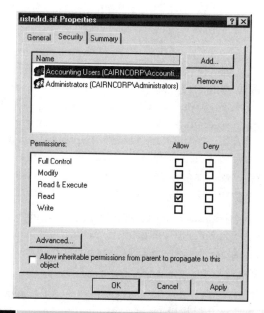

FIGURE 7-10   Assigning permissions to an answer file

CHECKPOINT

✔ **Objective 7.01:** Configure Active Directory to Support Remote Installation Services   Before you can successfully deploy Windows 2000 Professional using remote installation, you must have installed and configured the Remote Installation Services on a designated server (either a domain controller or member server), generated an installation image and answer file (either using the default CD image or through the RIPrep utility), and identified valid RIS clients that either conform to the PXE standard or have network cards that are supported by the RIS startup disk.

In addition, RIS requires that there be at least one DHCP server authorized in Active Directory, that Active Directory be enabled, and that DNS is available. The RIS server itself must be authorized in Active Directory through the DHCP management console.

✔ **Objective 7.02:** Configure RIS Options to Support Remote Installations   The remote installation process can be defined and modified through the properties of the RIS server itself as well as through Group Policy settings. At the RIS server level, you identify a naming convention and location for the new computer accounts that will be created, specify which answer files are associated with each image, and list any third-party maintenance and troubleshooting tools that can be made available to users as part of the installation process. Through Group Policy, you can specify which startup options are available to your users when they initiate a remote installation.

You can also choose to pre-stage the computers using the GUID associated with each computer to create a computer account in an appropriate OU. You can also identify which RIS server should host the installation.

✔ **Objective 7.03:** Configure RIS Security   You can enhance security for remote installations by using the Delegation of Control Wizard to identify those users and groups that have permission to create new computer accounts when initiating the remote installation process. You can also use NTFS permissions on the answer files associated with each image to restrict user access only to specific users and groups.

REVIEW QUESTIONS

1. You have decided to use RIS to install Windows 2000 Professional on several new computers in your organization. You have an authorized DHCP server in Active Directory. The computers will be located in various locations within your routed network. The computers and the DHCP server are not on the same local network. What else is required to enable successful use of RIS for the new computers?

   A. Authorize a RIS server in Active Directory.
   B. Enable a DHCP relay agent on the local network for each computer.
   C. Place the new computers in the same site as the RIS server.
   D. Pre-stage the new computers.

2. You are planning to install a RIS server in your domain. Active Directory has been installed, and a valid DNS server exists. What else will you need to do to successfully enable and configure RIS for use within your domain? Select all that apply.

   A. Authorize the RIS server in Active Directory.
   B. Pre-stage the new client computers.
   C. Authorize a DHCP server in Active Directory.
   D. Create RIS startup disks for the new client computers.

3. You have decided to install Windows 2000 Professional on new computers within your network. Some of the computers have network cards that are not PXE compliant. What is the easiest way to handle the computers that do not have PXE-compliant network cards?

   A. Pre-stage the computers.
   B. Install PXE-compliant network cards in those computers.
   C. Create RIS startup disks for those computers.
   D. RIS only supports PXE-compliant network cards.

4. You have decided to install Windows 2000 Professional on new computers within your network. The computers will be located in various locations within your routed network. The RIS servers and the DHCP server are not on the same local network as all the clients. You would like to accomplish the following goals:

- Ensure that all new computers will be able to locate the RIS servers.
- Reduce network traffic associated with RIS installations.
- Deploy a standard image to all new computers that includes standard applications.
- Have computer accounts already created in the appropriate OUs before installation takes place to reduce user interaction.

You decide to install the RIS servers using the default CD image in the same sites that the new computers will belong to, and you pre-stage the computers in their appropriate OUs. You also authorize a DHCP server in Active Directory. Which of your goals have you accomplished? Choose all that apply.

A. Ensure that all new computers will be able to locate the RIS servers.

B. Reduce network traffic associated with RIS installations.

C. Deploy a standard image to all new computers that includes standard applications.

D. Have computer accounts already created in the appropriate OUs before installation takes place to reduce user interaction.

5. You have configured a RIS server using the standard CD image and are testing the remote installation process on several computers. You notice that the computers' hard drives are being reformatted as one large NTFS partition rather than using the parameters set in the answer file you created. What can you do to ensure that the answer file parameters for partition formats are followed?

A. Set the Repartition value in the answer file to No.

B. Delete the Repartition value in the answer file.

C. Format the drives as you want them to be prior to remote installation.

D. Pre-stage the computers prior to remote installation.

6. You want to use RIS to deploy Windows 2000 Professional, but you want to minimize the amount of time it takes for the installation to take place and the amount of traffic that is generated. All the computers will require the same standard Registry and desktop settings as well. What can you do to accomplish your goals? Choose two.

A. Install RIS server with the standard CD image and modify the RIStndrd.sif answer file to install the standard Registry and desktop settings.

B. Place the RIS server in the same site as the new computers.

   C. Use RIPrep to generate an image from a source computer configured
   with the standard Registry and desktop settings.

   D. Pre-stage the computers.

7. You have used the RIPrep tool to create an installation image based on a standard source computer. You have copied this image to a RIS server. After you have
   deployed this image to some new computers, you decide that you need to modify some of the image's desktop and Registry settings. What should you do?

   A. Modify the settings on a new source computer and create a new image.

   B. Modify the settings on the original source computer and update the
   existing image.

   C. Open the existing image on the RIS server using RIPrep on a source
   computer, modify the settings, and save the image.

   D. Modify the settings through the image's answer file created by RIPrep.

8. You have configured a source computer to use with RIPrep to generate an
   installation image for RIS deployment. While testing the image, you find that
   after a user completes the remote installation through RIS, the desktop settings you configured on the source computer do not appear to have been
   applied. How would you troubleshoot this? Choose the *best* answer.

   A. Check the GPO for the OU in which the computer is being created to see
   whether the inheritance of settings is being blocked.

   B. Set permissions on the answer file for the image to allow users Read and
   Read & Execute permissions for the answer file.

   C. On the source computer, copy the administrator's profile to the All Users
   profile and then regenerate the image.

   D. On the source computer, copy the administrator's profile to the Default
   Users profile and then regenerate the image.

9. You are planning to deploy Windows 2000 Professional using RIS. You want
   to deploy three custom applications as part of the installation, prevent unauthorized RIS client computers from initiating a remote installation, load-
   balance server resource handling and network traffic related to RIS servers,
   and ensure that only authorized users can create the new computer accounts
   and install only images that they are authorized to install. Up to this point,
   you have not set any other GPO settings within the site, domain, or forest.

You decide to pre-stage the client computers and assign them to specific OUs. You use RIPrep to generate an image that includes the three custom applications, and you assign NTFS permissions for your answer files to the appropriate users. Which of the following goals will you accomplish? Select all that apply.

A. Deploy three custom applications as part of the installation.

B. Prevent unauthorized RIS client computers from initiating a remote installation.

C. Load-balance server resource handling and network traffic related to RIS servers.

D. Ensure that only authorized users can create the new computer accounts.

E. Ensure that users can install only images that they are authorized to install.

10. You are deploying Windows 2000 Professional using RIS. You have restricted the extent to which users can access Active Directory through the use of Site and Domain GPOs. However, you need to allow specific users the ability to create new computer accounts in their respective OUs when initiating a remote installation. What is the easiest way to ensure that the appropriate users can create their computer accounts?

A. Delegate control over creating computer objects to the users within their respective OUs.

B. Modify all the GPOs to allow users to create computer objects within their respective OUs.

C. Pre-stage the clients in their respective OUs.

D. Do nothing. All users can create up to ten computer accounts by default.

REVIEW ANSWERS

1. **B** Unless the new computers can obtain an IP address, they will not be able to contact the RIS server. Pre-staging (D) only creates the computer accounts before the installation and assigns an RIS server to handle the installation request. You do need to authorize the RIS server (A), but so what if the clients can't find it? Placing the clients in the same site (C) will reduce traffic, but again, being in the same site does not necessarily mean being on the same local network as the DHCP server.

2. **A** and **C** The RIS server must be authorized, and this can only be done through an authorized DHCP server. Pre-staging (B) and creating an RIS startup disk (D) can assist in the actual remote installation, but these actions have no real bearing on the successful configuration of RIS in Active Directory.

3. **C** RIS startup disks can be used for computers that have network cards that RIS supports, and RIS does support network cards that are not PXE-compliant (D) for this purpose. Pre-staging the client (A) creates the computer accounts ahead of time and assigns an RIS server to handle the installation, but if the client cannot connect in the first place, no installation can take place. You could certainly replace all the network cards with PXE-compliant cards, as suggested in B, but this is not the easiest, or even the most cost-efficient way, perhaps, to solve the problem.

4. **B** and **D** Installing RIS servers in the same sites as computers and pre-staging them accomplishes these goals. However, using the standard default CD image only deploys Windows 2000 Professional and does not install any other applications or custom settings (C). Simply authorizing a DHCP server does not ensure that clients on subnets other than the DHCP servers will be able to obtain an IP address and locate the RIS server (A). To do that, you'd need to install a DHCP proxy agent on each subnet that needed it.

5. **A** The Repartition value is set to Yes by default, resulting in the drive being reformatted as one large NTFS partition. Setting the value to No prevents this from happening and forces the use of any other drive settings in the answer file. Answer B is wrong because if the Repartition value is not specified, the drive will still be reformatted by default. Pre-staging the client (C) creates the computer account for the client ahead of time but does not affect drive partitioning. Partitioning ahead of time (D) will not override the Repartition value in the answer file.

6. **B** and **C** Placing the RIS server in the same site as the computers will help to reduce network traffic associated with the installation. Using RIPrep ensures that the image contains only the files and settings required to deploy the installation, thus reducing the time it takes to install as well as reducing traffic. Using the standard CD image and answer file (A) will result in a regular installation taking place, which will last longer and not do much to reduce traffic. Pre-staging the computers (D) creates the computer accounts beforehand, but again, this does not significantly affect the amount of time the installation will take or the traffic that will be generated.

7. **A** is the only correct answer. Once the image has been generated and copied to the RIS server using RIPrep, you cannot alter it in any way. The image can only be modified later by replacing it with a new image. Therefore, B, C, and D are incorrect.

8. **D** In order for you to configure the source computer, you would have to be logged on as an administrator, and the settings would be stored as part of the administrator's profile on the source computer. Copying the administrator's profile to Default Users (not All Users, as in answer C) makes it available to all users when they initiate the remote installation. Because the settings are part of the image itself, the GPO inheritance settings (A) would have no effect here, except whether to allow installation at all. Similarly, setting permissions on the answer file (B) only serves to designate which users can initiate a remote installation using that answer file.

9. **A B C D** and **E** Using RIPrep takes care of A. Pre-staging the client affects both B and C. Setting permissions on the answer file ensures E, and D is true by default (because the questions states that you haven't otherwise modified any GPOs). By default, all users can create up to ten computer accounts in Active Directory.

10. **A** Use the Delegation of Control Wizard to create that specific custom task. Although you can argue that modifying all the GPOs (B) would accomplish the same thing, that could take a lot more time and testing than delegating control. Pre-staging the computers (C) would ensure that the computer accounts were created beforehand, but the question specifically states that you need to enable users to create the accounts. Finally, D is factually correct. However, the question makes it clear that GPOs modify what users can do in Active Directory, and the implication is that through the GPOs, users cannot create computer accounts.

P A R T

IV

Managing, Monitoring, and Optimizing the Components of Active Directory

Managing Active Directory Objects

CHAPTER 8

	NEWBIE	SOME EXPERIENCE	EXPERT
ETA	6+ hours	4+ hours	2+ hours

Part III began a discussion of techniques for managing Active Directory. Specifically, Chapters 5, 6, and 7 dealt with change and configuration management and focused on managing users' environments through the use of Group Policy as well as the installation of standard Windows 2000 Professional computers using Remote Installation Service.

This part of the book continues the discussion of management techniques— this time specifically relating to objects and components of Active Directory itself, including optimizing its performance and recovering from failure. This chapter, in particular, explores using Active Directory to locate and manage objects as well as control who has access to what.

Locate Objects in Active Directory

Active Directory maintains numerous objects, many of which you have already seen in this exam prep. For example, each site, domain, and OU you create is an object in Active Directory. User, group, and computer accounts, as well as printers and other published resources, also are kept as objects in the Active Directory.

Every object in Active Directory has a set of attributes that define that object. For a user account, the attributes might include the user's phone extension, office number, e-mail address, manager's name, and so on. For a printer, the attributes might include the printer's physical location or the fact that it can perform certain functions, such as an envelope feed.

The attributes of each object are supplied by the administrator creating the object. Each object, along with a subset of its attributes, is stored in the global catalog and replicated to all other global catalog servers in a forest. This ensures that anyone can locate an object that exists in Active Directory anywhere in the forest.

When you create an object, therefore, it is wise to supply that object's more common attributes—that is, those attributes that users are most likely to search on when trying to locate the object. For example, users are likely to want to find printers that are closest to them, so entering information about a printer's location would facilitate the users' searches.

Active Directory objects are created and maintained by those who have been given administrative control over the objects. For example, in order to create a new user or group in a domain, you must be a member of the Domain Admins group for that domain. To create a new domain in the forest, you need to be a member of the Enterprise Admins group for the forest. Delegation of control is discussed in more detail later in this chapter.

However, any user can search for an object in Active Directory provided that user has Read access to the object (which users will have by default). Although Read access is a default, you can effectively hide an object from a user by removing the Read permission for that user or for a group that the user belongs to.

To quickly review, you create a new object by first selecting the location where the object will reside, such as a domain or OU container. Then, right-click the container, choose New and the type of object you want to create. The list of objects presented will depend slightly on the location you select. The New Object Wizard will ask for the required attributes for the object and generate it in the location you've selected.

The object's additional attributes can be accessed and modified by then viewing the object's Properties dialog box. Figures 8-1 and 8-2 display the Properties dialog boxes for a user and printer object, respectively, and some of the attributes that can be modified.

You can locate objects in Active Directory through the Active Directory Users and Computers console. You would start by selecting a domain or OU to search. On the Action menu in this console, you would next select Find and then enter the search criteria necessary to find the object, as you see in Figure 8-3.

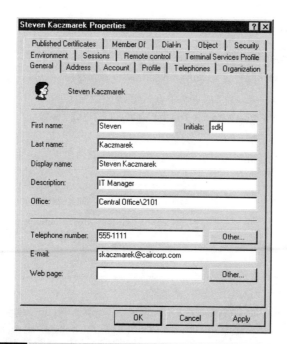

FIGURE 8-1   User object attributes

SCRUFFY-HP1100 Properties ? ✕

General | Managed By | Object | Security |

HP LaserJet 1100

Location: Central Office\2nd Floor\East

Model: HP LaserJet 1100

Description:

☑ Color

☐ Staple

☐ Double-sided

Printing speed: 4 ppm

Maximum resolution: 600 dpi

OK Cancel Apply

FIGURE 8-2 Printer object attributes

Exam Tip

This exam is not concerned with testing your ability to create objects; however, it assumes that you know how to do this. If you are not comfortable with or do not know how to create objects in Active Directory, you should spend some time practicing that task on a Windows 2000 server.

Travel Assistance

For detailed information concerning the creation of user and group objects, refer to the Microsoft Official Curriculum (MOC) number 2152, "Implementing Microsoft Windows 2000 Professional and Server."

Users would similarly use the Search menu option on the Start menu or the search menu commands in Windows Explorer, My Computer, or My Network Places to locate objects in Active Directory to which they have been given Read

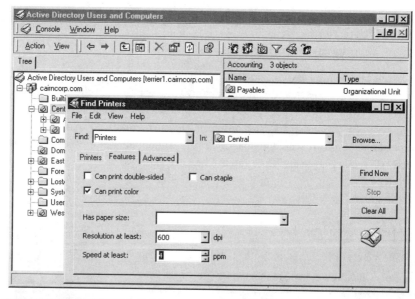

FIGURE 8-3   Searching for an object using Active Directory Users and Computers

Travel Assistance

The Active Directory Client for Windows 95 and 98 (dsclient.exe) is included on the Windows 2000 Server source CD in the \CLIENTS\WIN9X folder, whereas the client for Windows NT can be downloaded from the Microsoft site. A version of the Active Directory client is not yet available for Windows Me; installing any of the other versions of the client on Windows Me can cause the operating system to become unstable.

access. Only computers running Windows 2000 or an earlier version of Windows with the Active Directory Client installed can search Active Directory.

When you search for an object, begin by selecting the type of object you want to locate. You can search for the following object types:

- Users, contacts, and groups by name or description
- Computers by name, owner, or role
- Printers by name, location, or model

- Shared folders by name or keyword
- OUs by name
- More advanced search criteria can also be specified

You can customize your search to include other attributes that you may have specified for the object, and you can narrow your search from the entire Active Directory, which uses the global catalog, to specific domains and OUs.

Results of the search are listed onscreen and can be managed according to the type of object you are searching for, just as you would manage the objects through Active Directory Users and Computers. Users are managed like users, printers like printers, and so on.

Travel Advisory

The more attributes you fill in, the more criteria options users will have available to them to facilitate a search.

Exam Tip

Again, the main focus of this book and exam is not your ability to create users and groups. However, you should already be familiar with how to do that and the concepts associated with creating and managing users and groups and it will have been the focus of another core certification exam. As with all such material, Microsoft will expect you to know this, especially as it relates to questions in other exams. To that effect, here is a reminder about group management strategy: Microsoft recommends that you manage groups and object security by organizing users based on their needs into global groups within a domain. Optionally, use *nesting*—placing a global group into another global group—for greater flexibility (For example, you might place the IT Help Desk and IT Network Admin global groups into an IT Dept global group.) Add the global groups into domain local groups. Use the domain local groups to assign permissions to access network resources. Microsoft calls this the A-G-DL-P strategy: Accounts into Global groups into Domain Local groups assigned Permissions.

Move Active Directory Objects

When you create an object for the first time, such as a computer account or a user account, you will typically create that object within the Active Directory container (site, domain, or OU) in which the object will reside. This helps simplify administration of Active Directory objects. Objects cannot be members of more than one container at a time. Access to the object is defined, in part, by its container membership.

Nevertheless, things change, and it may happen that some objects will need to be moved from one container to another in Active Directory. Perhaps you are redistributing computers within the organization because of a reorganization of OUs. Perhaps a user has been promoted or reassigned to another department, necessitating a change for the user's account object in Active Directory.

The process of moving an object is quite straightforward. You right-click the account and select Move from the pop-up menu. In the Move dialog box, you browse for the container you want to move the object to and click OK. You can select and move several objects to another container in one action if necessary.

Permissions assigned to an object, such as a user or group, become part of that object's attributes. Because of this, any Active Directory permissions previously assigned directly to the object will remain with the object after you move it. Because the object will reside in a new container, it will inherit permissions from the new container and that container's parent containers. Previously inherited permissions will no longer apply to the object.

Publish Resources in Active Directory

The idea behind publishing resources in Active Directory is to make frequently accessed resources easily locatable by users who need them as well as to make them easily securable by the administrator. Actually, every object you create in Active Directory is automatically made part of the directory and is therefore published. Every Windows 2000 print server, for example, automatically publishes its shared printers in Active Directory.

Nevertheless, you can also publish resources that do not automatically appear in Active Directory. For example, you can publish a reference to a shared folder or a printer shared on a Windows NT 4.0 print server. Because objects in Active Directory are replicated to all domain controllers within a domain as well as to global catalog servers, you'll want to publish resources whose content remains static so as to keep network-replication traffic under control. Furthermore, as long as you update the published object's link to its physical location, you can physically move the object around within the network without having to notify users of the change.

Publishing a Printer

As mentioned earlier, printers installed on Windows 2000–based computers are automatically published in Active Directory. The server sharing the printer contacts a domain controller to create a print queue object for the printer in the server's computer object in Active Directory. If the printer is no longer shared or the print server is no longer active on the network, the print queue object is automatically removed from Active Directory.

Local Lingo

Printer In Windows 2000 networks, the term "printer" actually refers to the logical share, or print queue, for the print device. It consists of the device driver and software-management interface for the device.

If you'd rather not have printers published automatically (perhaps because you want to control which users have access to specific printers), you can control this action in two ways. When you share a printer, you will find the option List in the Directory on the printer's Sharing tab. This option is enabled by default. If you uncheck it, the printer will not be automatically published in Active Directory. If the printer has already been published, clearing this option will remove the object from Active Directory.

The other way to control automatic publishing is through—you guessed it— the use of a Group Policy. Printer publishing is a Computer Configuration setting that can be found under Administrative Templates | Printers in the GPO Settings window. In Figure 8-4, automatic printer publishing has been disabled for the Accounting OU.

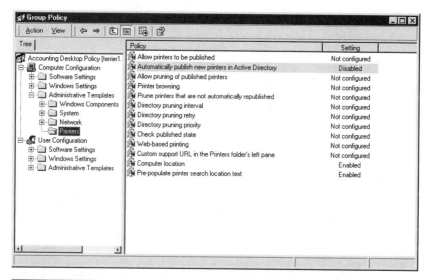

FIGURE 8-4 GPO—Disabling automatic printer publishing

If you need to publish a printer in Active Directory, particularly if the printer has been shared on a non-Windows 2000 server, you can do so by creating a printer object for it in the appropriate container. In Active Directory Users and Computers, right-click the appropriate container and choose New | Printer from the pop-up menu. Enter the universal naming convention (UNC) path to the printer and then click OK. Of course, you can then modify the printer's properties to facilitate searches and set security. You can also right-click the printer object to move, install, or open the print queue to manage jobs.

Local Lingo

UNC path A network locator to a shared resource that uses the following syntax: *servername**sharename*.

Active Directory provides a search feature specific to printers called *printer locations.* If you have at least one site and two or more subnets defined in Active Directory, you can take advantage of printer locations. This feature allows users to quickly find printers that reside in the same physical subnet as they do.

Each printer location name will correspond to an IP subnet and should represent as nearly as possible the physical location of the printer, because that is what the user will be most concerned about—where the printer is. For example, a printer located in the Accounts Payable department in the 222 building in Chicago might be called Chicago/Accounts Payable/222. Each name separated by slashes can be up to 32 characters long, for a total of 260 characters, so you can be quite descriptive. Of course, you should try to strike a balance between being too descriptive and making it easy for the user to locate a printer without having to type in too much information. Define a naming convention and adhere to it.

Travel Assistance

For information about creating and managing subnet objects, refer to Chapter 4.

In the Properties dialog box of each subnet object in Active Directory, on the Location tab, you need to enter the location name of that subnet using the naming convention to be defined, as shown in Figure 8-5.

Then, for each printer that resides in that subnet, modify the Location attribute on the General tab in the printer's Properties dialog box to include the

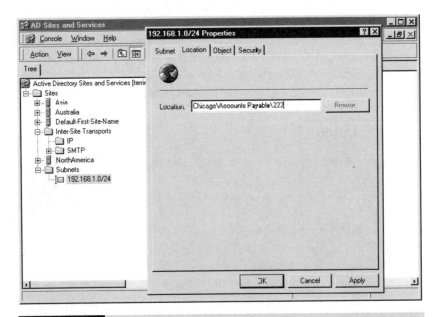

FIGURE 8-5   Location name for a subnet

same location name. Finally, you must enable printer location tracking through—well, what do you know—Group Policy. In the appropriate GPO's Properties dialog box, locate the Pre-populate Printer Search Location setting under Computer Configuration | Administrative Templates | Printers, as shown in Figure 8-4.

When a user searches for a printer, Active Directory finds the subnet object associated with the computer's location in a site, performs a search for all printers whose location value matches that of the subnet object, and returns a list of matching printers to the user. Of course, the user can search for printers located anywhere in Active Directory.

Travel Advisory

You can override the computer's location setting by setting a Group Policy for the OU the computer resides in that specifies which location value to use. In the printer's GPO settings, enable Computer Location and enter the location that should be used (refer to Figure 8-4).

Publishing a Shared Folder

As with printers, you can publish any shared folder that has a valid UNC path. Publishing a shared folder is even more straightforward than publishing a printer. You begin, as always, by selecting the container where the folder will be published and right-clicking that container. Choose New | Shared Folder from the pop-up menu and then enter the UNC path to the shared folder. Once the folder has been published, modify its properties to provide one or more keywords that a user can use to search for it (see Figure 8-6).

It is significant to note that the published folder or printer and the actual shared resource are two distinct entities. Because you are referencing the shared resource by its UNC path, it is a relatively easy task to physically relocate the shared resource. You need only update the UNC path for the corresponding object in Active Directory. If you move the published object from one container to another, the UNC path does not change, making it easy to relocate the object in Active Directory.

It is also important to realize that access to the shared resource itself is still managed by the permission list, or DACL (Discretionary Access Control List), set through NTFS and/or share-level permissions. Security set through Active Directory on the object referencing the shared resource reflects who has access

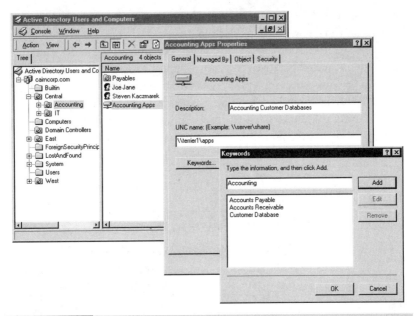

FIGURE 8-6 Published shared folder properties

to manage the object rather than who can actually access the resource itself. In Figure 8-7, for example, you can see the NTFS permissions for the shared folder Apps on the right and the object permissions for the published folder object Accounting Apps on the left. Note the difference in the permissions that can be set.

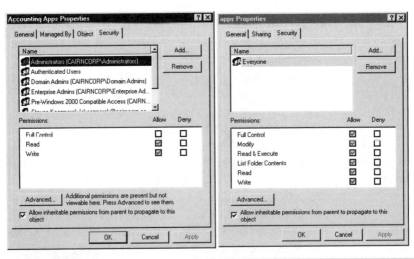

FIGURE 8-7 Object versus resource permissions

Objective 8.04

Create and Manage Objects Manually Using Scripting

If you have a large number of objects that you want to add to Active Directory, you may choose to add these in bulk to facilitate the process. Perhaps these objects already reside in a database format. Objects such as users, computers, and printers can be imported to Active Directory through the use of scripts.

Two tools are provided with Windows 2000 to facilitate bulk importing of objects: Comma-Separated Value Directory Exchange (CSVDE), used to add objects to Active Directory through the use of a comma-delimited text file; and Lightweight Directory Access Protocol Data Interchange Format Directory Exchange (LDIFDE), used to add, modify, and delete objects in Active Directory through the use of a line-separated text file. Most databases include tools that allow you to export records using one or both of these formats. You can also use ADSI and VBScript programming to create, modify, and delete objects in Active Directory.

Exam Tip

You can use ADSI and VBScript to add and modify objects in Active Directory. In fact, Windows 2000 includes a VBScript in the WINNT\System32 folder called pubprn.vbs that you can use to publish printers. However, the exam is more concerned that you know the basics about using CSVDE and LDIFDE.

The basic concept here is that you are creating or modifying object records in Active Directory. Therefore, you need to include information pertinent to the object as it is referenced in Active Directory. For example, when adding new user accounts, you must include the full Active Directory *distinguished name* (DN) of the user, because that's how Active Directory refers to the account. And, note that the object class is "user." You can populate any additional attributes of the object as well. The most common objects that you will import in bulk will likely be user accounts.

CSVDE uses a comma-delimited text file to define objects that will be imported into Active Directory. The first line will always identify the attributes of

Travel Advisory

When you're adding new user accounts using CSVDE or LDIFDE, the Password field is intentionally left blank so that the user must change it on their first logon. You cannot include a password in your import file. Also, by default, user accounts are left enabled. Because the user accounts have no password when added to Active Directory this way, you might want to set the accounts to be disabled when you add them and then enable them as you need to make them available.

the objects that you will be defining. Subsequent lines define each object's attribute values. Any value that contains commas in this case, such as the DN, must be enclosed in quotes. The following illustration is an example of a comma-delimited import text file.

```
distinguishedName,objectClass,userPrincipalName,displayName,scriptPath,home
Directory,userAccountControl
"cn=Steve
Kaczmarek,ou=IT,ou=Central,dc=Cairncorp.com",user,skaczmarek@Cairncorp.com,
Steve Kaczmarek,logon.bat,\\terrier1\home,512
"cn=Jane
Doe,ou=Accounting,ou=Central,dc=Cairncorp.com",user,jdoe@Cairncorp.com,Jane
Doe,logon.bat,\\terrier1\home,512
```

In this example, we are adding two new accounts. Each account includes the following attributes: distinguishedName, objectClass, userPrincipalName, displayName, scriptPath, homeDirectory, and userAccountControl. For the most part, the attributes should be descriptive enough. The userAccountControl attribute is used to enable or disable the account. The default value, 512, enables the account, whereas a value of 514 disables it.

To use this file to add the accounts to Active Directory, enter the following command at a Windows 2000 command prompt: **csvde -i -f import.cdf**. This command will also provide success or failure status and a reference to an error log file.

LDIFDE uses a line-separated text file to define objects that will be imported to, modified in, or deleted from Active Directory. Here are the same two accounts you saw earlier but presented in a line-separated format file.

Here, lines beginning with a pound sign (#) represent remarks and are not processed. This kind of format is somewhat easier to read. Notice, too, that the second entry represents a change to an existing account. To use this file to add, modify, or delete accounts, enter the following command at a Windows 2000 command prompt: **ldifde -i -f import.ldf**. You can use LDIFDE to export objects from Active Directory to help facilitate bulk modifications without having to create the file from scratch.

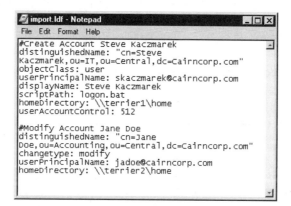

```
#Create Account Steve Kaczmarek
distinguishedName: "cn=Steve
Kaczmarek,ou=IT,ou=Central,dc=Cairncorp.com"
objectClass: user
userPrincipalName: skaczmarek@cairncorp.com
displayName: Steve Kaczmarek
scriptPath: logon.bat
homeDirectory: \\terrier1\home
userAccountControl: 512

#Modify Account Jane Doe
distinguishedName: "cn=Jane
Doe,ou=Accounting,ou=Central,dc=Cairncorp.com"
changetype: modify
userPrincipalName: jadoe@cairncorp.com
homeDirectory: \\terrier2\home
```

Travel Assistance

For more information about using LDIFDE and VBScript to make bulk changes to Active Directory, see the whitepaper titled "Step-by-Step Guide to Bulk Import and Export to Active Directory," which can be found under Technical Resources on Microsoft's Windows 2000 Web site (www.microsoft.com/Windows2000/techinfo/default.asp).

Objective 8.05   Control Access to Active Directory Objects

Remember that access to an object in Active Directory is different from access allowed to a shared resource such as a file, folder, or printer through NTFS or share permissions. In this case, we are examining access to the objects in Active Directory.

Windows 2000 provides security access in two main ways: through a valid logon process and through the use of object permissions. Object security is stored and managed as a property of the object rather than a property of the account and is stored as the object's security descriptor. Security principals (that is, user, group, and computer accounts) are assigned permissions in the DACL of the object and are represented in the DACL by their security identifiers, or SIDs. When you view the DACL for an object, however, the SIDs are resolved to their account names for ease of administration. Each account has its own *access control entry* (ACE) in the DACL. Some ACEs are globally available for all objects, whereas others are specific to the object in question.

When a user logs on and is authenticated through a valid user account and password, Windows 2000 creates an access token that contains, among other things, the user's account SID, group memberships, and group SIDs. When a user attempts to access an object through Active Directory—say, to view the properties of a printer or try to modify a user attribute—the user's access token is processed against the DACL of the object.

Permissions assigned explicitly to a user account or implicitly through group membership are determined, and the user's effective permission is cumulative. The only exception is if at any point, either explicitly or through group membership, the user is denied access. In this case, the user's effective permission is to be denied access to the object. If permission to perform an action is not explicitly assigned (to the user account or through group membership), that action is implicitly denied to the user.

Travel Assistance

For more detailed discussions of the logon process and the security processes surrounding object access, refer to Microsoft Official Curriculum 2154, "Implementing and Administering Microsoft Windows 2000 Directory Services," or search for the topic Security on Microsoft's Windows 2000 Web page (www.microsoft.com/Windows2000).

Inheritance of object permissions works quite the same way as inheritance of Group Policy settings. Objects within a container automatically inherit the permissions of that container. Containers inherit permissions from parent containers, and so on. You can tell which object permissions have been inherited when you view the Security dialog box for an object. Inherited permissions appear dimmed, as you see in Figure 8-8.

You can prevent permission inheritance similar to the way you can prevent GPO inheritance. As you see in Figure 8-8, the Security tab includes an option called Allow Inheritable Permissions from Parent to Propagate to This Object. This option is enabled by default. If you deselect this option and confirm it, you

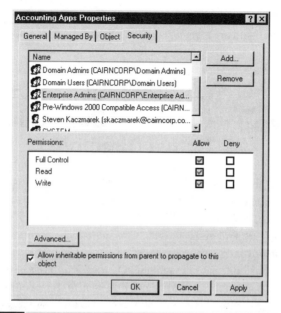

FIGURE 8-8 The Security tab for an object

will be asked whether you want to copy and retain the permissions that have been inherited or clear them. You should retain the permissions if, for the most part, they will stay the same (for example, if you plan to modify one permission). Clear them if you are effectively starting over.

Standard permissions include Full Control, Read, Write, Create All Child Objects, and Delete All Child Objects, which can be set either to Allow or Deny. A permission must be explicitly allowed to enable that level of access for the affected account. The Advanced button gives you an added level of granularity over setting permissions by allowing you to control access to specific attributes of an object. This level of granularity is generally discouraged because it is easy to set a permission in such as way as to inadvertently make the object unavailable to the user or the system.

Whoever creates an object in Active Directory is flagged as the owner of that object. Because administrators usually create objects, it is common for the owner of an object to be represented as the Administrators group. However, depending on how you have delegated control over the creation of objects, other user accounts may be represented as the owner of an object. The owner is displayed when you click Advanced on the Security tab of an object's Properties dialog box and select the Owner tab.

You cannot assign ownership of an object, but you can give an account permission to take ownership of the object. Any member of the Administrators group can take ownership of an object. However, any account that has been granted the advanced permission Modify Owner can also take ownership of the object.

On the Owner tab under Advanced settings, find your account (or Administrators, if you are a member of that group), select it, and choose OK to take ownership.

Delegate Administrative Control of Objects in Active Directory

Another way to control access to objects in Active Directory is by identifying which users should be able to perform specific tasks with designated Active Directory objects. This is accomplished by delegating control of tasks to designated users, who are sometimes referred to as *sub-administrators*.

Delegation of control was introduced to you in Chapter 5, in the context of delegating responsibility for managing GPOs at various levels in the site hierarchy, and in Chapter 7, in the context of allowing users to create computer accounts when performing RIS installations of Windows 2000 Professional. The same concepts apply in this chapter in the context of assigning responsibility for various management tasks to designated users or groups.

As you saw in the chapters mentioned, delegating control over objects begins at the container level, and management tasks over those objects fall into three areas:

- Modifying properties of the container itself
- Creating and deleting all or specific objects within the container
- Modifying properties of all or specific objects within the container

Assigning management tasks of these types is best accomplished using the Delegation of Control Wizard, although you could assign specific permissions in the DACLs of each object and of the container. The latter is not recommended because of the increased potential for error that is present when manually setting permissions.

As you have seen before, you can launch the Delegation of Control Wizard by right-clicking the container for which you are assigning a management task and choosing Delegate Control from the pop-up menu. On the Users and Groups screen, select the user or groups that you are assigning a task to and proceed to the Tasks to Delegate screen, as shown in Figure 8-9.

The following common management tasks can be assigned to a user or group and are self-explanatory:

- Create, delete, and manager user accounts
- Reset passwords on user accounts
- Read all user information

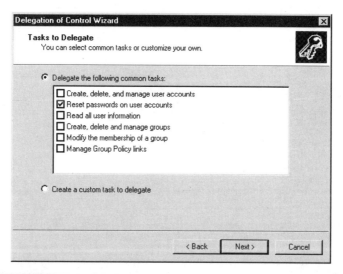

FIGURE 8-9   The Tasks to Delegate screen of the Delegation of Control Wizard

- Create, delete, and manage groups
- Modify the membership of a group
- Manage Group Policy links

You can also create custom tasks that allow you to assign more specific tasks to perform by clicking the Create a Custom Task to Delegate option on the Tasks to Delegate screen. When you select this option and click Next, the subsequent screen asks you to select the object type over which you are delegating control. This could be the OU itself, which effectively assigns control over all existing and new objects in the container, or specific objects within the container, such as users, computers, groups, and printers.

Then, you assign specific permissions to the user or group. Again, the permissions can be chosen from a common list or limited to the creation or deletion of new objects and the modification of specific object properties (see Figure 8-10).

Exam Tip

Microsoft recommends that control be delegated at the OU level, rather than becoming granular with task assignment, to more easily track and document which permissions have been assigned to which users and groups and to more easily troubleshoot problems relating to the delegation of tasks.

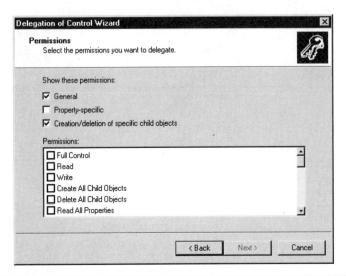

FIGURE 8-10   Permissions for custom tasks

All administrative tasks that involve Active Directory are performed through one of the many *Microsoft Management Consoles* (MMCs) provided with Windows 2000. When working with Active Directory objects of the kind we have been talking about here, you are using the Active Directory Users and Computers console to carry out management tasks.

When you delegate control of one or more administrative tasks to a user or group, those users still need to carry out their tasks using the appropriate MMC—in this case, Active Directory Users and Computers. Some tasks may involve the use of two or more different consoles. Because the default consoles show a lot more to the user than the user may have access to, the consoles may be confusing or overwhelming to the user. To this end, MMCs can be customized in a couple different ways to fit the delegation and administration needs of your sub-administrators. You can customize MMCs to include all the administrative consoles that the user requires, and you can narrow the focus of a custom console to display only tasks that the user is authorized to perform.

Customizing Consoles

You can create a customized MMC by first launching the MMC template. In the Start | Run menu option, enter **mmc** and click OK. All the available consoles are listed as snap-ins in the Add/Remove Snap-Ins dialog box. Add the appropriate snap-ins to the custom console—perhaps Active Directory Users and Computers and Active Directory Sites and Services. Set the console mode to User Mode, to limit the ability for changes to be made, or Author Mode, if you want administrators to be able to modify the console (perhaps as their responsibilities change).

When you create a custom console, you can modify which components of the console can be viewed when it is opened, such as the toolbar or console tree, and then save it. However, you cannot change how the snap-in is displayed. If you want to provide the users with an interface that displays only those tasks that they can perform, create a taskpad for them, as discussed next.

Obviously, the custom console must be distributed to the users who will be using it. How you choose to do that is entirely up to you. What is necessary, however, is that the designated user must have at least the Read permission to the console (for example, if the console is located on a shared network folder), and, perhaps more significantly, the snap-in itself must be installed on whatever desktop the user will be performing delegated tasks. The snap-ins can be installed through Add/Remove Programs using the installer program Adminpak.msi, which comes with the Windows 2000 Server products.

Creating Taskpads

You can, and probably should, take the customization of the administration console to the next level by creating taskpads for your sub-administrators. A *taskpad* essentially maintains shortcuts to specific tasks that the user can perform through the custom console.

For example, if a user is responsible for changing users' passwords and unlocking user accounts, you should create a custom console that contains the Active Directory Users and Computers snap-in and then modify it to display a taskpad with two shortcut buttons: one that lets the user change a password and another that lets the user unlock a user account.

Once you have created the custom console, you can create a taskpad by launching the New Taskpad Wizard. Right-click the item in the console tree for which the task applies and select New Taskpad from the pop-up menu. You'll be asked to specify the name, description, and appearance of the taskpad. You also will be asked to add and configure the task you want to assign. Tasks can also be configured to execute scripts, batch files, or other programs that can run from a command prompt. The resulting taskpad might look something like what's shown in Figure 8-11.

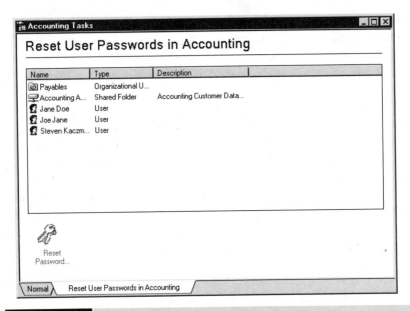

FIGURE 8-11　Example of a taskpad

Exam Tip

When you create a taskpad, you are modifying the custom console, so you must be in Author Mode to do so. However, be sure to modify the console view to remove the console tree so that only the taskpad is displayed, and then set the console back to User Mode, before distributing the console to your users.

After you have delegated control over specific tasks to specific sub-administrators, you can just sit back and relax, right? Wrong! You should monitor the actions of your designated sub-administrators and be sure that the tasks for which they are responsible are being carried out. You can make their jobs easier by creating taskpads, as you have seen. You can even add the custom console as a shortcut on their desktop or on the Start menu if that helps. Perhaps consider storing the custom consoles on a network shared folder so users can easily access them from any computer on which the snap-ins have been installed. You are still, after all, "the" Active Directory administrator.

CHECKPOINT

✔ **Objective 8.01: Locate Objects in Active Directory** Every object that you create in Active Directory contains a set of attributes that is used to define that object. The values of these attributes are supplied by the administrator creating the object. Each object, along with a subset of its attributes, is stored in the global catalog and replicated to all other global catalog servers in a forest. This ensures that anyone can locate an object that exists in Active Directory anywhere in the forest.

Therefore, when you create an object, it is wise to supply that object's more common attributes (that is, those attributes that users are most likely to search on when trying to locate the object).

Administrators can use Active Directory Users and Computers to search Active Directory for objects, whereas users can use the various search menu options available through their Windows 2000 computers (or Windows computers with the Active Directory Client installed).

✔ **Objective 8.02: Move Active Directory Objects** Objects cannot reside in more than one container at a time in Active Directory. You'll always begin by creating an object where you think it should reside. If you need to move the object to a new location later, you can easily do so. Keep in mind that any permissions assigned directly to the object will remain with the object after you move it. However, because the object will reside in a new container, it will inherit permissions from the new container, and that container's parent containers and previously inherited permissions will no longer apply to the object.

✔ **Objective 8.03: Publish Resources in Active Directory** All objects you create in Windows 2000 are automatically published in Active Directory and replicated to all domain controllers. All objects and a subset of their common attributes are also replicated to the global catalog server to facilitate forest-wide searches.

Some objects, such as printers shared on non-Windows 2000 servers, are not automatically published in Active Directory. Specifically, you can publish printers and shared folders in Active Directory to make it easier for users to locate these network resources.

✔ **Objective 8.04: Create and Manage Objects Manually Using Scripting**
Large numbers of objects, usually user accounts, can be imported into
Active Directory through the use of scripts. Scripts can be comma delimited
(using the CSVDE command-prompt tool to import objects), line delimited (using the LDIFDE command-prompt tool to create, modify, or delete
objects), or generated through ADSI and VBScript.

✔ **Objective 8.05: Control Access to Active Directory Objects** Object
security in Active Directory is different from, but complementary to,
resource security applied through NTFS and shared permissions. Resource
security defines who has access to the network resource and what level of
access is available (for example, who can send a print job to a printer and
manage print jobs sent to a printer). Object security in Active Directory
defines who has control over an object and its attributes and what level of
access is available (for example, who can create a printer object in Active
Directory and modify attributes of the printer object).

Object security is set by assigning permissions explicitly to users,
groups, or computers. These permissions are maintained in the DACL of
each object and are applied to users based on the access tokens created for
the users when they log on.

✔ **Objective 8.06: Delegate Administrative Control of Objects in Active
Directory** Often, specific users can and should be given responsibilities to
carry out specific tasks within their OUs or for specific objects in their OUs.
This can help to reduce calls to the main administrators to perform common tasks such as resetting a user's password as well as provide a sense of
purpose and responsibility to specific individuals in the organization. You
can delegate administrative tasks by using the Delegation of Control
Wizard to assign tasks and permissions to designated users and groups, and
then customize their administrative interface through the use of custom
MMCs and taskpads.

REVIEW QUESTIONS

1. Each OU in your organization has a user who will be responsible for performing common user account tasks, such as modifying user accounts, resetting
   passwords, and creating new users within the OU. You want to be sure that the
   users can perform these tasks within their individual OUs only and with the
   easiest interface. What three steps do you need to take to accomplish this goal?

   A. Create a taskpad that defines the tasks each user can perform.

   B. Delegate control over user objects to the user for each OU.

   C. Create a custom console for each user.

   D. Make each user a member of the Domain Admins global group.

2. You have published several printers in Active Directory and you want your users to be able to locate printers that are closest to them. Which of the following steps do you need to take to accomplish this goal? Select all that apply.

   A. Specify a location value for each subnet object.

   B. Specify a location value for each printer.

   C. Enable location tracking in Group Policy.

   D. Define a location naming convention.

3. You have created several computer and printer objects in the Central\ Accounting OU that now need to be relocated to the East\Accounting OU. Many of these objects have specific DACLs that outline explicit permissions for users. You want these permissions to remain the same while any OU-specific permissions are applied as defined for the target OU. What steps do you have to take after you move the objects? Select all that apply.

   A. Disable inheritance for the objects in the target OU.

   B. Enable inheritance for the objects in the target OU.

   C. Reconfigure the DACL for each object after you move it.

   D. Do nothing.

4. You have published several shared folder objects in the Central\Accounting OU that now need to be relocated to the East\Accounting OU. After you move the shared folders, what else will you need to do to ensure that users will still be able to access the network resource associated with the published folder?

   A. Modify the UNC path in the published folder so that it correctly points to the network resource.

   B. Modify the DACL on the shared folder so that users who were able to access it before can access it now that it has been moved.

   C. Modify the NTFS and share permissions of the network resource so that users who were able to access it before can access it now that the published folder has been moved.

   D. Do nothing.

5. When you're assigning permissions to users to access a network resource, such as a printer, or to access an Active Directory object, such as a printer or user, which of the following accurately represents the best way to assign those permissions?

   A. Assign the permissions explicitly to each user.
   B. Assign the permissions to a global group and then add the users to the global group.
   C. Assign the permissions to a domain local group and then add the users to the domain local group.
   D. Assign the permissions to a domain local group and then add global groups that contain the appropriate users to the domain local group.

6. You have been given the task of adding an OU to your domain for a company that has recently been acquired by your organization. You need to create user and group accounts for the new OU, but there are several hundred accounts to create. You know that the acquired company has an accurate employee database maintained in Access 2000 that can be exported to a comma-delimited text file. How can you simplify the creation of the user accounts for the OU you are creating?

   A. Import the accounts using the LDIFDE tool and the comma-delimited text file.
   B. Import the accounts using the CSVDE tool and the comma-delimited text file.
   C. Import the accounts using a VBScript that defines each account.
   D. Active Directory does not support bulk import of user accounts.

7. As you have created objects in Active Directory, you have also been diligently providing attribute values to facilitate the location of those objects by users. You support Windows 2000 Professional and Windows NT 4.0 clients in your network. The Windows NT 4.0 clients are running the Active Directory Client. Some of the users in the network complain that they cannot see all the objects they think they should when they search Active Directory. What is the likely cause?

   A. Only Windows 2000 clients can search Active Directory.
   B. Only Windows NT 4.0 clients with the Active Directory Users and Computers snap-in can search Active Directory.

    C. Users can only see objects that they have been given Read permission to.

    D. Users can only see objects they have been delegated control over.

8. You have created and published several printer objects in Active Directory. Now you would like to configure them so that your users can search for printers closest to their physical location. You define the location value for each subnet and enable location tracking in Active Directory. However, when users search for printers, some users are not seeing all the printers they should, and, in some cases, they see no printers at all in the search results. What is the likely cause?

    A. You need to publish the printers in the global catalog.

    B. You need to override the users' computer location so that they search printers defined in their OU.

    C. You need to modify the location value for each printer so that it matches the location value for the subnet the printer resides on.

    D. When you enable location tracking, it applies to new printers only, so you need to re-create the existing printers.

9. As you create new objects in a new OU, you notice that some of the security permissions for the objects are grayed out. What does this mean?

    A. Those permissions cannot be modified.

    B. Those permissions are inherited from the OU and/or its parent.

    C. Those permissions are default permissions and can be modified.

    D. Those permissions were copied with the objects when they were moved from another OU.

10. You plan to provide key users in each OU in your organization with the ability to control printing tasks. You have created custom taskpads to facilitate these tasks. What else do you need to do to ensure that users can perform their tasks in their respective OUs? Choose the *best* means to accomplish your goal.

    A. Delegate control over print objects to the appropriate users in their OUs.

    B. Assign permissions to each printer object in each OU to the appropriate user.

    C. Have each user create the printers they need to manage so that they become the owner of the printer.

    D. Make each user a member of the Printer Operators group on each print server.

REVIEW ANSWERS

1. **A** **B** and **C** To ensure that the users have control over users in their own OU, you use the Delegation of Control Wizard. Taskpads can create an easy interface for the users by defining shortcuts to specific tasks, and taskpads must be created in custom consoles. D does not ensure that the users have access only within their own OU and is therefore incorrect.

2. **A** **B** **C** and **D** You should always start by defining a naming convention for your location values. Then set the location value for each subnet, identify each printer with an appropriate matching location value, and enable the location-tracking setting in Group Policy.

3. **D** You don't need to do anything else. When you move an object, any permissions set in the DACL for the object remain with the object, so you do not have to reconfigure them (C). By default, inheritance is enabled for the object in the target OU, which means that any OU permissions will be applied by default (B). If you disabled inheritance, the target OU's permissions would not be applied (A).

4. **D** When you move any published object in Active Directory, its attributes move with it. That means that the UNC path will stay the same, so you don't have to modify it (A), and its permissions remain the same, so you don't have to modify them (B). Moving the object in Active Directory has no effect on the network resource associated with it (C).

5. **D** Remember that Microsoft's recommended best practice is to place user accounts into global groups, place global groups into domain local groups, and assign permissions to the domain local groups (a.k.a. A G DL-P). All the other answers will accomplish the same task, but none is the "best" way to do this as far as Microsoft and the exam are concerned.

6. **B** Because the Access database can export the employee data to a comma-delimited file, you can use the CSVDE tool to import the accounts after you make whatever syntax changes might be necessary in the file. LDIFDE, as suggested in A, could be used as well, but it only recognizes line-delimited file formats. You could use VBScript, as in C; however, that answer does not take advantage of the fact that the data can be easily exported to a file. Because Active Directory obviously does support bulk import, answer D is incorrect.

7. **C** When you set permissions on an object in Active Directory, only users who have been given Read permission can view the object when performing a search. Although it is true that Windows 2000 clients can search Active

Directory, Windows clients (such as Windows NT 4.0) running the Active Directory Client can also search Active Directory, making A incorrect. Installing the snap-in (B) does not help users if the Active Directory Client is not also installed. Delegation of control (D) defines which users have control over creating, modifying, and deleting objects, but not necessarily searching for them.

8. **C** The location value for each printer must match that of the subnet in which it physically resides in order for the search to display that printer in the results window. When you enable location tracking, it applies to all printers, not just new printers, making D incorrect. When you create or publish a printer, it is automatically placed in the global catalog, so A does not apply. B might be correct if the question had noted that the location values for the printers matched that of a subnet. However, in the context of this question, B is not likely correct.

9. **B** When permissions for objects are dimmed, it means those permissions were inherited. If you disable the security option Allow Inheritable Permissions from Parent to Propagate to This Object, you can retain, clear, and modify those permissions, making A incorrect. These are not necessarily default permissions because they may have been inherited, and they are not necessarily part of the original permissions if the objects were moved, making answers C and D incorrect.

10. **A** Although each answer can result in accomplishing your goal, the best answer is A. Microsoft recommends using the Delegation of Control Wizard to assign common tasks, such as managing printer objects, because it is easy and less prone to error.

Maintaining
Active
Directory

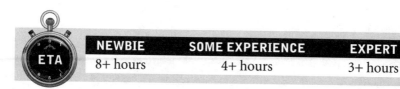

	NEWBIE	SOME EXPERIENCE	EXPERT
ETA	8+ hours	4+ hours	3+ hours

In Chapter 8, you explored various methods of managing objects in Active Directory. Most of the tasks you reviewed were perhaps more mundane—searching for objects, moving and publishing objects, and controlling access to objects.

In this chapter, you will look at a different aspect of managing Active Directory. Here you will explore how to manage performance and replication of Active Directory as well as how to perform an effective recovery of Active Directory in the case of system failure or loss of data.

Objective 9.01
Monitor, Optimize, and Troubleshoot Active Directory Performance and Replication

In Chapter 4, you studied the form and function of Active Directory replication. You saw how you can use sites, subnets, site links, site link bridges, and connection objects to control how and what kind of replication takes place among domain controllers.

In review, sites generally define computers installed on subnets that are connected by high-speed, reliable network connections and because of that may contain domain controllers from different domains. Sites are generally used to localize logon traffic and control replication traffic within the forest.

Sites use site links, site link bridges, and connection objects to determine a replication topology among sites in a forest. Once you have created your sites and site links, Active Directory can use the *Knowledge Consistency Checker* (KCC) to generate a replication topology. However, you can customize or create your own replication topology to optimize network traffic, or you can create alternate routes by building your own connection objects, site link bridges, and designated bridgehead servers.

Travel Assistance

Go back and review Objective 4.02 in Chapter 4 for a complete treatment of Active Directory replication and the creation and configuration of sites, site links, and connection objects to generate, manage, and optimize a replication topology.

After you have created your replication topology, you can just sit back and enjoy the benefits of a faster, more efficient Active Directory, right? Wrong. Just as many major cities periodically review traffic patterns within their urban transportation grids, you should periodically review and adjust Active Directory replication based on traffic needs and changes. This is all part of the ongoing challenge of creating an optimal replication topology. Your primary tool in dealing with Active Directory replication is Active Directory Sites and Services. However, Windows 2000 offers a couple other tools to help you review and assess replication performance: Replication Monitor and its companion, the Repadmin command-line utility.

Replication Monitor

The Replication Monitor is an administrative console tool that displays the replication topology of connections between servers (domain controllers) within a given site. Included among the several things you can do with this tool are the following actions:

- Identify replication partners
- Display replication statistics such as the *update sequence number* (USN), which helps to determine what data needs to be replicated, objects that need to be replicated, failed replication events, reasons for failure, and replication flags
- Schedule a polling interval to obtain up-to-date information
- Regenerate the replication topology through the KCC
- Force a replication to synchronize replication between two domain controllers

The Active Directory Replication Monitor is part of the Windows 2000 Support Tools and can be launched from the Windows 2000 Support Tools program group on the Start menu after the Support Tools have been installed from the Windows 2000 source CD. When you first launch this tool, no servers will be monitored by default. You will need to add the server or servers that you want to monitor to the interface. To do this, follow these steps:

1. Choose Options from the View menu to display the Active Directory Replication Monitor Options properties dialog box.

2. On the Status Logging tab, enable the option Display Changed Attributes When Replication Occurs to ensure that the interface is updated after subsequent replication events and then click OK. You may set other options as well, such as notification when replication fails a specified number of times, how notification should take place, and debug logging.

3. Right-click the entry Monitored Servers and select Add Monitored Server from the pop-up menu, or you can choose the Search the Directory for a Server to Add option to browse for a server.

4. In the wizard, select Add the Server Explicitly by Name, click Next, enter in the name of the domain controller you want to monitor, and then click Finish.

5. Repeat steps 3 and 4 for each additional domain controller you want to monitor.

The Replication Monitor interface will look similar to what you see in Figure 9-1. The Replication Monitor can be used to view server-specific data, such as operations master roles, TCP/IP configuration, inbound replication connections, and other server roles (time server, certificate server, and global catalog server). Among many other tools, it has the ability to display a graphic flowchart of the replication topology as well as Group Policy object status information and the version data for Active Directory objects.

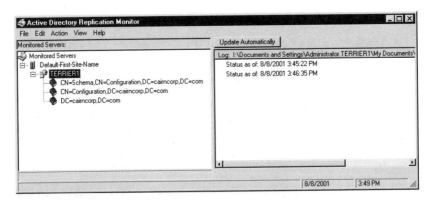

FIGURE 9-1   Active Directory Replication Monitor

Repadmin

An alternate command-line tool available for you to use when evaluating replication performance within your forest is the repadmin command. Although not as nice looking as the Replication Monitor, this command can also be used to perform the following actions:

- Identify replication partners
- Display the update sequence number, objects that need to be replicated, failed replication events, reasons for failure, and replication flags
- Show connection objects for a domain controller
- Force a replication event
- Create and modify the replication topology

The general format of the command is: **repadmin** /*command* [/u:[*domainname\ username* /**pw**:{*password*|*}], where *command* represents a specific task for repadmin to perform and the options in brackets represent the means of performing the task in the context of a user who has the appropriate permissions. For example, as you see in Figure 9-2, the command **repadmin /showconn terrier1.cairncorp.com** displays the connection objects for the domain controller terrier1.

Additional repadmin command switches include the following:

- **/showreps**   Displays replication partners for each naming context on the domain controller. When used with /full, it forces a full replication.
- **/showmeta**   Displays object information such as version number and USN.
- **/kcc**   Performs a knowledge consistency check.

```
I:\WINNT\System32\cmd.exe                                              _ □ X

I:\>repadmin /showconn
Show Connection Objects
CN=Default-First-Site-Name,CN=Sites,CN=Configuration,DC=cairncorp,DC=com:
     TERRIER1\TERRIER2
          enabledConnection: TRUE
          fromServer: Default-First-Site-Name\TERRIER1
          TransportType: intrasite RPC
          ReplicatesNC: CN=Configuration,DC=cairncorp,DC=com
          Reason: RingTopology
          ReplicatesNC: CN=Schema,CN=Configuration,DC=cairncorp,DC=com
          Reason: RingTopology
          ReplicatesNC: DC=cairncorp,DC=com
          Reason: RingTopology
          whenChanged: 20010705161049.0Z
          whenCreated: 20010705155955.0Z
```

FIGURE 9-2   Results of repadmin command

Modifying Replication

As you recall from Chapter 4, Active Directory uses the KCC to create connection objects for each domain controller and generate a replication topology that conforms to its requirements—namely, that there are no more than three replication hops between domain controllers. As you add domain controllers to the mix, or if a failure occurs at one of the domain controllers, the KCC regenerates the replication topology, creating additional connection objects if needed.

However, you can create your own connection objects to adjust the way that replication occurs—again, as you saw in Chapter 4. For example, you may want to ensure that there are no more than two replication hops between domain controllers for redundancy or for alternate replication connections for the KCC to use should one or more domain controllers fail. You might also choose to have the KCC generate a topology based on connection costs that you have assigned rather than the defaults.

Any connections that you manually create, however, are managed by you. KCC, for example, will not remove a connection object that you created for a domain controller if the domain controller is removed. Also, the KCC will not create any additional connection objects for a domain controller once you have created a manual connection object for it.

Regarding other ways to optimize replication and make it more efficient, you should have at least one domain controller in each site, including a global catalog server. This will ensure that authentication can take place within a site, reducing logon traffic across a WAN as well as reducing traffic pertaining to accessing and searching for directory information that would otherwise have to be done outside the site. In a similar fashion, you should have at least one DNS server in each site to reduce the need for traffic outside the site pertaining to name resolution.

Defragmentation

There is probably not an administrator in the real world who has not heard the term "defragmentation" before. Usually, you associate defragmentation with the process of rearranging the data on a computer's hard disk so that data files reside in contiguous sectors, making data access more efficient and improving overall disk performance. Defragmentation can also help to reduce the potential for data corruption on the hard disk. Active Directory data can also benefit from a periodic defragmentation of its data files.

Active Directory uses its database engine, the *Extensible Storage Engine* (ESE), to maintain the directory database. Whenever you add, delete, or modify objects in Active Directory, ESE is in use. ESE uses the database, transaction, and log files created when you implement Active Directory to carry out its tasks. These files include the following:

- **NTDS.dit** This is Active Directory's directory database, which is stored in *systemroot*\NTDS on the domain controller.
- **EDB*.log** Used as the transaction log when NTDS.dit is updated. EDB*.log is 10MB in size and is renamed EBD*xxxx*.log when full, where *xxxx* represents an increasing number.
- **EDB.chk** Used as a checkpoint file by ESE, EDB.chk tracks data not yet written to NTDS.dit and determines where to begin recovering data in the case of failure.

ESE caches requests for Active Directory changes in memory to increase performance by minimizing disk I/O. The transaction is written to the log file. When the database is updated, the transaction is updated in the checkpoint file so that ESE "knows" where to pick up in case data recovery is required.

However, ESE does not make the best use of space when writing data back to NTDS.dit. This results in the directory database becoming fragmented. The same concepts apply in this scenario as they do for hard disks regarding defragmentation. Periodically defragmenting the directory database will result in the data being rewritten to contiguous sectors, thus optimizing data storage space and providing space in the database for new objects.

Happily, the database is automatically defragmented during the garbage-collection process, which will be described in more detail later in this chapter. This is referred to as *online defragmentation*.

However, you can also manually defragment the directory database. This offline defragmentation results in a new, compacted, and potentially smaller version of the directory database. The main difference between online and offline defragmentation is that with offline defragmentation, a new file is created and written to a new location (specified by the administrator) and then copied over the original file.

Offline defragmentation is one of several tasks that must be performed in what is known as *Directory Services Restore mode*. You can enter this mode on a domain controller by restarting it, pressing the F8 key during restart to display the Windows 2000 Advanced Options menu, and selecting Directory Services Restore Mode.

After logging on as the local administrator, you enter **ntdsutil** at the command prompt and then enter the command **files** to be placed at the files prompt. Next, type the command **compact to** *path*, where *path* represents a drive path to a folder on a drive with enough disk space for the directory database file. A new NTDS.dit file will be created in the location specified. Enter the command **quit** twice to exit to the command prompt. The final step is to replace the original NTDS.dit file with the new NTDS.dit file you just created and then restart the domain controller.

Travel Advisory

Before performing any administrative task involving NTDS.dit or its related files, it is strongly recommended that you first back up Active Directory as a precaution.

Moving the Directory Database

Typically, once Active Directory has been implemented and the directory database established, you will not want to mess with NTDS.dit or its related files. It may happen, however, that for various reasons (most likely to place NTDS.dit on a separate or faster disk drive), you may choose to move the database to a different location.

This is also accomplished using the Directory Services Restore mode and the ntdsutil command-line utility.

Restart the domain controller in Directory Services Restore mode and launch ntdsutil, as described for performing an offline defragmentation, proceeding to the files prompt. Next, type the command **move DB to** *path*, where *path* represents a drive path to a folder on a drive with enough disk space for the directory database file. The existing NTDS.dit file will be moved to the location specified. Enter the command **quit** twice to exit to the command prompt. Finally, restart the domain controller.

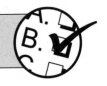

Exam Tip

You can likewise move the transaction log files to a new location using the ntdsutil files prompt command move logs to *path*.

Troubleshooting Tips

As always, a good place to begin troubleshooting events in Windows 2000 is the Event Viewer. The Windows 20000 Event Viewer records replication events in the Directory Service Event log. For example, if the KCC could not complete generation of a replication topology for a site, that event would be recorded in the Directory Service Event log.

By default, only the most important events are logged by the KCC. However, you can modify a couple Registry entries to increase the number and detail of events that are recorded. In HKEY_Local_machin\System\CurrentControlSet\Services\NTDS\Diagnostics, find and increase the value of the nine Internal Processing and one Knowledge Consistency Checker entries to 3. At the next attempt by KCC to generate a replication topology, additional detail will be recorded to assist your troubleshooting.

Probably your best (or worst) source for information regarding the efficiency of your replication topology will be from users themselves. Clients and users who complain of slow logon response, or slow responses to directory searches and such, should probably have their site membership reviewed. Remember that if a client has to go outside the site to authenticate or perform searches, network traffic will be adversely affected and response will likely be poorer than if all such traffic remained within the site. Perhaps you need to place additional domain controllers or global catalog servers within the site to accommodate users' needs.

Exam Tip

Recall from Chapter 4 that sites should represent domain controllers in subnets connected by reliable, high-speed network communications. Because the replication traffic within the site is uncompressed and cannot really be scheduled, you want to make sure the network connections within the defined site will have enough available bandwidth to support replication and logon traffic. Also, you want to make sure user-generated traffic, such as authentication and directory searches, remains within the site to take advantage of the reliable, high-speed network communications.

Finally, check and recheck your replication schedules as determined by site links. If you do not have site links or site link bridges such that the sites can replicate information to each other, or if the topology and schedule of existing site links is such that replication data is slow to propagate, the result can be an incomplete replication or one that takes more time than intended to complete.

Objective 9.02

Back Up and Restore Active Directory

It should not be necessary to point out the benefits of performing regular back-ups of any kind to a seasoned network administrator. Any backup procedure is, of course, useless without a periodic check of the restore process. You only need that one time in your career when a server crashes and you do not have a cur-rent—or any—backup with which to recover important data to convince you that backups are a vital part of your network's survival.

The same, therefore, is true as far as Active Directory is concerned. A regular and current backup of Active Directory can be of great assistance in helping you recover lost or corrupted data and to repair the directory database.

The backup utility that comes with Windows 2000 Advanced Server has been updated and enhanced from its Windows NT version. In particular, the Windows 2000 Backup utility allows you to back up not only data files and the Registry but also the system state data. The system state data on a domain controller, which is the focus of this discussion, consists of the following items:

- Active Directory database
- Class registration database (information about Component Services applications)
- Certificate Services database (if the server is also a certificate server)
- SYSVOL shared folder
- Registry
- System startup files

Exam Tip

The system state data will not contain Active Directory or the SYSVOL shared folder unless the server is a domain controller.

System state data can be backed up along with other data as part of a regular full backup, or it can be backed up by itself. It can also be backed up while the domain controller is online. Also, although the Windows 2000 Backup utility pro-vides a convenient and built-in method of backing up the system state data, sev-eral third-party backup products are available that can do so as well. The advantage of using third-party backup/restore applications is that you get addi-tional functionality.

For example, third-party backup applications typically provide a means of backing up one or more remote servers as part of a single backup process. The Windows 2000 Backup utility can only back up the local server. Third-party backup applications also typically provide a means of backing up other Windows 2000 enterprise applications, such as Exchange and SQL Server.

Exam Tip

Because Windows 2000 backup can only back up the local system state data, it is only backing up Active Directory on the local domain controller. However, copies of Active Directory reside on all domain controllers, and modifications may have been made on one domain controller that have not yet been replicated to all the others. For this reason, you have not really backed up Active Directory in the forest unless you have backed up the system state data on all domain controllers.

The Windows 2000 Backup utility can be accessed through the Accessories | System Tools program group on the Start menu of the domain controller. You can direct the backup process to back up the system state data in one of three ways:

- On the What to Back Up screen, select the option Only Back Up the System State Data, as you see here. The default is to backup everything.

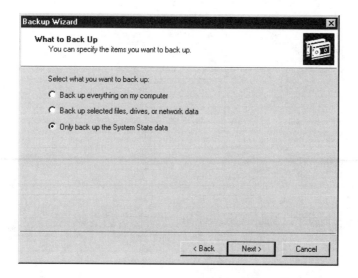

- Select Backup Selected Files, Directories, or Network Data on the What to Backup screen and click Next. Then on the Items to Back Up screen, select the System State check box under My Computer, as you see here.

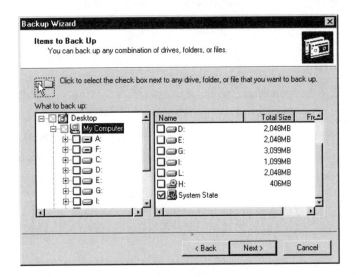

- On the Backup dialog box's Backup tab, select the System State check box under My Computer, as you see here.

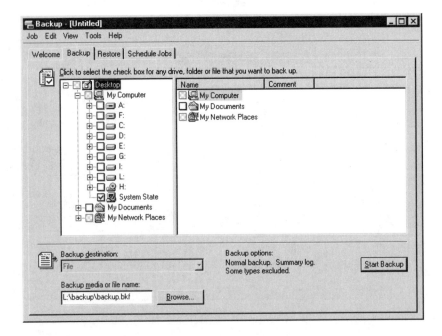

You can then set your other regular backup options and configure backup parameters such as verification of data, compression, type of backup, location of media, and, of course, the backup schedule.

Exam Tip

In order to perform a backup, you must be a member of the Administrators, Backup Operator, or Server Operator group on the domain controller.

Data restoration is also performed through the Backup utility. However, there is more to restoring Active Directory than just recovering from a current backup as you will see in the next section.

Perform an Authoritative and Non-Authoritative Restore of Active Directory

Objective 9.03

In the event that the directory database becomes corrupt or lost due to hardware or software failure, you can rebuild the data in a couple ways. In the case that the domain controller itself fails, if there are other domain controllers that have been implemented, you might just reinstall the domain controller that has failed and let Active Directory replication rebuild the directory database on the restored domain controller.

If the domain controller itself is up and running, but the directory database needs to be recovered, you can then restore Active Directory using either an authoritative or non-authoritative restore method. An authoritative restore is generally used when you need to recover a specific object that had been deleted or corrupted. A non-authoritative restore is generally used when you need to recover Active Directory fully as of its last backup.

Authoritative Restore

As just mentioned, an authoritative restore is used when you need to recover a specific object in Active Directory. When you delete an object from Active Directory, that object is flagged for deletion. This flag is called a *tombstone*. The object is not immediately removed from the directory database when you delete it. Every 12 hours, tombstones are evaluated and deleted through a process known as *garbage collection*. As you saw earlier, the garbage-collection process also ensures that the database is defragmented as well.

Because a copy of Active Directory resides on every domain controller, it is necessary that the fact of the deletion (the tombstone) have enough time, called the *tombstone lifetime*, to be replicated to all the domain controllers in the forest. After this happens, the object is removed from the directory database. Active Directory determines how data should be replicated, including which objects should be deleted, by using version numbers, as reviewed in Chapter 4. Data with the highest version number is considered current, or *authoritative*.

If you need to recover an object that was improperly deleted, basically you need to mark the version of the object that does not carry the tombstone flag as being current. When you use an authoritative restore, you are actually assigning the object a higher version number than other versions of that object that may have been already replicated, including the tombstone version. In practice, when you perform an authoritative restore, the object's versions number is incremented by 100,000 for each day since the last time a backup was performed to ensure that the restored object has the highest version number and will be replicated as restored to all the domain controllers.

Travel Advisory

The tombstone lifetime is, by default, 60 days. If your last backup is older than the tombstone lifetime, you will not be able to restore Active Directory.

Travel Advisory

Authoritative restores follow a non-authoritative restore of Active Directory from a current backup. It is possible that the non-authoritative restore from backup might recover the object as well, particularly if you only have one domain controller or if replication of the deletion has not yet taken place. However, if the object has been replicated to another domain controller, or if any change was made to the object since it had been backed up, it would necessarily have a higher version number than that on the backup. This is where the authoritative restore comes into play—to ensure that the restored object's version number is the highest.

Authoritative restores must be performed with the domain controller restarted in Directory Services Restore mode, as described earlier when you reviewed defragmentation. Suppose you need to restore the Accounting OU, which resides in the Central OU in Cairncorp.com, because it was erroneously deleted. Figure 9-3 shows what the version number of the Accounting OU was prior to being deleted (using the command **repadmin /showmeta OU=Accounting, OU=Central, DC=Cairncorp, DC=Com** to display the version number).

Use the Backup utility to restore the system state data from the most current backup. Then at a command prompt, run ntdsutil.exe. At the ntdsutil prompt, enter **authoritative restore**. At the authoritative restore prompt, enter **restore subtree** *object-dn*, where *object-dn* represents the distinguished name of the specific object you want to restore. For this example, because you need to restore the Accounting OU, which resides in the Central OU in the domain cairncorp.com, you would enter **restore subtree OU=Accounting,OU=Central, DC=Cairncorp, DC=Com**, as shown here.

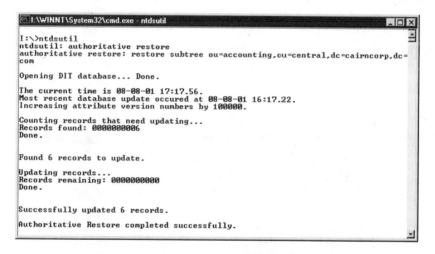

FIGURE 9-3   Version number for the Accounting OU before deletion

Figure 9-4 shows what the version number of the Accounting OU is after being authoritatively restored. Note that it is 100,000 higher than before. For this figure, the Replication Monitor console was used to display the Accounting OU's object information.

Exam Tip

An authoritative restore cannot be used to restore changes made to the Active Directory schema.

Non-Authoritative Restore

A non-authoritative restore is essentially a restoration of data from a current backup. Active Directory is merely restored to the state it was in when the last backup occurred. For example, if the hard disk crashes and needs to be replaced, after you reinstall Windows 2000 and Active Directory, you would restore the Active Directory database from the last backup. Of course, this also means that the version numbers of the restored objects will likely be lower than those for the same objects that had been replicated to other domain controllers.

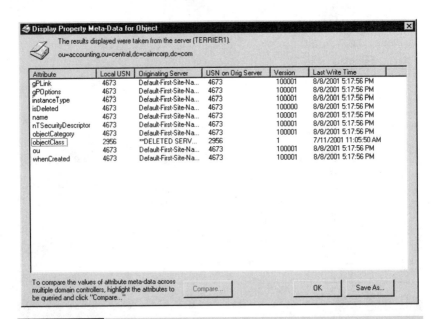

FIGURE 9-4   Version number for Accounting OU after an authoritative restore

To ensure that the restored data is synchronized with the other domain controllers, after the non-authoritative restore is completed, Windows 2000 automatically performs a consistency check on the data and updates the directory database on the restored domain controller as necessary from its replication partners.

Like an authoritative restore, a non-authoritative restore must be performed with the domain controller restarted in Directory Services Restore mode. After you log on, start the Backup utility and restore the system state from the last backup. Then restart the domain controller.

Travel Advisory

As with any backup, any changes that may have occurred since the last backup was performed will be lost when the last backup is used to restore the system. Take this into account when determining how frequently you should back up system state data.

Objective 9.04 # Recover from a System Failure

This particular topic is almost a miscellaneous category. You have already studied most of what you need to know to recover Active Directory in the event of a system failure. One of the things that has come up several times so far is the Directory Services Restore mode, which is an advanced startup option. Some network administrators will already be familiar with a variation of advanced startup from their work with Windows 99 and 98.

Several options are available to select from when you perform an advanced startup by pressing the F8 key when the system restarts besides the Directory Services Restore mode. They can be used to help you diagnose and troubleshoot startup problems, driver problems, and service problems. Table 9-1 describes these options.

Another Windows 2000 tool that can be useful when you're trying to diagnose and troubleshoot problems on a computer is the Recovery Console. The Recovery Console is a command-line tool that is launched from the operating system startup menu that displays when you boot a Windows 2000 computer (boot.ini). Some of the tasks that you can perform using the Recovery Console include starting and stopping services, accessing data on local disks, formatting disks, performing checkdisk operations, repairing the master boot record, logging on to a Windows 2000 installation, creating and deleting folders, and so on.

TABLE 9.1   Advanced Startup Options

Advanced Startup Option	Description
Debugging Mode	Enables debugging data to be sent to a remote computer via a serial connection.
Directory Services Restore Mode	Starts the domain controller without enabling Active Directory to facilitate restoration and maintenance.
Enable Boot Logging	Generates a log file called ntbtlog.txt in the systemroot folder that records drivers and services loaded during startup.
Enable VGA Mode	Starts the computer using a generic VGA driver to bypass existing video drivers.
Last Known Good Configuration	Starts the computer using Last Known Good configuration in the Registry.
Safe Mode	Launches Windows 2000 with only those basic devices and drivers required to start the computer—mouse, keyboard, disk, base video, but no networking. Used for troubleshooting drivers and services.
Safe Mode with Command Prompt	Loads basic devices and drivers, as in Safe mode, but launches a command prompt instead of the Windows interface.
Safe Mode with Networking	Launches Windows 2000 as in Safe mode and also enables networking.

The Recovery Console is not installed by default. You can install it by running the command **winnt32 /cmdcons** in the I386 folder of the Windows 2000 source CD. This will add it to the startup menu. You can also access it by booting with a Windows 2000 startup disk and selecting the Repair option.

Travel Assistance

Although not, strictly speaking, a part of this exam, fault-tolerant volumes, mirrored volumes, and RAID-5 volumes (striping with parity) all provide hardware-based ways to improve your chances of recovering data in the event of a system failure on Windows 2000 servers. For more information on setting up and recovering systems using fault-tolerant volumes, refer to Microsoft Official Curriculum 2152, "Implementing Windows 2000 Professional and Server," as well as other Windows 2000 online and Web-based documentation.

Objective 9.05

Seize Operations Master Roles

In Chapter 4 you learned that there are five single master operations roles. Two of these roles, schema master and domain naming master, are specific to the forest. The other three roles—infrastructure master, PDC emulator, and RID master—are specific to each domain.

Travel Advisory

The first domain controller in the forest gets assigned all five of the operations master roles since it not only represents the forest but the first domain as well. The first domain controller in each subsequent child domain gets assigned the RID, infrastructure, and PDC emulator roles. Because that could result in excessive performance demands on the domain controller—especially the first domain controller in the forest—Microsoft recommends that some of the roles be transferred to another domain controller in the domain. Therefore, initially you may choose to transfer some roles, but after the roles have been moved to the appropriate domain controller, you will usually not have to reassign them.

After the operations master roles have been assigned, you typically do not have to reassign them. However, the occasion may arise when you have to demote a domain controller that has been assigned one or more of the five operations master roles back to member server status, bring online a new server better suited for the role, or modify the placement of global catalog servers (which can affect the domain naming master and infrastructure master roles).

In Chapter 4, you saw how to transfer the operations master roles yourself prior to making any changes. For example, when you demote a domain controller to the role of member server, any operations master roles that it was performing will automatically be reassigned to another domain controller, but perhaps not a domain controller that you would have chosen yourself. However, by transferring the role(s) yourself first, you can eliminate the possibility of an inappropriate server being assigned the role(s). Both domain controllers must be available and able to communicate with each other for the transfer to complete successfully.

However, it may happen that a domain controller fails prior to you being able to transfer an operations master role. As you saw in Chapter 4, each of the operations master roles must be assumed by some domain controller in the forest or domain, depending on the role. If an operations master is unavailable, some functions may become unavailable in the forest or domain. Sometimes, the loss of an operations master does not have any noticeable short-term effect. Other times, it may affect the users' ability to access the network.

For example, if the PDC emulator is unavailable, users on Windows 9x or Windows NT computers will not be able to modify passwords, and logons that fail due to a bad password will not be able to be resolved. Because the infrastructure master is responsible for tracking object references in other domains (such as adding a global group from one domain into a domain local group in another), if it becomes unavailable, you won't be able to track such movement—perhaps not too significant if you don't need to move large numbers of objects in the short term.

If the domain naming master, RID master, or schema master is unavailable, you will lose its functionality, but users will typically not be directly affected its absence, and you can probably function just fine for a period of time without any of them. For example, if the domain naming master is unavailable, you won't be able to add or delete domains in the forest. Unless you have a really pressing need to add or delete domains and can't wait for the server to be brought back online, or if the server that had that role will never be available again, you can probably survive without it for the short term.

If a domain controller holding one or more operations master roles does fail and cannot be recovered at all or in a reasonable length of time—that is, in a period such that the loss of the operation master(s) will not adversely affect the network—you may need to forcibly assign the role(s) to another domain controller. This is known as *seizing the role*.

Before you seize the operations master role, you should check to see which servers are holding which master roles and, in particular, the role you want to seize (see Chapter 4). Whenever possible, you should attempt to transfer a role before seizing it—for example, if the server is still up but showing signs of failure (data loss, intermittent blue screens, and so on), or if the server can be brought up long enough to transfer the role.

Travel Advisory

Before seizing an operations master role, be sure to disconnect the failed server from the network to ensure that it cannot accidentally be brought back online and thus conflict with the server to which you will assign the role.

The PDC emulator, RID master, and infrastructure master roles can be seized through the Active Directory Users and Computers console connected to the domain controller that will assume the role you are transferring. In that console, you need to right-click the entry Active Directory Users and Computers and then select Operations Masters from the pop-up menu. Select the tab for the operations master role you want to seize and click Change. Because the server holding the role can no longer be contacted, a message will appear indicating that the role cannot be transferred. Confirm the message and then click OK twice to confirm that you want to forcibly transfer the role. Similarly, you can use the Active Directory Domains and Trusts console to seize the infrastructure master role, and you can use the Active Directory Schema Admin console to seize the schema master role.

You can also use the ntdsutil command-line tool to seize an operations master role. At a Windows 2000 command prompt, launch ntdsutil and then type **roles** to enter the fsmo maintenance prompt. At the prompt, enter the command **connections** to get to the server connections prompt and then type **connect to server** *server*, where *server* represents the FQDN of the server that will assume the new role. Type **quit** to go back to the fsmo maintenance prompt.

At the fsmo maintenance prompt, type the command to seize the appropriate role—**seize domain naming master, seize infrastructure master, seize PDC, seize RID master**, or **seize schema master**—then type **quit** twice to exit from ntdsutil. Always verify that the role has been properly assigned after seizing or transferring it.

Local Lingo

FSMO Flexible single master operation—another, albeit older, term for operations master.

CHECKPOINT

✔ **Objective 9.01: Monitor, Optimize, and Troubleshoot Active Directory Performance and Replication** Sites, site links, and connection objects can be used to create and influence a replication topology and optimize network traffic. Windows 2000 provides tools that can help you monitor replication performance. The Replication Monitor tool is a graphic utility that among other things lets you identify replication partners, display replication statistics, display objects that need to be replicated, regenerate a replication topology, and force replication between two domain controllers. The repadmin tool lets you accomplish many of the same tasks through the command line.

   In addition to these tools, regular defragmentation of the directory database will result in a more efficient use of storage space and provide more room for database objects, increase the performance of Active Directory searches, and minimize the potential for corruption of Active Directory. You can also consider moving the directory database to a separate disk drive to improve performance related to disk I/O.

✔ **Objective 9.02: Back Up and Restore Active Directory** Backing up the system state data on a regular basis on all your domain controllers will ensure that Active Directory is fully and completely backed up. Frequent backups will make recovery easier and more complete.

✔ **Objective 9.03: Perform an Authoritative and Non-Authoritative Restore of Active Directory** If Active Directory becomes corrupt on a server, or if you have to rebuild the server, you might just let the Active Directory database on that server be rebuilt through the normal replication process from other domain controllers. However, you can also recover data through either a non-authoritative or an authoritative restore.

   A non-authoritative restore simply restores Active Directory to the state it was in when the last backup occurred. Objects in the Active Directory database will likely have version numbers that are lower than those for the same objects in other copies of Active Directory. Through the regular replication process, the Active Directory database will be synchronized with the domain controller's replication partners.

If you need to recover a specific object—for example, because it was accidentally deleted—you will additionally need to perform an authoritative restore through the ntdsutil command-line utility. An authoritative restore ensures that the object's version number is higher than that of any replica objects, including the object originally marked for deletion.

✔ **Objective 9.04: Recover from a System Failure**   Other than performing backup and recovery to restore Active Directory, you can also use the advanced startup options to start the computer in various modes to facilitate troubleshooting of a startup, device, or service-related problem. You can also use the Recovery Console to help you troubleshoot problems and perform basic tasks, such as starting and stopping services, accessing files, and so on.

✔ **Objective 9.05: Seize Operations Master Roles**   There are five single master operations roles. Two of these roles—schema master and domain naming master—are specific to the forest. The other three roles—infrastructure master, PDC emulator, and RID master—are specific to each domain. Usually, once the roles have been assigned to one or more domain controllers, they will not be changed. However, changes does happen, and whenever possible, you should try to perform a transfer of a role from one domain controller to another to ensure an orderly transition of power.

In the event of server failure, however, you may need to forcibly transfer a role from the failed server to a different domain controller. This action is called *seizing the role*. Before seizing a role, you should determine which server had the role previously and disconnect it from the network, seize the role through an administrative console or through the ntdsutil utility, and then verify that the role was properly transferred.

REVIEW QUESTIONS

1. In the course of upgrading a Windows 2000 server, you add a new device and driver. Upon restarting the server, you receive the infamous blue screen STOP error message. How can you resolve the problem?

   A. Restart the server with the Windows 2000 startup disk and choose the repair option to remove the driver.

    B. Restart the server displaying the advanced startup options menu, select Safe Mode, and then remove the driver.

    C. Restart the server displaying the advanced startup options menu, select Directory Services Restore mode, and then use ntdsutil to remove the driver.

    D. Reinstall Windows 2000 on the server.

2. While performing some basic administrative tasks, one of the administrators of the Accounting OU accidentally deleted that OU. Which of the following steps would you need to perform to recover the deleted objects? Select all that apply.

    A. Use ntdsutil to perform an authoritative restore of the deleted OU.

    B. Start a domain controller in Directory Services Restore mode.

    C. Perform a non-authoritative restore of Active Directory from a current backup.

    D. Replicate the restored OU to the other domain controllers.

3. Which domain controller becomes the PDC emulator for a domain by default?

    A. The first domain controller in the forest.

    B. The first domain controller in the domain.

    C. The global catalog server.

    D. Whichever domain controller you assign the role to.

4. You need to perform some hardware maintenance on a domain controller in the forest that holds the PDC emulator and infrastructure master operations roles. What should you do to ensure that the functions served by those operations roles will continue to be available to the network?

    A. Transfer each role to another domain controller.

    B. After you shut down the domain controller, seize the roles on another domain controller.

    C. Before you shut down the domain controller, seize the roles on another domain controller.

    D. Do nothing. Active Directory will automatically reassign the roles to another domain controller.

5. Which of the following actions can help to improve the performance of Active Directory? Select two.

    A. Increase the tombstone lifetime interval.

    B. Move the directory database to a different disk drive.

    C. Perform an offline defragmentation of the directory database.

    D. Back up the system state data regularly.

6. You have recently joined your company as the Active Directory network administrator. You find that system state data is regularly backed up on all domain controllers every Friday evening. This morning, one of your assistants indicates that she accidentally deleted five printer objects that you created on Monday. How can you recover the deleted objects?

    A. Perform a non-authoritative restore of Active Directory using the most current backup.

    B. Perform an authoritative restore of the deleted printer objects.

    C. Select Undo Delete from the Action menu for each printer in the Windows 2000 Recycle Bin.

    D. Re-create the printer objects.

7. Which of the following repadmin commands can you use to display the version information of an object in Active Directory?

    A. Repadmin /showconn

    B. Repadmin /showmeta

    C. Repadmin /kcc

    D. Repadmin /showreps

8. You have organized your domain controllers into three sites within your forest. The global catalog server is on a domain controller in one of the sites. You would like to improve user response time when searching Active Directory and minimize WAN traffic. What two steps can you take to accomplish this goal?

    A. Create a global catalog server in each site.

    B. Make sure all users can authenticate on at least one domain controller within the site they are members of.

    C. Back up the system state regularly.

    D. Increase the garbage-collection interval.

9. Which of the following tasks cannot be performed by the Windows 2000 Backup utility?

    A. Backup of the Registry.

    B. Backup of the system state data.

C. Backup of remote servers.

D. Backup of data to a tape backup device.

10. The domain controller currently holding the PDC emulator role has crashed and will be unavailable for a unspecified period of time. Your network consists of a mixed-client environment—Windows 98, Windows NT 4.0 Workstation running the Active Directory Client, and Windows 2000 Professional computers. Which of the following accurately describes the problems you may face?

A. Users on Windows 2000 clients will not be able to process password changes.

B. Users on Windows NT 4.0 Workstations will not be able to process password changes.

C. Users on Windows 98 clients will not be able to process password changes.

D. Users on non-Windows 2000 clients will not be able to process password changes.

REVIEW ANSWERS

1. **B** Safe mode starts the server with only the basic drivers and services needed to start up. In this mode, you can remove the suspect driver and then try to start normally again. The repair option suggested in A lets you perform repair tasks such as fixing a corrupted boot record or restoring the Registry. Although you might be able to remove the driver this way, most likely this option would not be very helpful. Directory Services Restore mode (C) is used to restore Active Directory objects. Booting with this option would likely not ignore the offending driver. Rebuilding the server (D) is the last resort.

2. **A B C** and **D** You need to start a domain controller in Directory Services Restore mode, recover Active Directory from a current backup (non-authoritative restore), and then use ntdsutil to mark the deleted OU as authoritative. When you restart the domain controller, you can let Active Directory replication take place as always, or you can force replication to take place to ensure that the OU is restored to all domain controllers.

3. **B** The PDC emulator is a domain-wide operations master role. By default, the first domain controller in a domain will assume that role, making all other answers incorrect.

4. **A** Whenever possible, you should transfer an operations master role to another domain controller when you know that a current domain controller that has the role will be unavailable for an extended period of time. Active Directory will not automatically reassign any operations master roles, making D incorrect. You should only seize an operations master role if transferring the role is not possible. Because transferring each role is possible in this case, answers B and C are incorrect.

5. **B** and **C** Moving the directory database to a different disk drive, especially if it is faster, will improve Active Directory performance related to disk I/O. Also, defragmentation rewrites data in contiguous sectors and compacts the database, resulting in a potentially smaller, more efficiently accessible database. A only results in deleted objects lasting longer before they are permanently deleted. D, although extremely important for disaster recovery, does not really affect the performance of Active Directory one way or another—unless you consider not being able to recover the Active Directory at all something of a performance inhibitor.

6. **D** You must re-create the printers. Since the last backup occurred before you created the printer objects, a non-authoritative restore will be of no use, making A incorrect. Because you must perform a non-authoritative restore before you can perform an authoritative restore, B won't work. C is incorrect simply because no such command exists, and Active Directory objects are not sent to the Recycle Bin.

7. **B** The /showmeta command argument followed by the fully distinguished name of the object in question displays information about that object, such as the version information. The /showconn command argument (A) displays connection objects for a specified domain controller. The /kcc command (C) performs a knowledge consistency check of the replication topology. The /showreps command (D) displays replication partners for a specified domain controller and lets you initiate a replication event.

8. **A** and **B** Because the global catalog server plays a significant role when searching Active Directory, you should place at least one in each site so that users can search for a global catalog server within their site rather than across the WAN. This will also increase the response time to their searches. Placing a domain controller that a user can authenticate with within each site will also reduce WAN traffic so that the user doesn't have to look for an authenticating server outside the site. C is significant for being able to recover Active

Directory but doesn't really affect user or network performance. Increasing the garbage-collection interval (D) will result in deleted objects taking longer to be permanently removed from Active Directory and the online defrag process taking place less frequently, which in itself could decrease performance of Active Directory.

9. **C** If you need to perform remote backups of other servers, you need to obtain a third-party backup solution. All the other tasks can be performed by the Windows 2000 Backup utility, making A, B, and D incorrect.

10. **C** Because non-Windows 2000 clients use the PDC emulator to process password changes, you would expect the Windows 98 and Windows NT 4.0 Workstation clients to experience a problem. However, because the Windows NT 4.0 clients are running the Active Directory Client service, they do not need to rely on the PDC emulator. Therefore, B and D are incorrect. A is incorrect because Windows 2000 clients can process password changes at any domain controller.

P A R T

V

Configuring, Managing, Monitoring, and Troubleshooting Security in a Directory Services Infrastructure

Managing Security

	NEWBIE	SOME EXPERIENCE	EXPERT
ETA	3+ hours	2+ hours	1+ hour

275

Throughout this book, you have been exploring how to implement and configure Active Directory to help organize, standardize, manage, and troubleshoot your network and user desktop environments. This final section explores one more facet of Active Directory—security.

Apply Security Policies Using Group Policy

Objective 10.01

As you have sent throughout this book, Active Directory supplies a healthy set of tools for managing your network environment as well as your users' desktop environment. Group Policy plays a significant role in helping you to configure and implement both standard and custom environments.

A significant element of any networked environment is its security. It should be of no surprise, therefore, that Windows 2000 provides policies and utilities that facilitate the implementation of security settings for computers within your Active Directory environment. Just as you can implement a Group Policy to standardize a desktop, set service startup options, or deploy software, you can create a Group Policy that prevents users from modifying a computer configuration and protects sensitive areas of your network. These latter settings are known specifically as *security templates*.

Security template settings can be applied locally to each individual Windows 2000 computer or to computers at large in your network through Group Policy. Local security settings can be configured through the Local Security Policy tool located in the Administrative Tools program group on Windows 2000 Server computers. You would launch the Local Security Policy console on the computer in question, browse for the item you want to modify a security setting for, select it, find the policy you want to configure for that item, double-click it, and then change the setting, as you see in Figure 10-1.

Travel Advisory

If you want to modify local security settings on Windows 2000 Professional computers, you will need to add the Local Security Policy snap-in to a new Microsoft Management Console (MMC) on that computer.

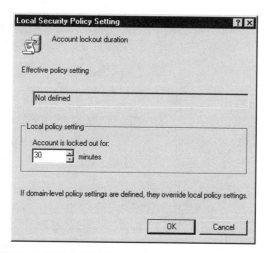

FIGURE 10-1   The Local Security Policy Setting dialog box

Exam Tip

Group Policy settings are always applied in the following order: local settings, site settings, domain settings, and OU settings. Therefore, keep in mind that any security settings you configure locally will be overwritten by conflicting settings at the site, domain, or OU level.

Obviously, if you want to configure security settings for computers based on their site, domain, or OU membership, you will do so through an appropriate Group Policy object (GPO) in Active Directory. These settings are configured like any other GPO policies and can be found under Computer Configuration | Windows Settings | Security Settings or User Configuration | Windows Settings | Security Settings in the GPO. You can see the similarities and differences between the GPO settings, shown in Figure 10-2, and the local security policy settings, shown in Figure 10-1. Table 10-1 describes the types of security settings that can be configured either locally or through a GPO.

Exam Tip

Public-key policies are the only settings available under User Configuration | Windows Settings.

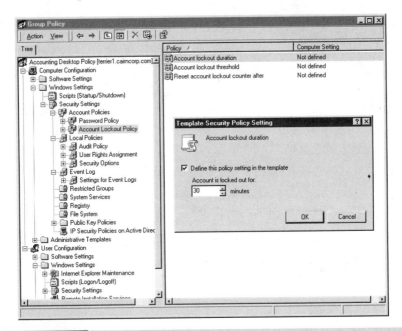

FIGURE 10-2　GPO Security Settings

TABLE 10.1　Security Settings

Method Name	Description
Account	Configure password policies and other account policies such as lockout and Kerberos v5 protocol policies (both locally and through GPO)
IPSec	Configure IP security for your network (both locally and through GPO)
Local	Configure auditing, user rights and permissions, and other local security options (both locally and through GPO)
Public Key	Configure encrypted data-recovery agents and trusted certificate authorities (both locally and through GPO)
Event Log	Configure Event Viewer log settings such as log size, retention parameters, and access (GPO only)

(Continued)

TABLE 10.1 *Continued*

Method Name	Description
File System	Configure security for specific file paths (GPO only)
Registry	Configure security for specific Registry keys (GPO only)
Restricted Groups	Configure membership for specific security groups such as Administrators, Power Users, Server Operators, Domain Admins, and so on (GPO only)
System Services	Configure security and startup settings for services such as file and print, telephony, Internet, and so on (GPO only)

Travel Advisory

If you want to configure security policy settings that will be applied at the domain level, you can do so by modifying the Default Domain Policy GPO through Active Directory Users and Computers, as you have seen earlier in this book, or by using the Domain Security Policy console, which can be found in the Administrative Tools program group on the domain controller. Similarly, you can modify the Default Domain Controller Policy GPO by using the Domain Controller Security console in Administrative Tools.

Exam Tip

The Default Domain Policy GPO security settings always override local domain controller settings. For example, if you set an account lockout duration of 15 minutes at one domain controller, but the default setting is 30 minutes, the effective account lockout setting at that one domain controller will remain 30 minutes. Similarly, Default Domain Controller Policy settings always override domain policy settings. For example, if users are allowed to log on locally through a domain policy but are restricted through the Default Domain Controller Policy GPO, users will be restricted.

You can modify these security settings yourself, or you can use one of several security templates that come with Windows 2000. Windows 2000 provides four predefined levels of security that can be applied through the use of a security template:

- **Basic** Represents the default level of security applied to all new installations of Windows 2000 on an NTFS partition
- **Compatible** Provides a higher level of security than Basic but still ensures that standard applications will run successfully under the local user's security context
- **Secure** Adds an additional layer of security to Compatible that may restrict some functionality of standard applications
- **Highly Secure** Provides a maximum layer of security for network traffic and communication protocols without consideration for applications running on the computer

All predefined security templates are located by default in the systemroot\ security\templates folder.

Exam Tip

The Basic security template settings are applied by default only to new installations of Windows 2000 running NTFS. This template is not applied automatically to Windows NT 4.0 computers that are upgrading to Windows 2000, nor to Windows 2000 computers installed using the FAT file system. If you upgrade a Windows NT 4.0 computer to Windows 2000 (especially if that computer is a server), you might consider applying the predefined Basic security template to that computer.

There are three Basic security templates designed for use with specific computer types: Basicwk.inf is the default workstation template, Basicsv.inf is the default server template, and Basicdc.inf is the default domain controller template. These Basic templates are applied to installations of Windows 2000 as stated earlier; however, they can—and it is strongly recommended that they should—be applied to computers that have been upgraded to Windows 2000. The Basic security templates are also intended as a means to return a computer back to its default security settings from a different security template. When used in this fashion, only the user rights settings are not reset so as not to interfere with any changes made through application setup programs.

There is one Compatible-level template, called compatws.inf. This template can be applied to either workstations or servers. The default Windows 2000 settings allow all users to successfully run Windows 2000–certified applications but only allow power users the ability to successfully run noncertified applications. However, many organizations make local users power users to get around this security. The Compatible template is designed to accommodate this scenario while still providing extra security over what users can do.

There are two Secure-level templates designed to be used with either a workstation or server or a domain controller. These are called securews.inf and securedc.inf, respectively. Again, this level of template adds an even tighter level of security to the desktop, to the degree that some functions of standard applications may not run.

There are similarly two Highly Secure-level templates that can be applied to workstations and servers or to domain controllers. They are called hisecws.inf and hisecdc.inf, respectively. This template is intended for use in high-security areas or with specifically designed applications. This template would not be used on the average user's desktop, for example, but it may be used in a sensitive lab environment.

Any of these security templates can be applied to their respective computer types, either locally or through a GPO. You can apply a security template to a local computer using the Security Configuration and Analysis console. Template settings are hosted in a database file with the extension .sdb. In the console, right-click the entry Security Configuration and Analysis, select Open Database from the pop-up menu, and either select an existing database from the list or enter the name of a new database that you will create. Next, click the Import Template button, select one of the security templates from the list, and click Open. Finally, right-click the entry Security Configuration and Analysis once again and select Configure Computer Now from the pop-up menu.

Travel Advisory

See the discussion about analyzing template settings before applying them in Objective 10.02 later in this chapter.

If you want to use one of the predefined security templates as part of a GPO, you must import that template into the appropriate GPO. You can import a security template using either the Active Directory Users and Computers console (for domain- and OU-specific GPOs) or through Active Directory Sites and Services (for site-specific GPOs).

In the properties of the appropriate GPO, expand Computer Configuration\ Windows Settings to find and select Security Settings. Right-click Security Settings and choose Import Policy from the pop-up menu. Select a template from the list and click Open to apply the settings to the GPO. The next time the computer starts or the GPO is refreshed, the settings will be applied.

You can also create your own custom security templates if none of the predefined templates adequately meets your needs. There are two ways you can create your own customized security templates: by exporting a modified template through the Local Security Policy console or by using the Security Templates snapin to create a new or modify an existing security template.

Exporting a Modified Template Through Local Security Policy

There are really three parts to this method. The first involves importing an existing security template and applying it to a local computer. The second part involves modifying the settings on the local computer and then exporting them to a new template file. The third part involves importing the new template and applying the new settings appropriately.

So, you begin by importing an existing security template to a local computer through the Local Security Policy console on that computer. You could also import it at the domain policy level and let it be applied to a local computer that way. On the local computer, through Local Security Policy, you can see both the local setting and the effective setting, as shown in Figure 10-3.

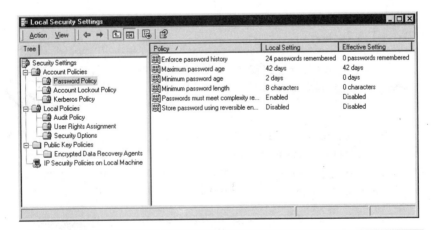

FIGURE 10-3 Local versus effective settings

Basically, what you can do now is compare the effective settings to those you actually want the computer to have and make the changes appropriately. If you based the local policy on a domain policy, you can use differences you find between the desired local settings and the effective settings applied at the domain level as a checklist for modifying the conflicting settings in the default domain GPO.

When you have modified the local settings as you want them, right-click the entry Security Settings in Local Security Policy and then select Export Policy from the pop-up menu. You can choose to export either the local policy settings or the effective policy settings. Select Local Policy or Effective Policy and then enter a name for the new (modified) policy template, as shown in Figure 10-4. You can now apply the new security policy settings by importing the template into a GPO at the site, domain, or OU level.

Exam Tip

An alternative method that accomplishes the same result just discussed is to use the Security Configuration and Analysis console, which is discussed in Objective 10.02 later in this chapter.

Creating a New Policy Using the Security Templates Snap-In

You can create a new security policy or modify a copy of an existing security template policy using the Security Templates snap-in. Begin, of course, by creating a new MMC using the Security Templates snap-in.

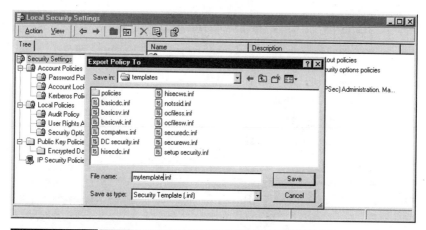

FIGURE 10-4   Exporting settings to a template

If you want to create a new template, simply right-click the template storage location path in the Security Templates console and select New Template from the pop-up menu. The default location path is systemroot\security\templates. Give the new template a name; then select it from the list on the screen, as you see in Figure 10-5. Similarly, if you want to modify an existing template, in the Security Templates console, expand the template storage location path and browse for the template you want to modify. Right-click it and choose Save As to create a copy of the template that will serve as your working copy.

Expand the template in question and modify the settings as you desire by selecting a policy setting and double-clicking it to configure it. When you have finished making your changes, save the template. You can now apply the new security policy settings by importing the policy into a GPO at the site, domain, or OU level.

Exam Tip

The Security Templates console allows you to copy and paste any of the seven major policy areas from other templates into your new template. You simply right-click the policy area—for example, Local Polices or Account Policies—in the source template and select Copy. Then right-click the corresponding policy area in the target template and select Paste to merge the settings from the source template with those of the target template.

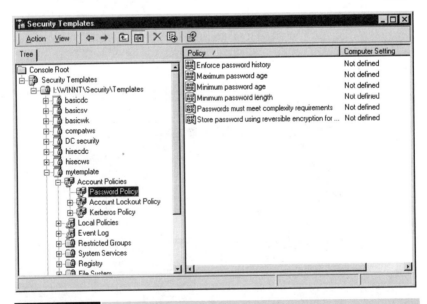

FIGURE 10-5   Security Templates console

Create, Analyze, and Modify Security Configurations Using the Security Configuration and Analysis Snap-in and the Security Templates Snap-In

Objective 10.02

As stated many times throughout this book, it is imperative that you test any GPO before rolling it out to a production environment to ensure that you obtain the results you expect. This advice is even more significant when it comes to implementing a security policy. Not only are you looking for any unexpected or adverse results to computers, programs, or resource access due to the application of the security policy, but you are also looking for potential gaps in security as well.

Windows 2000 provides the Security Configuration and Analysis snap-in to facilitate your analysis of your security policies. This tool performs a comparison of the local security policy of a given computer against a proposed security policy imported from a template file and generates a report stored as a database file with an .sdb extension.

Because the Security Configuration and Analysis console tool is a snap-in, you have to add it to an MMC. Once you have done this, you can launch the console on the computer on which you will perform the analysis and then begin. It is also essential that the computer on which you will perform the analysis is configured with the security settings you expect your computers to ultimately have; other- wise, the analysis will be an exercise in time mismanagement.

In the Security Configuration and Analysis console, right-click the entry Security Configuration and Analysis and select Open Database from the pop-up menu. You can either select an existing database file (perhaps from a previous analysis) or enter a new name to generate a new database file. Then click Open. If you are creating a new database, you'll need to import a template to analyze. Otherwise, the template associated with the database you selected will be displayed.

Now, right-click the Security Configuration and Analysis entry again, this time selecting Analyze Computer Now from the pop-up menu and entering a location for the analysis log file to be written. When you click OK, Windows 2000 will proceed to compare the local computer's settings against those of the imported template. When the processing is finished, browse the Security Settings tree to see how the settings compare, as you see in Figure 10-6. Settings that are consistent are marked with a green checkmark icon. Discrepancies are marked

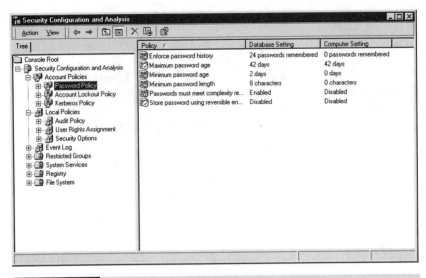

FIGURE 10-6   Security Configuration and Analysis console

with a red flag icon. Any setting that is not marked has simply not been configured as part of the local policy settings.

The most important part of the analysis is yet to come. This element, of course, involves you the administrator. It is now up to you to check the discrepancies and reconfigure your proposed template settings to match those of the local computer. However, you probably should also check the consistencies and nonconfigured settings to be sure that those are actually configured the way you want them.

You might choose to import another template file and perform another analysis, or you might build on the current analysis by merging the new template's settings into the current database. You can also export the settings to a separate template file that you can later import to a GPO in production or apply the settings to the local computer.

Using the Secedit Command-Line Utility

Windows 2000 provides command-line alternatives to many of its console tools that provide similar or additional functionality. Secedit.exe is a command-line utility that performs many of the same functions as the Security Configuration and Analysis console, plus some additional functions that the console does not offer. Six main command options can be used with Secedit, and these are described in Table 10-2.

| **TABLE 10.2** | Command Options |

Command Options	Description
/Areas	Allows you to identify specific areas of security settings to configure on a computer or export. Valid areas include securitypolicy, group_mgmt, user_rights, regkeys, filestore, and services.
/Analyze	Performs the same function as the Analyze Computer Now option in Security Configuration and Analysis. It is used with **/db** to specify a database to use and **/cfg** to specify a template to import. You can also append the **/verbose** switch to detail the analysis in a log file or **/quiet** to have it run in the background.
/Configure	Like its counterpart in Security Configuration and Analysis (Configure Computer Now), this command lets you apply a template's settings to the local computer. It is used with **/db** to specify a database to use and **/cfg** to specify a template to import. You can also append the **/verbose** switch to detail the analysis in a log file or **/quiet** to have it run in the background.
/Export	Used to export template settings to a new template file as you can do with Security Configuration and Analysis. It is used with **/db** to specify a database to use. You can also append the **/verbose** switch to detail the analysis in a log file or **/quiet** to have it run in the background.
/Refreshpolicy	Not available through Security Configuration and Analysis. This command allows you to force GPOs associated with the computer to be refreshed. When it's used with the **/enforce** switch, GPOs are refreshed regardless of whether they have been modified.
/Validate	Verifies the syntax of a template created through the Security Templates console.

For example, if you want to analyze template settings that you've stored in a database called mytemplate.sdb (in the i:\winnt\security\database folder) against the local security policy and want to write a detailed log file called mytemplate.log in the folder i:\winnt\security\logs, at a Windows 2000 command prompt you would enter the command **secedit /analyze /db i:\winnt\security\database\ mytemplate.sdb /log i:\winnt\security\logs\mytemplate.log /verbose.** Some of the results of this command can be viewed in Figure 10-7. You can then open the log file that is created with any text editor, review the results in more detail, and perform your analysis.

Travel Assistance

The full syntax of Secedit.exe, along with other command-line utilities provided by Windows 2000, can be reviewed with examples through the Windows 2000 online Help on any Windows 2000 server.

```
I:\WINNT\System32\cmd.exe                                               _ □ ×
See log i:\winnt\logs\mytemplate.log for detail info.

I:\WINNT\logs>secedit /analyze /db i:\winnt\security\database\mytemplate.sdb
/log i:\winnt\logs\mytemplate.log /verbose
Completed 14 percent (450/3147)          Process Privilege Rights area
Completed 14 percent (451/3147)          Process Privilege Rights area
Completed 14 percent (452/3147)          Process Privilege Rights area
Completed 14 percent (453/3147)          Process Privilege Rights area
Completed 14 percent (454/3147)          Process Privilege Rights area
Completed 14 percent (455/3147)          Process Privilege Rights area
Completed 14 percent (456/3147)          Process Privilege Rights area
Completed 14 percent (457/3147)          Process Privilege Rights area
Completed 14 percent (458/3147)          Process Privilege Rights area
Completed 14 percent (459/3147)          Process Privilege Rights area
Completed 14 percent (460/3147)          Process Privilege Rights area
Completed 14 percent (461/3147)          Process Privilege Rights area
Completed 14 percent (462/3147)          Process Privilege Rights area
Completed 14 percent (463/3147)          Process Privilege Rights area
Completed 14 percent (464/3147)          Process Privilege Rights area
Completed 14 percent (465/3147)          Process Privilege Rights area
Completed 14 percent (465/3147)          Process Group Membership area
Completed 14 percent (466/3147)          Process Group Membership area
Completed 14 percent (467/3147)          Process Group Membership area
Completed 14 percent (468/3147)          Process Group Membership area
Completed 14 percent (469/3147)          Process Group Membership area
Completed 14 percent (470/3147)          Process Group Membership area
Completed 14 percent (471/3147)          Process Group Membership area
Completed 15 percent (472/3147)          Process Group Membership area
Completed 15 percent (473/3147)          Process Group Membership area
Completed 15 percent (474/3147)          Process Group Membership area
Completed 15 percent (480/3147)          Process Group Membership area
```

FIGURE 10-7   Results of the secedit command

CHECKPOINT

✔ **Objective 10.01:** Apply Security Policies Using Group Policy   Because securing your network and your users' desktop environments can be a significant part of your overall Active Directory structure, Windows 2000 provides policies and utilities that facilitate the implementation of security settings for computers within your Active Directory environment. Just as you can implement a Group Policy to standardize a desktop, set service startup options, or deploy software, you can create a Group Policy that prevents users from modifying a computer configuration and protects sensitive areas of your network.

You can use one or more of the predefined security templates to apply security settings to your network or computers by importing them into a new or existing GPO, or you can create your own custom templates by using the Security Templates console or the Local Security Policy console.

✔ **Objective 10.02:** Create, Analyze, and Modify Security Configurations by Using the Security Configuration and Analysis Snap-in and the Security Templates Snap-In   Creating, importing, and applying security policy settings through a GPO is never recommended without first testing and analyzing the potential results of that policy. Windows 2000 provides several tools that can assist you in analyzing and configuring security templates before implementing them enterprise-wide.

The Security Configuration and Analysis console snap-in provides you with the means of comparing local security settings that you expect a computer to have against settings you configured in a template. It shows you where the settings match and where they conflict. Based on these results, you can tweak your template settings so that all computers to which the security settings will be applied have them applied as you expected.

The Secedit command-line utility offers an alternative method for analyzing and configuring security settings, as well as additional functions not available through the Security Configuration and Analysis console, such as the ability to forcibly refresh GPO settings on a given computer.

REVIEW QUESTIONS

1. You need to set up three kiosk computers running Windows 2000 and a secure company information program for customers in the lobby of your building. You need to make these computers as secure as possible. Which security template should you apply?

   A. Basicwk.inf
   B. Compatws.inf
   C. Securews.inf
   D. Hisecws.inf

2. Which of the following tools will allow you to import and apply template settings to a local computer? Select all that apply.

   A. Basicwk.inf Security Configuration and Analysis
   B. Secedit.exe
   C. Local Security Policy
   D. Active Directory Users and Computers

3. You want to give a specific user the ability to log on locally at a designated domain controller to perform a file-maintenance function on a folder that has not been shared. You decide to modify the User Rights security settings for that domain controller to enable the user to log on locally. What is the result of this action?

   A. The user can log on locally at the domain controller.
   B. The user will not be able to log on locally at the domain controller.
   C. The user will be able to log on as an administrator.
   D. The user will only be able to log on through a share point.

4. You need to apply the same set of security settings to all Windows servers in a particular domain. The predefined secure template comes closest to the actual settings you want. Which of the following represent steps necessary to apply the desired security settings to all the servers? Select all that apply.

   A. Import the secure template into the local security policy on one of the servers.
   B. Modify the security settings as desired.
   C. Export the settings to a custom template.
   D. Import a custom template to each server.

5. Which of the following policy types can be configured locally on each computer as well as through a GPO? Select all that apply.

  A. Account
  B. File System
  C. Local
  D. Registry

6. You would like to customize security settings for all domain controllers in the domain. Which utility would you use to perform this action? Select two.

  A. Use Active Directory Users and Computers to create a custom GPO for each domain controller.
  B. Use the Domain Security Policy Administrative tool to customize the settings for each domain controller.
  C. Use Active Directory Users and Computers to customize the Default Domain Controller Policy GPO.
  D. Use the Domain Controller Security Policy Administrative tool to customize the settings for the Default Domain Controller Policy GPO.

7. You would like to create a custom security template that will be applied through a GPO to all Windows 2000 Professional workstations in your organization. Which of the following tools gives you the ability to create and/or customize a security template and make it available to be imported to a GPO?

  A. Secedit
  B. Security Configuration and Analysis
  C. Security Templates
  D. Local Security Policy

8. You are creating a custom security template that consists of Account settings from one existing template and Registry settings from another template. Which of the following tools will let you easily merge those two policy areas into the same custom template?

  A. Secedit
  B. Security Configuration and Analysis
  C. Security Templates
  D. Local Security Policy

9. Which of the following utilities will allow you to force Group Policy to be refreshed on a computer?

    A. Secedit

    B. Security Configuration and Analysis

    C. Security Templates

    D. Local Security Policy

10. Which of the following utilities is best used to analyze and note discrepancies among the local security settings on a computer against the proposed settings in a security template?

    A. Secedit

    B. Security Configuration and Analysis

    C. Security Templates

    D. Local Security Policy

REVIEW ANSWERS

1. **D** Basicws.inf (A) provides default workstation settings, which allow users access to most programs. Compatws.inf (B) provides a higher level of protection, and securews.inf (C) still higher, but hisecws.inf provides the highest level.

2. **A** and **B** Both of these tools allow you to both import and apply template settings to a local computer. Local Security Policy (C) lets you import a template for comparison purposes so that you can modify the local settings to match and then export them to a template file, but you cannot apply the template settings themselves directly. Active Directory Users and Computers (D) lets you import a template into a GPO, but the settings are applied to a computer on the next policy refresh or when the computer restarts.

3. **B** The user will not be able to log on locally because the Default Domain Policy GPO will always override the local policy on any given domain controller and the default GPO does not allow users to log on. Therefore, A is incorrect. No mention is made of changing the user's group membership, as implied in C, and we know the folder in question is not shared, as implied in answer D.

4. **A** **B** **C** and **D** You would import the security template into the local security policy of one of the servers, modify the local settings as desired, export those settings to a new custom template, and then apply that template to each of the servers using the Security Configuration and Analysis console.

5. **A** and **C**   Account (password, account lockouts, and so on) and local (user rights and permissions) policies can be modified both locally and through a GPO. File system (security for file paths) and Registry (security for Registry keys) are configurable only through a GPO, making answers B and D incorrect.

6. **C** and **D**   A and B are incorrect because domain security settings are overwritten by the Default Domain Controller Policy GPO, so the settings should be configured through the Default Domain Controller Policy GPO.

7. **B** **C** and **D**   Each of these allows you to access a template, modify settings, and export the settings as a new template that can be imported by a GPO. A is wrong because although secedit does have an export command option, you can't use it to modify settings.

8. **C**   The Security Templates snap-in allows you to quickly copy a policy area from one template and paste it into the corresponding area in another. Although Secedit (A) does have an Areas command option, it is used to determine which portion of a template should be applied to a computer or exported. It can't be used to merge settings into an existing template. Both answers B and D only let you modify settings, not copy and paste between templates.

9. **A**   Secedit includes the Refreshpolicy command option, which can be used to force Group Policy to be refreshed on the computer on which you run the command. None of the other three utilities provides this function.

10. **B**   Security Configuration and Analysis analyzes proposed settings against current settings on a computer and displays consistencies and discrepancies with a green checkmark and red flag, respectively. Secedit (A) can do this also, but it's not as efficient because after you run it, you will have to read through a log file to determine the discrepancies. Security Templates (C) does not perform any analysis. Although Local Security Policy (D) does display local settings and template settings side by side, it doesn't mark them as consistent or discrepant. You still have to go through all the settings and compare them yourself.

Monitoring Security

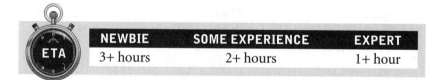
	NEWBIE	SOME EXPERIENCE	EXPERT
ETA	3+ hours	2+ hours	1+ hour

In Chapter 10, you began your review of security management by exploring how to use Group Policy to configure and implement a security policy for computers in your network, including the analysis of the effective result of applying proposed security settings. In this final chapter, the discussion of security will come full circle as you examine how to audit, monitor, and analyze security events.

Objective 11.01   Implement an Audit Policy

You saw how to implement a security policy in Chapter 10. Another type of policy you can create that can compliment your security policy is an *audit policy*. In essence, an audit policy provides a means to perform an ongoing assessment or analysis of your overall security strategy by tracking the activities, or events, of users and the operating system.

Just as you use Group Policies and security policies to configure and manage users' desktops, network access, and computer security, you use audit policies to define which events and activities you want Windows 2000 to record. Audit events are written to the Security log of the Event Viewer on the computer where they took place. Through an audit policy, you can do the following:

- Track and log logon attempts, including account lockouts due to bad passwords
- Track and log the successful and failed attempts to access network resources, such as printers and files
- Track and log administrative changes, such as modifications to user accounts or the creation of new objects
- Track and log changes made to other Active Directory objects and security settings
- Track and log system shutdown and reboot events and identify the users who performed these actions

By collecting this kind of audit information, you can then monitor the use of resources, create records of activity, and hopefully spot and correct unauthorized activity before it can be harmful to the network. Table 11-1 outlines the various types of events and activities you can track and log through an audit policy.

Obviously, then, you need to determine which events you want and/or need to audit and develop an audit strategy. Implementing an audit policy will necessarily result in an increase in system resources expended on the system being audited. Therefore, it is essential that you carefully choose those activities and events that are to be audited as well as the computers on which the auditing is to take place.

TABLE 11.1 Audit Events	
Auditable Event	**Enabling This Event Allows You To...**
Account Logon	Track and log the success or failure of user authentication against either the local security database of a computer or the domain security database.
Account Management	Track and log the success or failure of creation, modification, or removal of a user or group account.
Directory Service Access	Track and log the success or failure of access made to specified Active Directory objects.
Logon	Track and log the success or failure of simple logons to a local computer or the connection or disconnection of network resources.
Object Access	Track and log the success or failure of access made to specified file, folder, or printer objects.
Policy Changes	Track and log the success or failure of changes made to user security settings, such as passwords, user rights, and audit policies.
Privilege Usage	Track and log the success or failure of events related to user rights and permissions, such as modifying the system clock, starting or stopping services, and so on.
Process Tracking	Track and log the success or failure of a program to execute a process. Process tracking is used mainly by developers when troubleshooting application issues.
System	Track and log the success or failure of actions that affect security or the Security log, such as system restarts or shutdowns.

For example, do you need to audit account logons to determine whether there are any attempts by unauthorized persons to access the network? Then you might audit account logon events on domain controllers. Are you trying to determine whether the appropriate users and groups can successfully gain access to network resources after changes are made to resource permissions? Then you might choose to audit object access on the computer where the resources reside. Are you trying to get a feel for which administrators are managing user accounts and what they are doing? Then you might choose to audit account management events. You get the idea.

When you enable the auditing of an event, you must choose also whether to audit only success events, failure events, or both. For example, when auditing account logon events, you might only be interested in recording when an account logon fails, because that is more likely to highlight gaps in security. When auditing object access, you might be more interested in recording success events, because these events identify the users and groups that should be able to access the resource. When auditing account management, you might choose to record both success and failure events to create an audit trail of account-related activity.

Auditing for some events can be implemented by simply creating and applying an audit policy. Other objects—notably file, folder, and printer objects—require the creation of an audit policy and then the configuration of the object in question. Both will be discussed next.

If you want to implement an audit policy for a particular computer, you need to configure those settings in the Local Security Policy console for that computer. If you want to apply the same audit policy settings to several computers, you can create a GPO, modify the audit settings there, and then assign the GPO to the computers in question. Either way you choose, the policy settings are the same. You are most likely to need to audit-specific events on specific computers, so this discussion will focus on implementing an audit policy on the local computer.

Audit settings are actually part of security settings, so you can access and modify the settings using any of the tools or methods outlined in Chapter 10. You can simply modify the local settings using the Local Security Policy console on the computer itself, create a security template that holds the audit policy settings and then use the Security Configuration and Analysis console or Secedit to apply them to the local computer, or import the template into a GPO. You can also use the Group Policy snap-in first mentioned in Chapter 5.

However you go about it, you will find audit policy settings under Computer Configuration | Windows Settings | Security Settings | Local Policies | Audit Policy in the policy. You can see the nine event types in Figure 11-1 with no settings selected by default. Select an event type that you want to audit, right-click that entry in the console, and select Security from the pop-up menu.

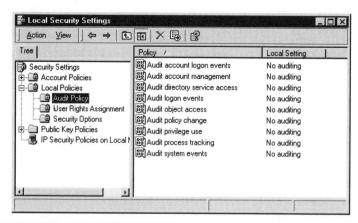

FIGURE 11-1 Audit policy event types

If you want to audit successful events of the type selected, check the Success option box. If you want to audit failures of events of the type selected, check the Failure option box. To disable auditing for an event, make sure both options are deselected. In Figure 11-2, success and failure account logon events have been enabled, and failed access to network resources (object access) has been enabled.

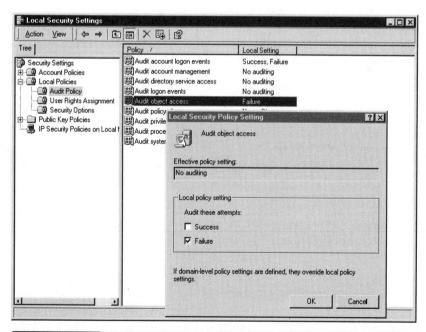

FIGURE 11-2 Enabling audit events

Exam Tip

You must be a member of the local administrators group to configure audit policy settings for the local computer.

Activities such as user logons, account management, policy changes, and system events, when enabled, will record success and failure events directly into the Security log of Event Viewer on the computer on which auditing was implemented. In addition, access to resources such as file, folder, and printer objects requires that you identify and configure auditing options for the specific file, folder, and printer object you want to audit. You still must first have enabled auditing for object access through an audit policy.

When you configure auditing for each specific object, you will identify whether you want to track and record success and/or failure events for each file, folder, and printer object individually. Furthermore, you must identify the user(s) and/or group(s) whose activity you want to audit. For example, if only the Accounting group should be able to send print jobs to the printer, you may want to restrict your auditing to members of the Accounting group. Restricting auditing in this way helps to minimize the resource requirement on the computer.

As you can see, if you take the time to think carefully about what you want and need to audit and develop a sound strategy, you can record and track much relevant information without placing too great an additional resource burden on the computer in question.

Exam Tip

You can only implement auditing for file and folder objects that exist on an NTFS partition. File and folder auditing is a function of NTFS.

Figure 11-3 shows the different object-specific events you can choose to track and record for printer objects. Note that auditing of success and failure events for print actions has been enabled for the Everyone group, whereas all successful and failed activities related to administrative tasks (Full Control operations) has been enabled for the Administrators group.

In Figure 11-4, you can see the configurable audit events for a file object. In this example, failed attempts by the Everyone group to read the file will be recorded, as well as success and failure events for Read and Change actions for members of the specific security group Accounting Users.

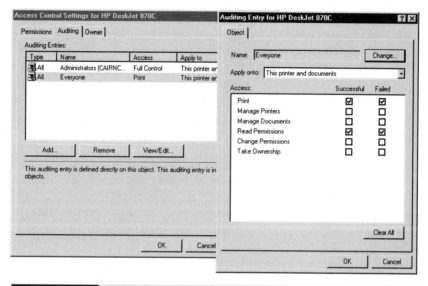

FIGURE 11-3   Auditable events for printer objects

You configure auditing on specific objects by viewing the Security tab on the object's Properties dialog box. On the Security tab, click the Advanced button and then the Audit tab. Here, you can modify existing entries by double-clicking the user or group in the Auditing Entries list to display the list of auditable events. Find the event you want to audit, select Success or Failure, and then click OK.

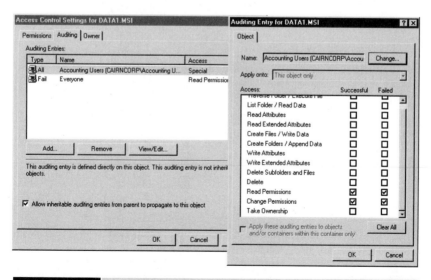

FIGURE 11-4   Auditable events for file objects

You can add additional users or groups to the list by clicking Add to display a browse window from which you can select the user or group you want to add. You then make your selection and configure the event you are auditing for that user or group. Any one list can contain users and groups for which you are auditing different events.

The audit event list is known as the *System Access Control List* (SACL) for the object. Similar to the *Discretionary Access Control List* (DACL) described in Chapter 8, the SACL represents the security descriptor for auditing information for the object. The SACL identifies the following items:

- The group or user accounts to audit when the object is accessed
- The access events to be audited for each group or user, such as reading a file or managing a printer
- A Success or Failure attribute for each access event, based on the permissions granted to each group and user in the object's DACL

Active Directory objects can also be audited to determine who has performed certain activities on them. Many of the auditable events are the same as those for file, folder, and printer objects, such as reading an object's attributes, creating, deleting, or changing ownership, and so on. However, as with file, folder, and printer objects, there are also events that are specific to the SACL of that object, such as the default inherited permissions shown in Figure 11-5 for a user object.

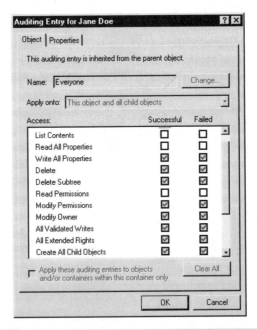

FIGURE 11-5   Auditable events for a User object in Active Directory

You can use auditing to monitor who has modified or deleted an OU, added child objects, or changed the password on a specific user account. In Figure 11-6, you can see some of the auditable events available when configuring the auditing of an OU.

You can use the Active Directory Users and Computers console to configure auditing for an Active Directory object. You find the Active Directory object that you want to configure auditing for and then view the Security tab on the object's Properties dialog box. Next, click the Advanced button on the Security tab and then click the Audit tab. Finally, either modify the entries in the Audit Access list, click Add to add more entries, or highlight an entry and click Remove to delete it from the list.

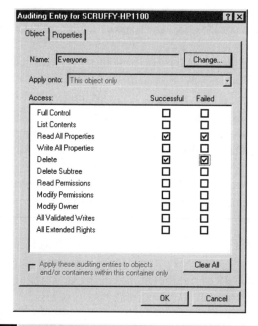

FIGURE 11-6 Auditable events for an OU object in Active Directory

Monitor and Analyze Security Events

Your choice of tracking success or failure events, in part, will help you develop an effective strategy for monitoring security-related activities. Here are some Microsoft-suggested best practices when determining whether to audit for success or failure events:

- Tracking failure events for Read access to file and folders objects helps you to determine whether unauthorized persons have attempted to gain access.
- Tracking both success and failure events for permission changes made to objects, especially restricted or secure objects, as well as taking ownership of objects helps you to identify potentially malicious attempts to modify security to gain unauthorized access to objects.
- Tracking failure events for account logons in general can help you determine whether anyone might be attempting to hack a logon account.
- Tracking success and failure events for logons on specific shared computers can help you determine whether appropriate personnel are using that server to access the network.
- Tracking success and failure events for any operation performed by an account or group that has been designated as having limited or secure access to specific areas of the network, such as a guest account, external client access, and so on, can help you determine whether only authorized personnel are actually accessing those areas.
- Tracking failure events for restricted objects, such as expensive or dedicated-use printers, can help you determine whether unauthorized print jobs are being sent or other unauthorized printer-related events are taking place.
- Tracking success events for print job deletions can help you to be sure that print jobs were deleted by authorized personnel rather than as a result of hardware error or inappropriate access.
- Tracking success and failure events for Active Directory objects can help you determine whether authorized administrators have access to delegated OUs.

You might need to configure and reconfigure auditing on some objects several times before you determine the appropriate settings. Planning, configuring, and monitoring the effect of audit settings has the same strategic significance as planning, configuring, and monitoring object permissions.

Audit Setting Inheritance

As you have seen, audit settings are subject to inheritance similar to that of GPOs. When you configure auditing on a parent object (such as a folder or OU), objects created beneath that parent automatically inherit the same audit settings. For example, if you configure auditing of Read and Write access by the Accounting group for the folder Accounting Data, any new files or new subfolders will also have auditing of Read and Write access by the Accounting group configured.

There are several ways in which you can modify the inheritance of audit settings. When you first configure success and failure audit events for an object, you will find the option Apply These Auditing Entries to Objects and/or Containers Within This Container Only, as you see in Figure 11-7. If you want to propagate the audit settings to all existing child objects, select this option. If you only want the audit settings to apply to that specific object (or in the case of an OU, to certain types of objects such as computers or users), select This Folder Only, or the appropriate object, from the Apply Onto list box (also shown in Figure 11-7).

It may happen that the audit settings you configure at a parent object should apply to most child objects, but not all. In that case, select each child object that

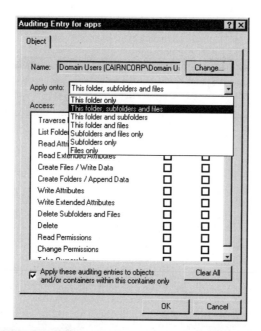

FIGURE 11-7 Configuring audit setting inheritance

should not inherit the audit settings, view the Security tab in the object's Properties dialog box, click Advanced, and then select the Auditing tab. As you see in Figure 11-8, the option Allow Inheritable Auditing Entries from Parent to Propagate to This Object is enabled by default.

When you deselect the option, you will be asked whether you want to retain or remove the inherited settings, as you see here.

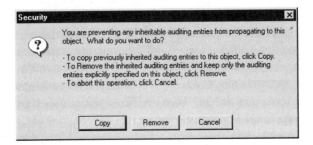

If you choose to remove the settings, the object will no longer inherit audit settings from the parent object and no audit settings will be applied. If you choose to retain the settings, any inherited settings will still be in effect. You can then either delete the existing audit settings by clicking Remove or modify the settings to better fit the audit requirements for that object by clicking View | Edit.

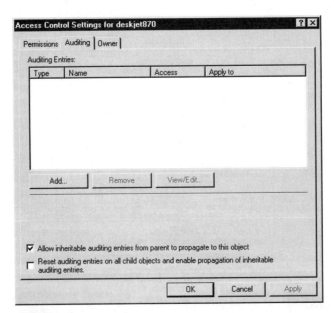

FIGURE 11-8   Disabling inheritance for a child object

> **Travel Advisory**
>
> Inheritance does not affect printers whose security and audit settings you configure through the regular Printers folder. However, inheritance does affect Active Directory printer objects like any other Active Directory objects.

For folder objects, as you see in Figure 11-8, you also have the option of resetting auditing settings on all child objects and effectively reenabling inheritance of audit settings from the parent folder.

> **Exam Tip**
>
> As you learned with Group Policy inheritance in Chapter 5, it is an important part of any audit strategy that you monitor inheritance of audit settings to ensure that objects that should be audited are and that the extent of auditing is appropriate for the object in question. If you set Read event auditing for the Accounting group on a parent folder, files created in that folder will inherit that audit setting. If a particular file also needs Write event auditing, it is up to you to monitor the file and determine that Write event auditing is required and is configured.

Viewing Audit Events

After you have configured auditing of events for various objects, success and failure events are recorded in and can be tracked through the Security log in the Event Viewer utility. Obviously, the events that appear in the Security log depend on how you have configured audit settings—that is, are you recording both success and failure events, or just one or the other? Are you recording actions taken by any user or for specific user or groups? Are you recording network-based actions, such as logons, or object-specific actions, such as Read access to a file? You can find the Event Viewer logs by opening the Computer Management console and expanding Event Viewer under the System Tools entry.

The Security log in Event Viewer is your best tool for monitoring the effect of your audit settings, analyzing events that have occurred, and determining whether any additional action must be taken, such as further refining audit settings, modifying object permissions, or tightening security policies in general.

Exam Tip

The Security log has a predefined size of 512KB. In addition to monitoring the audit events and other events recorded in this log, you should also check to ensure that you don't run out of log space. By default, when the log fills up, old entries are removed as new entries are recorded. This is a fine self-maintenance activity. However, you may be also be losing valuable security-related information.

It may be necessary to increase the log size to accommodate the amount of information you intend to keep track of. You can also choose to archive old log file information so as to have an audit trail of activity to refer back to. This can also assist you in spotting or developing trends in activities.

You can modify the size of the log by right-clicking the Security entry under Event Viewer in the console and then selecting Properties from the pop-up menu. Next, modify the value in the Maximum Log Size text box, as you see in Figure 11-9. Here, you can also choose to modify what happens to existing log entries when the log file fills up.

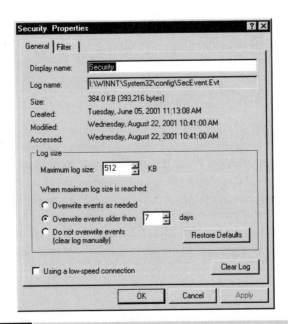

FIGURE 11-9 Security Properties dialog box

You can archive old log data by right-clicking the Security entry, selecting Save Log File As from the pop-up menu, and then entering a path and name for the log file. Saved log files can later be viewed by right-clicking Security and selecting Open Log File from the pop-up menu.

A typical Security log audit entry will detail the action that was performed and the user account associated with the action, the success or failure of the event (depending on what you chose to record), and other pertinent information (for example, in the case of a logon event, the computer the logon event occurred on). Figure 11-10 provides an example of a file access event. You can view audit events by double-clicking the entry you want to view in the Security Log window.

You can also locate specific events by selecting Find from the View menu in the Event Viewer and then identifying the criteria you want to use to locate an event. Typically, you would enter a category, which represents an event type such as account logon, directory services access, object access, and so on, and perhaps the user or computer involved in the action. If you know the specific event ID, you can be even more narrow in your search. The Find feature here works similarly to the Find options on the desktop. When you click Find Next, the log entry that matches your criteria is highlighted in the Event Viewer log window. With the criteria selected in Figure 11-11, you would be looking for failed logon attempts by the user account skaczmarek.

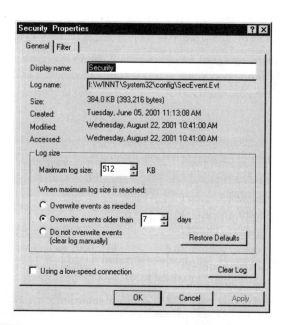

FIGURE 11-10   Sample Security log entry for a file access event

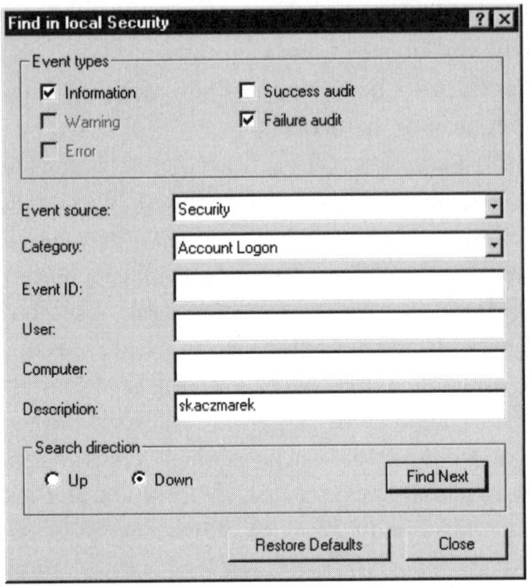

FIGURE 11-11   Example of an event lookup

Travel Advisory

The User field is deceptive because it represents the account that actually recorded the event. With most object access, the user account would be represented in this field. However, with account logons, security events are actually recorded by the account NT Authority\System. The value you place in this field must be an exact match; otherwise, your Find operation will fail. If you are not sure about the way a user account— or any other value you might be searching for—is actually recorded by the account NT Authority\System, enter the text value that you do know in the Description field. The Description field is used to match any text string that appears in the Description area of a log event. In Figure 11-11, because you are interested in failed logon attempts by a particular account, you enter that account name in the Description field rather than the User field.

Exam Tip

It is strongly suggested that you set up a regular review of Security log activity as part of your regular administrative tasks. This allows you to be more proactive in your approach to dealing with security issues rather than reactive.

CHECKPOINT

✔ **Objective 11.01: Implement an Audit Policy**   Audit policies provide you with a means to perform an ongoing assessment or analysis of your overall security strategy by tracking and recording specific activities and events performed by users and the operating system. Audit policies define which events and activities you want Windows 2000 to record. Audit events are written to the Security log of the Event Viewer on the computer where the events took place.

You can configure nine categories of audit events, including auditing of account logons and account management, system-related activities, such as a shutdown, and access to objects such as files, folders, printers as well as Active Directory objects such as OUs and accounts.

By collecting this kind of audit information, you can then monitor the use of resources, create records of activity, and hopefully spot and correct unauthorized activity before it can be harmful to the network.

✔ **Objective 11.02: Monitor and Analyze Security Events**   Your choice of audit settings will determine just how helpful tracking audit events can be as part of your overall network security strategy. Therefore, it is important that you regularly monitor and review your settings to ensure that you are recording accurate, valuable, and constructive information.

Your best tool for monitoring and analyzing audit events as they relate to security is the Security log in the Event Viewer utility. Use the Security log to determine the effectiveness of your audit settings, generate trends of activity, and document events for future reference and analysis.

REVIEW QUESTIONS

1. Which of the following audit event types would you need to configure if you want to track and record activity related to file and folder access on a network server?

   A. Account Logon
   B. Directory Service Access
   C. Object Access
   D. Privilege Usage

2. Which of the following audit event types would you need to configure if you want to track and record changes made to user accounts in Active Directory?

   A. Account Logon
   B. Directory Service Access
   C. Object Access
   D. Privilege Usage

3. The executive secretary for the director of IT in your organization has indicated that when she logs on to her computer in the morning, she frequently receives a message that her account has been locked out. You suspect that someone is trying to access the network using her account during the evening. What can you do to monitor this activity?

   A. Configure an Account Logon policy for her computer to track successful and failed logon attempts.
   B. Configure an Account Logon policy for the OU in which her computer is a member and apply the policy to all computer objects.
   C. Configure a Directory Services Access policy to monitor the activity of her user account.
   D. Set up a video camera to monitor her computer.

4. You want to monitor and record Read and Write activities within a particular set of folders on a server. You modify the audit settings for each folder to audit Read and Write activities for the Domain Users group. However, when you view the Event Viewer Security log later, you find that no security events have been recorded. What is the likely reason?

   A. No one has tried to access the folders.
   B. No one has tried to perform Read or Write activities within the folders.
   C. You need to audit Read and Write for the Everyone group instead.
   D. You need to configure an audit policy for Object Access.

5. You want to monitor and record Change activities related to a specific set of OUs in Active Directory. You have configured an audit policy that enables success and failure event tracking for Directory Service Access. However, when you view the Event Viewer Security log later, you find that no security events have been recorded. What is the likely reason?

   A. No one has tried to change the object properties of the OUs.
   B. You need to configure an audit policy for Object Access.

> **C.** You need to configure which events you want to audit for each OU object in Active Directory.
>
> **D.** You need to specify the users or groups you want to audit when you configure the Directory Services Access audit policy.

6. You need to enable auditing for a set of files and folders on a network server. However, when you view the properties of each file and folder, you cannot find the audit settings. What should you do?

   A. Move the files and folders to an NTFS partition.

   B. Move the files and folders to an NTFS or FAT32 partition.

   C. Apply the audit settings to the files and folders as a Group Policy.

   D. You must enable the audit policy for Object Access to track events before the audit settings become available.

7. Where can you view the accounts you are auditing, events to be audited, and whether you're tracking success or failures of any given file or folder object?

   A. In the object's SACL

   B. In the object's DACL

   C. In the object's Active Directory properties

   D. In the Object Access audit policy settings

8. You suspect that someone is trying to use the executive secretary's logon account, jdoe, to gain unauthorized access to the network. You have enabled account logon auditing to help you track logon attempts using that account. However, there are hundreds of events recorded in the Security log of Event Viewer. Which of the following steps would you take to locate logon attempts using the account jdoe? Select all that apply.

   A. Choose Find from the Event Viewer menu.

   B. Choose Filter from the Event Viewer menu.

   C. Enter jdoe in the Users field.

   D. Enter jdoe in the Description field.

9. In which of the following Event Viewer logs can you find audit events relating to Active Directory object access?

   A. Application log

   B. Directory Services log

   C. Security log

   D. System log

10. You have configured audit settings for a set of folders and their files and sub-folders. There is one particular subfolder that needs to have a different set of audit settings from the rest. How can you arrange this?

   A. Copy the folder to a new location and modify the audit settings.

   B. On the Audit properties tab for the subfolder, deselect the option Allow Inheritable Audit Entries from Parent to Propagate to This Object.

   C. On the parent folder, enable the option Apply These Auditing Entries to Objects and/or Containers Within This Container and then select the subfolder from the Apply To list.

   D. Do nothing. Audit settings are not inherited.

REVIEW ANSWERS

1. **C** You must configure success and/or failure events for Object Access to track activities related to folders and files on a computer. Account Logon (A) tracks and logs the success or failure of user authentication. Directory Service Access (B) tracks and logs activities related to accessing Active Directory objects. Privilege Usage (D) tracks and logs events related to the use of user rights.

2. **B** You must configure success and/or failure events for Directory Service Access to track activities related to Active Directory object access. Account Logon (A) tracks and logs the success or failure of user authentication. Object Access (C) tracks and logs activities related to files and folders. Privilege Usage (D) tracks and logs events related to use of user rights.

3. **B** Although A would work as far as monitoring logon attempts from her particular computer, her account could be locked out due to failed logon attempts at any computer, so you'd want to monitor all computers that could be used to see which one is being used to try to log on with her account. C would track changes made to her account, such as password changes and group membership, but wouldn't monitor logon activity. D might work, too, if you could narrow the logon attempts to her computer only.

4. **D** When auditing events related to file, folder, and printer objects, in addition to configuring the audit settings at the object level, you must also configure an audit policy setting—in this case, Object Access. Although it may be possible that no one has tried to access the folders or has performed the

activities you are monitoring, as suggested in A and B, or that someone outside the Domain Users group is accessing the folders, as in C, nevertheless, unless you enable the Object Access audit policy, nothing will be recorded in Event Viewer.

5. **C** When auditing events related to Active Directory objects, in addition to configuring an audit policy, you must also identify for each object that you want to monitor which events to monitor. You must do this at the object itself; you can't do it when you configure the audit policy, as suggested in D. Also, although it is possible that no one has tried to access the objects, as in A, nevertheless, nothing will be recorded in Event Viewer unless you configure auditing for each object. B is incorrect because it refers to the wrong audit policy type. Object Access enables auditing for file, folder, and printer objects.

6. **A** You can only implement auditing for file and folder objects that exist on an NTFS partition because auditing is a function of NTFS. You cannot apply file and folder auditing as part of Group Policy, as suggested in C. It is not necessary to have first enabled an Object Access audit policy, as in D, although you must do so eventually if you want to actually capture and record any auditable events.

7. **A** These elements are set and stored in the object's SACL (Security Access Control List). The DACL (Discretionary Access Control List), B, contains the object's permissions. These audit settings are not defined in either Active Directory or the Object Access audit policy (C and D).

8. **A** and **D** The only locate feature of Event Viewer is Find. There is no Filter option, as suggested in B. You must enter the user name in the Description field rather than the User field. The User field (C) represents the account that recorded the event. For logon attempts, the event is recorded by the operating system using the account NT Authority\System.

9. **C** The Application log (A) records events generated by applications. The Directory Services log (B), although it might seem correct, records events related to Group Policy activity. The System log (D) records general system events relating to operating system activity.

10. **B** The option Allow Inheritable Audit Entries from Parent to Propagate to This Object is enabled by default. When you disable it, you stop inheritance of audit settings from the parent folder. Although you could copy the folder

to a new location, as suggested in A, that would not be the most efficient way to handle the situation. C is incorrect mostly because you cannot select individual folders in the Apply To list. Also, if you select this option, changes will be applied to all folders, not just one. Finally, D is incorrect because audit settings are obviously inherited by default.

About the CD-ROM

APPENDIX A

Mike Meyers' *Certification Passport* CD-ROM Instructions

To install the *Passport* Practice Exam software, perform these steps:

1. Insert the CD-ROM into your CD-ROM drive. An auto-run program will initiate, and a dialog box will appear indicating that you are installing the Passport setup program. If the auto-run program does not launch on your system, select Run from the Start menu and type *d*:\setup.exe (where *d* is the "name" of your CD-ROM drive).
2. Follow the installation wizard's instructions to complete the installation of the software.
3. You can start the program by going to your desktop and double-clicking the Passport Exam Review icon or by going to Start | Program Files | Passport | Directory Services.

System Requirements

- **Operating systems supported**   Windows 98, Windows NT 4.0, Windows 2000, and Windows Me
- **CPU**   400 MHz or faster recommended
- **Memory**   64MB of RAM
- **CD-ROM**   4X or greater
- **Internet connection**   Required for optional exam upgrade

Technical Support

For basic *Passport* CD-ROM technical support, contact Hudson Technical Support:

- Phone: 800-217-0059
- E-mail: mcgraw-hill@hudsonsoft.com

For content/subject matter questions concerning the book or the CD-ROM, contact MH Customer Service:

- Phone: 800-722-4726
- E-mail: customer.service@mcgraw-hill.com

For inquiries about the available upgrade, CD-ROM, or online technology, or for in-depth technical support, contact ExamWeb Technical Support:

- Phone: 949-566-9375
- E-mail: support@examweb.com

Career
Flight Path

The Microsoft Windows certification program that you will be joining when you take your 70-217 exam includes an extensive group of exams and certification levels. Passing the Windows 2000 Directory Services Infrastructure exam is all that is required for Microsoft's baseline certification—the Microsoft Certified Professional (MCP).

Microsoft's premier certification is the Microsoft Certified System Engineer (MCSE), and the 70-217 exam is a great place to start on this certification. In total, passing seven exams is required to obtain the MCSE, and these are broken down as follows: 4 core exams; 1 core elective exam; and 2 elective exams.

Core Exams

There are 4 exams that every MCSE candidate must pass. These exams test your knowledge of Windows 2000 both as a server and as a client OS, and also test your ability to implement a network based on Microsoft technologies. The core tests are

- **70-210**   Installing, Configuring, and Administering Microsoft Windows 2000 Professional
- **70-215**   Installing, Configuring, and Administering Microsoft Windows 2000 Server
- **70-216**   Implementing and Administering a Microsoft Windows 2000 Network Infrastructure
- **70-217**   Implementing and Administering a Microsoft Windows 2000 Directory Services Infrastructure

Core Elective Exam

The four core required exams test your ability to do, whereas the core elective exam tests your ability to plan. These core elective options are sometimes referred to as the "Designing" exams. The four options available for you to choose from are the first point at which you can begin to customize your MCSE certification around the topics that interest you. Choose one:

- **70-219** Designing a Microsoft Windows 2000 Directory Services Infrastructure
- **70-220** Designing Security for a Microsoft Windows 2000 Network
- **70-221** Designing a Microsoft Windows 2000 Network Infrastructure
- **70-226** Designing Highly Available Web Solutions with Microsoft Windows 2000 Server Technologies

Those interested in working as an Active Directory specialist, a security specialist, a network designer, or an Internet specialist will find that this decision is obvious. For those not so sure, exam 70-220 might be your best bet, as knowledge of network security is always a valuable commodity.

Elective Exams

With the core elective/design exam you are given a bit of choice, but with the last two elective exams, you can really customize your MCSE around your interests and knowledge. Microsoft lists more than 20 exams to choose from, and these can include any of the unused design exams, or any of a number of Microsoft server applications.

If you have a particular interest in SNA server (exam 70-085) or SMS server (exam 70-086) then go for it. In most cases, though, a certification seeker who is looking to make themselves marketable to a broad range of employers should concentrate on a core group of elective exams that relate to Microsoft's most common server applications. Probably the two best electives for MCSE candidates who are on a job hunt are these:

- **70-028** Installing, Configuring, and Administering Microsoft SQL Server 2000 Enterprise Edition
- **70-224** Installing, Configuring, and Administering Microsoft Exchange 2000 Server

There are, as mentioned, numerous other exams available. To check the complete list, refer to http://www.microsoft.com/trainingandservices. For those interested in testing on the quickest—"easiest"—set of electives, consider Proxy Server 2.0 (70-088) or Site Server (70-056). They are generally considered to be extremely easy, but because of this they also raise a warning flag in the minds of employers familiar with the MCSE program. Users with Windows NT 4.0 knowledge can leverage this into their Windows 2000 MCSE by taking exam 70-244, which covers support and integration of Windows NT 4.0 networks.

.NET and Beyond

One thing to remember, of course, is that computer technology changes rapidly, and most certifications therefore require you to regularly update your certifications. With the Windows 2000 MCSE you are actually getting a reprieve, as Microsoft has declared that the .NET and 2000 exams can be used interchangeably, so re-certification for XP/.NET won't be necessary. See the Microsoft Web site for more information on which Windows 2000 exams map to which XP/.NET exams.

Good luck with your future adventures, and it has been nice traveling with you through this small region in the world of certification. Enjoy the trip!

MCSE 2000 Exam Requirements

4 Core Exams—Required	
70-210	70-216
70-215	70-217

-OR-

70-240 If you already passed 3 Windows NT 4.0 Exams: 70-067, 70-068, and 70-073.

+

I Elective Core Exam Selected From:	
70-219	70-221
70-220	

+

2 Elective Core Exams Selected From:	
70-219	70-222
70-220	70-223
70-221	70-227
Any current valid NT 4.0 MCSE elective exam.	

Index

INTERNATIONAL CONTACT INFORMATION

AUSTRALIA
McGraw-Hill Book Company Australia Pty. Ltd.
TEL +61-2-9417-9899
FAX +61-2-9417-5687
http://www.mcgraw-hill.com.au
books-it_sydney@mcgraw-hill.com

CANADA
McGraw-Hill Ryerson Ltd.
TEL +905-430-5000
FAX +905-430-5020
http://www.mcgrawhill.ca

GREECE, MIDDLE EAST,
NORTHERN AFRICA
McGraw-Hill Hellas
TEL +30-1-656-0990-3-4
FAX +30-1-654-5525

MEXICO (Also serving Latin America)
McGraw-Hill Interamericana Editores S.A. de C.V.
TEL +525-117-1583
FAX +525-117-1589
http://www.mcgraw-hill.com.mx
fernando_castellanos@mcgraw-hill.com

SINGAPORE (Serving Asia)
McGraw-Hill Book Company
TEL +65-863-1580
FAX +65-862-3354
http://www.mcgraw-hill.com.sg
mghasia@mcgraw-hill.com

SOUTH AFRICA
McGraw-Hill South Africa
TEL +27-11-622-7512
FAX +27-11-622-9045
robyn_swanepoel@mcgraw-hill.com

UNITED KINGDOM & EUROPE
(Excluding Southern Europe)
McGraw-Hill Education Europe
TEL +44-1-628-502500
FAX +44-1-628-770224
http://www.mcgraw-hill.co.uk
computing_neurope@mcgraw-hill.com

ALL OTHER INQUIRIES Contact:
Osborne/McGraw-Hill
TEL +1-510-549-6600
FAX +1-510-883-7600
http://www.osborne.com
omg_international@mcgraw-hill.com

ExamWeb is a leader in assessment technology. We use this technology to deliver customized online testing programs, corporate training, pre-packaged exam preparation courses, and licensed technology. ExamWeb has partnered with Osborne - McGraw-Hill to develop the CD contained in this book and its corresponding online exam simulators. Please read about our services below and contact us to see how we can help you with your own assessment needs.

www.examweb.com

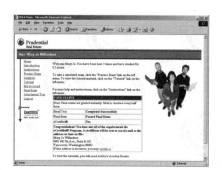

Corporate Assessment

ExamWeb can customize its course and testing engines to meet your training and assessment needs as a trainer. We can provide you with stand-alone assessments and courses or can easily integrate our assessment engines with your existing courses or learning management system. Features may include:

✓ Corporate-level access and reporting

✓ Multiple question types

✓ Detailed strength and weakness reports by key subject area and topic

✓ Performance comparisons amongst groups

Technology Licenses and Partnerships

Publishers, exam preparation companies and schools use ExamWeb technology to offer online testing or exam preparation branded in their own style and delivered via their websites. Improve your assessment offerings by using our technology!

Check www.examweb.com for an updated list of course offerings.

click. study. pass.™

Coming soon:

CCNA™ Passport / A+™ Passport / Server+™ Passport / Network+™ Passport / Java™ 2 Passport
MCSE Windows 2000™ Professional Passport / MCSE Windows 2000™ Server Passport
MCSE Windows 2000™ Directory Services Passport
MCSE Windows 2000™ Network Infrastructure Passport

For more infomation, please contact corpsales@examweb.com or call 949.566.9375